A WORKBOOK IN THE
RORSCHACH TECHNIQUE EMPHASIZING
THE BECK AND KLOPFER SYSTEMS

Publication Number 663
AMERICAN LECTURE SERIES®

A Monograph in
The BANNERSTONE DIVISION *of*
AMERICAN LECTURES IN PSYCHOLOGY

Edited by
MOLLY HARROWER, Ph.D.
Professor of Research in Clinical Psychology
Department of Psychiatry
Temple University School of Medicine
Philadelphia, Pennsylvania

A WORKBOOK IN THE RORSCHACH TECHNIQUE EMPHASIZING THE BECK AND KLOPFER SYSTEMS

By

JOHN E. EXNER, JR., Ph.D.

Chairman, Department of Psychology
Director of Training in Clinical Psychology
Bowling Green State University
Bowling Green, Ohio

CHARLES C THOMAS • PUBLISHER
Springfield • Illinois • U.S.A.

Published and Distributed Throughout the World by
CHARLES C THOMAS • PUBLISHER
BANNERSTONE HOUSE
301-327 East Lawrence Avenue, Springfield, Illinois, U.S.A.
NATCHEZ PLANTATION HOUSE
735 North Atlantic Boulevard, Fort Lauderdale, Florida, U.S.A.

© 1966, by CHARLES C THOMAS • PUBLISHER
Library of Congress Catalog Card Number: 66-25152

With THOMAS BOOKS *careful attention is given to all details of
manufacturing and design. It is the Publisher's desire to present books
that are satisfactory as to their physical qualities and artistic possibilities
and appropriate for their particular use.* THOMAS BOOKS *will be true
to those laws of quality that assure a good name and good will.*

Printed in the United States of America
0-5

Preface

THE impact of the Rorschach on clinical psychology during the past thirty years has been quite dramatic. In spite of its many critics, the use of the technique has grown and flourished widely. There are, of course, many questions yet to be settled concerning the Rorschach—including even the basic one as to whether it is really as useful as its advocates infer. Before approaching this question, the beginning student should become as proficient as possible in the administration and interpretation of the technique. Such proficiency is dependent upon both knowledge and experience. While the latter can come only with time, knowledge of past and contemporary thinking about the Rorschach is not difficult to derive, assuming adequate motivation. It is easy, however, for the complacent student to neglect the variety of ideas concerning the technique and instead adopt one approach or one attitude. This workbook is offered in the opinion that such a narrow approach is erroneous and harmful — that instead, it behooves the student to strive toward the broadest scope of information on any given technique as is within the realm of possibility. If this workbook contributes in even a minor way toward this goal for either the student or the instructor, its development will have been worthwhile.

This effort has not been an individual project. The assistance of many people has brought the project to closure. In particular, thanks should go to Robert Dies, William Eull, Lawrence Brown, Thomas Endress and Martin Levy, who aided considerably in the selection of the large pool of responses from which the three hundred listed responses were selected. Many students, too numerous to mention, individually aided in the annotations of the bibliography. If there are instances where it seems inadequate, the inadequacy is not due to a lack of effort. A note of thanks is also required for the several secretaries who worked on the project, which, at times, with its peculiar lingo must have seemed like a painstaking and almost insurmountable task. Finally, to Samuel Beck and Bruno Klopfer a special appreciation is required. Without their advice, comment and encouragement the project could not have been completed.

J. E. E., Jr.

ACKNOWLEDGMENT

The Rorschach location sheets on which the practice responses are numbered have been reproduced with the kind permission of Hans Huber Publishers, Berne, Switzerland.

Contents

TABLES

A WORKBOOK IN THE
RORSCHACH TECHNIQUE EMPHASIZING
THE BECK AND KLOPFER SYSTEMS

Chapter I

Introduction

THE student beginning his first course in Rorschach justifiably may sense a feeling of excitement. But he should not be misled. The first course in the Rorschach method is but a beginning and by no means creates a desired level of proficiency. Unfortunate as it may seem, most of the projective methods, and particularly the Rorschach, are of such complexity that considerable training and practice are required before proficiency can be anticipated. The Rorschach is one of the most complex of the projective methods. In part this complexity is created by the characteristics of the technique, in that it attempts to provide a standardized technique of coding or scoring of a subject's complicated response to a complicated ambiguous stimulus. Additionally, the technique is made more complex by the fact that we have only modest agreement between authorities on systems of scoring and interpretation. As a result, there are several systems commonly taught and used today.

One basic purpose of this workbook is to bring together a sizable number of responses of varying levels of difficulty on which the student, beginning in the Rorschach technique, can practice a method of scoring skills. The basic scoring principles of both Beck (1961) and Klopfer (1954) are included and the "Response Key" in the Appendix lists acceptable scorings for each of the practice responses to both of these methods. The rationale for inclusion of both the Beck and Klopfer systems of scoring rests on the fact that these two, while certainly not the only acceptable methods of scoring

Rorschach, are probably the most widely used in teaching and practice. In fact, the alert clinician is almost compelled to be proficient in his understanding of both systems in order to provide adequate communication with other Rorschachers, to appraise Rorschach research intelligently and to translate easily, into his own preferred method, quantitative summaries and interpretations based on another method.

A word of caution should be given the student, however, against neglecting other Rorschach systems. Particularly those of Hertz (1951), Piotrowski (1950, 1957) and Rapaport-Schafer (1945, 1954) have much to offer and are not uncommonly used. It seems impractical to believe that anyone could gain a full appreciation of Rorschach theory, research and practice without adequate familiarity with all systems of scoring and interpretation.

As a second word of caution, it should be noted that the material presented herein is not intended as a substitute for primary source material. There are many aspects of the systems of either Beck or Klopfer which cannot be covered easily without direct reference to the original source of material. The subtle discriminations of Movement responses, the Klopfer Form Level Ratings and the Beck Z scores are but examples of complex material where reference to primary sources is essential.

It seems worthwhile to make some comment on the historical and theoretical basis of the differences between the Klopfer and Beck systems. Rorschach died quite prematurely in 1922, at a time when only the first bits and pieces of his experiment with inkblots were falling into place. His book, *Psychodiagnostics,* was published posthumously through the efforts of his friend and colleague, Emil Oberholzer. After that time, no one directly carried on Rorschach's experiment. To be sure, Oberholzer manifested considerable enthusiasm for Rorschach's work but did not take an active leadership role in publication or, more particularly, research concerning the technique. Neither Klopfer nor Beck had any direct experiences with Rorschach. Klopfer received his Ph.D. from the University of Munich in 1922 but did not gain familiarity with the Rorschach until 1924 and had no formal study or experience in Rorschach technique until 1933.

Beck was introduced to the Rorschach by David Levy, who had previously trained under Oberholzer and is usually regarded as the person responsible for bringing the Rorschach to America. Beck completed his doctoral dissertation on the Rorschach in 1932 at Columbia University and in 1933 studied directly with Oberholzer on a Rockefeller Foundation Fellowship in Zurich, Switzerland. Interestingly, in the same year Klopfer was studying in Zurich at the Psychotechnic Institute.

But the differences began long before their actual introduction to Rorschach. The differences arose more from theoretical training. Klopfer, having been educated in Europe, was strongly committed to the phenomenological approach. This continental psychology is, of course, much more qualitative and subjective than the more rigorous positivistic attitudes manifest in American psychology, particularly in behaviorism, which was the tradition in which Beck was trained. Beck's undergraduate years were spent at Harvard, followed by graduate work at Columbia. In each school, he found himself oriented to a strong sense of behaviorism dedicated to scientific objectivity. Very possibly, the Beck system is more closely related to Rorschach's own original ideas, although certainly modified to some extent by Oberholzer, who had a very strong Freudian psychoanalytic orientation. Klopfer also manifests a psychoanalytic orientation, but much

more influenced by Jung than Freud. Thus, in developing their respective systems, Beck and Klopfer have maintained a certain consistency with their backgrounds. Beck striving for objectivity and understanding of individuals, both as persons and as contrasted with other persons, Klopfer striving for a more subjective understanding of the individual for himself, with less emphasis on his comparison to others.

In comparing the Beck and Klopfer techniques, the student of the Rorschach will readily identify agreement between the methods on several fundamental scoring issues. Differences will be noted in other areas of scoring. Some of these differences are modest and even vague, whereas in other instances the differences are quite extreme. The existence of such differences makes for difficulty in comparing interpretations. A quantitative summary derived by one scoring method cannot be legitimately approached in the same interpretative manner as a quantitative summary derived by another scoring method, even though the summaries pertain to the same protocol, and even though, hopefully, the conclusions derived from each would yield a high degree of similarity.

In that such complexity and disagreement appears to exist concerning the Rorschach, the student may well question why the technique is still so frequently used. Sundberg (1961) has pointed out that the Rorschach is among the most frequently used techniques in clinical work in the United States. This fact is particularly astonishing in light of a number of studies which have produced negligible or even negative results concerning the validation of the technique. Most dedicated Rorschachers, however, would maintain that the analysis of a protocol does yield valid data but that appropriate techniques to understand this type of validity have yet to be developed. Some suggest that the qualitative analysis of the response carries major weight in final conclusions, yet few have denied the importance of a well-scored and well-summarized record. It is toward proficiency in this latter task that most introductory Rorschach courses are orientated.

A sizable bibliography is included in the

Workbook, with most of the references accompanied by an annotation. This annotation is not to be mistaken for a comprehensive review of the article or of the literature pertaining to a given variable. These references have been selected because they relate most directly to the different scoring symbols with which the student will be familiarizing himself in a beginning course. The annotations are presented merely to give the student some quick reference material in order, hopefully, to stimulate further interest and reading in each of the given areas. There has been far too much literature published on the Rorschach to anticipate full coverage in one semester or even in a single year. Klopfer, Ainsworth, Klopfer and Holt (1956) list nearly 2,700 books and articles pertaining directly to the Rorschach. Certainly that number has increased considerably since 1956, and, in fact, it may be realistic to postulate that more than 4,000 articles and books on the technique exist today. In structuring the bibliography, no effort was made to present a section on diagnosis or interpretation, although obviously many of the articles listed pertain to these areas. The section pertaining to examiner interaction with the subject should be of particular interest to the beginning student.

The section of the Workbook on scoring and scoring symbols is designed for quick reference. As previously noted, it does not represent a comprehensive review of any scoring symbol. It should be sufficiently inclusive, however, to be readily useful to the student scoring the majority of the practice responses listed here.

Finally, it should be emphasized that the level of sophistication of Rorschach interpretation will not only be contingent upon the quality of the interpreter's training and experience in Rorschach but also the quality of his knowledge in the areas of personality and psychopathology. The translation of raw data from a Rorschach protocol into meaningful statements about a human being is a serious task. It should be taken neither lightly nor with fanatical conviction. Unfortunately, clinical psychology has not yet discovered the perfect technique of diagnosis or personality appraisal; thus the student, in aproaching the Rorschach, as with any test, must do so in a serious minded and highly ethical manner, dedicating himself first and foremost to the client and the client's well-being. If, perchance, the student has not familiarized himself comprehensively with the Ethical Standards for Psychologists as listed by the American Psychological Association (1953, 1959) he should do so.

INSTRUCTIONS AND THE TEST RELATIONSHIP

It is doubtful that any test is ever taken under stress-free conditions. Even those which are perceived by the subject to be challenging and worthwhile probably have stressful aspects. It also seems probable that the more ambiguous the stimuli, the greater the tendencies, correspondingly, toward perceiving the situations as stressful. It is therefore quite important that the examiner attempt to provide a pretest structuring of the situation in such a manner as to minimize the stressful effects. This is not to infer that some 'magical rapport' must be elicited by the examiner before he can begin the test, for such a relationship might well have a negative influence on the data to be collected. The subject should be comfortable and reasonably at ease. Most students beginning the Rorschach technique will have administered other tests and should by this time have some realistic idea of adequate rapport. But there is more to the relationship than may be covered under the heading of 'rapport.'

The influence of the examiner on the subject cannot be sufficiently stressed. The Rorschach experience is one of uniqueness for the subject, and it is quite unusual that the subject does not have some notion that the technique is designed for appraisal of personality or behavioral characteristics. Adding to this knowledge is the examiner himself, not so much in terms of the pretest information he reveals to the subject, but in terms of his very existence as an examiner. For many subjects the examiner is perceived as an awesome threat, for others as a friendly confidant, and still for others as some mystical all-knowing force. The examiner's own personality can, to a large extent, dictate the subject's interpretation of the situation, and, as Schafer (1954) has pointed out, the impact of one person on another in a highly sensitized private situation as Rorschach testing is such that it requires careful study and especially that it requires keen awareness by the examiner of his dynamic relation to the subject. A number of studies are cited in the annotated bibliography which suggest that the examiner's approach, attitude, instructions and emotional tone can all influence the length of a protocol and even create modification in the types of percepts given. Every beginning student of the Rorschach Technique no doubt can profit enormously from a thorough study

of the section on interpersonal dynamics in Schafer's book, *Psychoanalytic Interpretation in Rorschach Testing*.

The instructions suggested by Beck include the phrase: ". . . be sure to tell the examiner everything you see on the card as you look at it." Other authorities on the Rorschach, including Klopfer, do not include this emphasis in their instructions. It is difficult to predict whether change in emphasis will produce significantly more responses in a protocol. It seems practical, however, to suggest that this may be the case, since there are many studies which find variability in both number of responses and content of responses to be dependent upon the approach of the examiner. Whether or not this is the case, the examiner should use the instructional method recommended by the authority whose system he intends to use for a protocol.

RECORDING THE RESPONSE

All responses should be recorded verbatim by the examiner. The careful examiner will include notation for pauses, changes of facial expression and other important observational notes, as well as those standard notations for card turning and reaction times.

The recording of the material derived from the inquiry will appropriately note each question offered by the examiner. Both Beck and Klopfer stress the importance of the inquiry, suggesting that the scoring of any response is based on the combination of S's responses in the free association period and in the inquiry period. When the inquiry to a response is limited, so too is the available material on which to base accurate scoring. At the same time, an excessively long inquiry will often provoke information concerning the response which was not originally involved in percept. Naturally, the questioning is always nondirective. The basic orientation of the inquiry is to determine the location of the response by knowing exactly what part of the blot has been employed by the subject and to determine the absence or presence of every potential scoring

determinant. Even though it is desirable to keep the period of inquiry as short as possible, the examiner is often compelled to ask more questions than have been anticipated because of S's reluctance to give information or because of new information elicited from S by a preceding question. While the extensive inquiry can complicate decisions on scoring a particular response, *a general rule of thumb which seems realistic is that the earlier in the response process information occurs concerning the existence of a determinant, the more assured the scorer may be that the determinant is actually a legitimate part of a response and not one provoked by excessive questioning.*

In addition to the period of inquiry, the examiner may feel it necessary to gain additional information concerning the S's percept. Both Beck and Klopfer offer suggestions for this new procedure which may include an Analogy Period, or one of the several methods for 'Testing the Limits.' These variations should not, however, be used indiscriminately, and the student should be thoroughly familiar with the rationale underlying them as well as their

procedures before their employment.

Rorschachers, especially beginners, often find the problem of recording the subject's verbalization verbatim a difficult one. For this reason, most Rorschachers are prone to use logical abbreviations. While there is no standardized listing for abbreviations, some of those more commonly used are shown in Table I.

TABLE I

ABBREVIATIONS COMMONLY USED IN RECORDING RORSCHACH RESPONSES

Abbreviation Used	Meaning
a. t.	anything
ll	looks like
flwr	flower
st	something
stndg	standing
bc	because
wm	woman
cb	could be
j	just
Bf	butterfly
w	with

Use of Any Letter Which Sounds Like a Word Such as

r	are
g	gee
c	see
b	be
u	you

Use of Any Natural Scoring Content Abbreviations Such as

H	human
A	animal
Cld	cloud
Ls	landscape

The object, of course, is to minimize work and time, but at no expense to the requirement that all verbalizations be recorded verbatim. Thus, a subject's response, "This looks like a woman with a butterfly costume with her arms in the air," might be recorded by the examiner as: this ll a wm w. a Bf costum w her arms in the air.

Each examiner will naturally include his own abbreviations, but it should be emphasized that the protocol should be easily readable to any other Rorschacher at a later time.

Chapter II

Scoring of the Response

ALL Rorschach responses are scored for three characteristics—*Location, Determinants* and *Content.* In addition, some responses are also scored in a manner that indicates the commonness or popularity of the responses or the originality or the uniqueness of the responses. Rorschach scoring really represents a process of classification. Quantification is accomplished in a sense of compiling a frequency distribution for each of the different scoring symbols used.

SCORING FOR LOCATION

Location scores deal with the configurational properties of the percept. S is permitted to select any portion of the blot for his response. The location scoring thus refers to that part of the blot actually used. In some instances, the entire blot may be used, while in other instances only parts of the blot are involved. Both Beck and Klopfer have numbered the different parts of each blot, each in accordance with his own scoring rationale. There is considerable overlap in this numbering; however, the student should not be deceived to the point of believing that they are identical, for this is not the case. Information concerning the location of a percept is typically derived in the inquiry, although occasionally it is given in the free association period. In some instances, S will be vague, and it is not uncommon for the examiner to have S to trace the area involved with his finger or even draw the area on a location sheet, although this should not be a routine practice.

Beck Scoring for Location

W: *The Whole response.* S uses the entire blot in his percept. Some W responses seem formed instantaneously, while others ap-

pear to manifest a synthesizing process. While they are qualitatively different, both are scored W.

Example: A butterfly (using all of Card I).

Example: Two people picking up something. They might be at a party with decorations all around (using all of Card III).

D: *The Detail response.* D relates to portions of the blot usually responded to by S. Beck's list of D areas has been defined by the frequency of usage. Most D areas encompass sizeable portions of the blot; however, some small parts which are commonly attended to by S are also considered to be D areas. Thus, the size of an area does not necessarily dictate whether or not it will be scored D.

Example: Two humans (using all of Card III except the red parts).

Example: Two hands (using the top middle projections on Card I — numbered as Area D1 by Beck).

Dd: *The Rare Detail response.* S uses a portion of the blot to which responses are not commonly given. In most instances, the Dd

area will be small but not necessarily so.

Example: Two mountains (using the rounded projections in the top of the middle of Card I — numbered as Area Dd 22 by Beck).

Example: A bell (using the lower half of the middle portion of Card I — numbered by Beck as Area Dd 24)

s: *The White Space response.* S uses a white space area in his percept. In the Beck System, the scoring of s is always combined with another location score, i.e., Ws, Ds, Dds. When the white space used is statistically rare but involved with a W or D response, the Ws or Ds is recorded in the scoring with a marginal note of Dds.

DW: *The DW response* (Rorschach's Secondary W). In the free association S attends to one detail but then attributes the content of the response to the entire blot.

Example: These (D2) are wings, so I guess it's a bat (W) on Card 1. This type of response might also be scored DdW if the important detail is a Dd area, or DdD if the important detail is a Dd area and then generalized to a D portion of the blot rather than the whole blot.

Example: A map (all of Card 1) because these (Dd23) are islands—Score DdW.

Example: A clothing store mannequin (all of D1) because this (Dd27) is the belt buckle — Score DdD.

The DW type response should not be confused with the concepts of "confabulated" or "contaminated" response. Some DW type responses are obvious confabulations, suggestive of psychic disintegration; however, Beck notes that the DW type response may also appear in almost any personality group, including the healthy and even superior types.

Klopfer Scoring for Location

W: *The Whole response.* Same as Beck's W.

W̶: *The Cut-Off Whole response.* S uses almost all of the blot but *deliberately* omits certain portions which do not fit the basic concept. A minimum of two thirds of the blot is involved.

Example: A pelvis (on Card 1) but these pointed parts on the outside aren't included (Klopfer's area d1).

Klopfer indicates that W̶ responses are typically marked by the S's spontaneous mention of the parts of the blot to be disregarded. The exceptions to this rule occur on Cards II and III where a W̶ can be assumed when S omits the red portions of the card without a specific statement to this effect.

D: *The Large Usual Detail response.* S uses a large, commonly responded-to area which is clearly marked off from the remainder of the blot by form, shading or color. This is similar to Beck's D, except it is restricted only to large areas. Some differences exist between the Beck and Klopfer concepts of usual. For instance, on Card 1, Beck's Area Dd 24 is Klopfer's Area D4.

d: *The Small Usual Detail response.* S uses a small, commonly responded-to area, clearly marked off from the remainder of the blot by form, shading or color. In contrasting this symbol to the Beck system, it would appear that Klopfer attempts to give accord to both the frequency to which an area precipitates a response as well as the actual size of that area. Some Klopfer d Areas are Dd for Beck, while others are D for Beck.

Dd: The symbol Dd is *not used* by Klopfer to score. He does use the symbol to denote a special category of scoring symbols, all of which refer to unusual details. This category has four basic subdivisions.

1. dd: *The Tiny Detail response.* S uses areas comparable in size to the d areas but which occur so infrequently as to be considered unusual.

2. de: *The Edge Detail response.* S bases

his percept on the contour of the edge of the blot. None of the shaded portion is used. Profiles which exclude the shaded portions and coastlines are the most common types of de responses.

3. di: *The Inside Detail response.* S uses a shaded portion of the blot, disregarding the edges, to specify concepts which are not obvious. This involves internal areas of the blot that are ordinarily perceived by the majority of subjects as an unbroken surface. For instance, the light grey details near the center line of Card VI are scored d rather than di, since most subjects do not regard this area as an unbroken surface.

3. dr: *The Rare Detail response.* S uses an unusual location *which is not scorable by any other symbol.* dr responses may encompass very large areas of the blot, including, for instance, a very unusual combination of D areas or much smaller areas which border on the dd response.

S: *The White Space Response.* Same as Beck's S, although Klopfer uses capital letter S.

Unlike Beck, Klopfer scores S by itself as the location score when only white space is used. In fact, Klopfer does not combine symbols for location as does Beck in the use of Ws, Ds, or Dds. Instead, Klopfer uses a concept of Main and Additional Location scores, so that when more than one location scoring is applicable, the portion of the blot primary to the concept is listed first, followed by a comma, followed by a symbol for the secondary location scoring.

Example: Lakes (white space on Card 1) surrounded by landscape (using whole blot) — scored S, W.

Example: A Halloween face (all of Card 1) white spaces are the eyes and mouth — scored W, S.

DW: *The Confabulatory Whole response.* Klopfer's definition of the DW response is practically identical to that given by Beck. The differences between the two systems lie in the interpretation, wherein, as previously noted, Beck does not consider all DW responses as manifestations of disintegration, whereas Klopfer does feel that they are always a poor match for the blot.

DETERMINANT SCORING

The nucleus of the scoring of a response is the determinant. It refers to the characteristic(s) of the blot that cause S to see the percept as he does. In fact, much information derived concerning S, whether derived through a quantitative or qualitative interpretation, is heavily weighted by the determinants revealed in the protocol. Unfortunately, the information on which determinant scoring is based usually has to come directly from S. Were he able to answer the question: "What about the blot reminds you of a . . . ?" completely, the task of the scorer and interpreter could be much more elementary than is now often the case. In some instances, this completeness occurs; while in others exhaustive inquiry by the examiner (always using nondirective questions, i.e., "Tell

me more about it," "Can you describe it more") still leaves some doubt. Both Beck and Klopfer have suggested some general rules for scoring determinants which should be followed closely in order to avoid unnecessary ambiguity. As in the instance of Location Scoring, Beck and Klopfer often use the same symbols in much the same way; however, they also differ quite significantly in some areas. There are four main classifications used in scoring determinants, each of which has subclassifications. These four are Form, Movement, Color and Shading.

Beck Scoring for Form

F: *The Form response.* Whenever S's percept is based on the outline or shape of a blot area, Form becomes involved. In many instances the outline or shape is the sole determinant of the percept; thus F is the only symbol involved in the Determinant scoring. In other cases, the outline or shape, together with other determinants such as color or shading, establish a "multiple" determination of the percept. In either instance, the symbol F is used. Beck reports that almost all Form responses can be defined as either good form, wherein a + is added to the symbol F, or as bad form, wherein a − is added to the symbol F.

F+: *The Good Form response.* Beck's designation of good form is based on an extensive frequency distribution, wherein form responses given by a fairly large number of subjects in essentially good mental health are tabulated. In essence, the good form response is one which manifests an outline reasonably similar to that reported by S.

F−: *The Poor Form response.* The Poor Form response has also been largely determined on the basis of frequency distribution. Essentially, the poor form response is one in which the outline of the area is inconsistent with the percept given. Beck notes that there is an obvious continuum from the best of form to the worst of form, the latter being given by the most severely disturbed subjects.

F: *The Undetermined Form response.* This is a rarely used scoring in the Beck method, yet is necessary because of the possibility of those few occasions when a response is not clearly plus or minus. Beck suggests that these types of response will typically be of a Dd nature and will be far too few in any record as to have weighty significance. He also notes that the Rorschach (and also included in the Rapaport-Schafer 1945, 1954) system included the symbols ± to score responses which are not clearly plus or minus but have more plus characteristics and ∓ for responses which have more minus characteristics. The scorer using the Beck method will find an exten-

sive listing of Good and Poor Form responses by location area for each card in Beck's *Rorschach Test*, Volume I.

Klopfer Scoring for Form

F: *The Form response.* Klopfer does not differentiate form responses as plus or minus. All responses in which there are no other main determinants such as movement, shading, or color, are scored F. The differences between vague, indefinite or abstract form or the realities of the form are accounted for in Form Level Rating, which is discussed in a later section of the manual.

Beck Scoring for Movement

M: *The Movement response.* M represents the experience of movement for Beck. Essentially, it denotes a human experience but may occur in nonhuman percepts, provided certain criteria are met. M is scored whether the movement is active, i.e., running, fighting, reaching, jumping, or passive, i.e., sitting, thinking, looking. Any percepts in which the content is human-involving activity are scored M. Any animal content percepts in which the type of activity attributed to an animal is within the normal repertoire of the human are also score M, i.e., bears boxing (bears fighting is not scored M), rats plotting, bugs having an argument, a spider laughing. Animal percepts involving activity common to the animal is *not* scored M. Abstract emotion is also scored M, i.e., anger, depression, fear, even though the percept is marked by an absence of form. Also, in some associations S reports activity in inanimate objects that could be a type in which a human engages or it is described vividly enough to infer S is identifying with it. In each instance M is scored.

Example: A bullet moving swiftly.

Example: A terribly cold wintry blizzard with intense wind.

The guidelines for scoring M or not scoring M are far from simple in many responses. As Beck states: "The burden of proof regarding M or not M is always on the individual response." Cautiousness, experience and continual reference to the primary source material will aid the scorer considerably.

Klopfer Scoring for Movement

M: *The Human Movement response.* S infers a kinesthetic quality in a human concept. This concept applies not only to perceptions of humans but also to descriptions of human-like figures, i.e., drawings, statues, caricatures. The concept is also applicable for human-like movement in animals similar to the use of M in animal percepts described by Beck.

→M: *The Tendency to Movement.* The tendency to movement scoring refers to those responses in which M is not clearly delineated by S but instead is elicited in the inquiry under "fairly directive questioning." The M tendency is also used in those response situations in which the movement is not firmly established, i.e., the kinesthetic element is reluctant, mournful eyes, a surprised dog. The latter refers to situations in which an animal is attributed with a human-like expression but not human action.

FM: *The Animal Movement response.* S attributes movement to animals which is of an animal-like nature. This scoring is used even if the movement is attributed to caricatures, drawing or ornaments of animals.

Example: A dog standing proudly.

Example: A frog croaking.

Example: A deer leaping.

→FM: *The tendency to Animal Movement.* S acknowledges animal movement with reluctance, either with considerable doubt expressed or only after considerable inquiry.

m: *The Inanimate Movement response.* This category refers to the experience of movement in inanimate objects. This category contains three subdivisions.

Fm: *Form Dominated Inanimate Movement.* The object perceived as moving has a definite form, i.e., a falling maple seed, airplane flying, top spinning, bullet in flight. Fm is also used for a phallic force accompanying a phallic symbol, i.e., an erect penis. Fm is also scored for human or animal faces or masks that are horrible, frightening or sinister, even when the wording of the response suggests that the facial expression is the basis for the effect. The use of Fm rather than M is based on the idea that the percept involves an abstract or evil force.

Fm is also used whenever human detail is used abstractly or symbolically, i.e., the arm of the law, the fist of justice.

mF: *Inanimate Movement of Semi-definite Forms.* In this percept S refers to objects which imply some shape but which have no definite consistency to the shape, i.e., clouds moving, atomic explosions, burst of flame.

m: *Form Free Inanimate Movement.* S's percept involves no form, only the force of movement. The concept may be kaleidoscope or abstract, i.e., everything is falling apart, there's a sense of pull, a strong wind.

The Symbol F and the Scoring of Movement in the Beck and Klopfer Systems

Unlike the color and shading scoring categories, the symbol F is never used when M is scored in either the Beck or Klopfer Systems. Form is assumed to always exist in the Movement response for Beck, thus the signs of + and − for good and poor form are always added to the symbol M. In the Klopfer System the symbol F may or may not be used in conjunction with the symbol for inanimate object movement (m), depending upon the presence or absence of form in the percept; however, as Beck's method it is never used conjointly with M. It will be noted in the sections on color and shading responses that the symbol F may not be present, depending upon the actual existence of form in the percept.

Beck Scoring for Color (Chromatic)

C: *The Pure Color response.* The determinant of S's response is only color. It is a form-free percept in which the basic content is shapeless, i.e., blood, fire. A Pure C response is relatively infrequent and sometimes difficult to establish. S's free association is the primary guide as to whether the percept is C or CF. C is not scored in instances where S refers to form, even though somewhat vague; i.e., blood spot is not scored C.

CF: *The Color-Form response.* S's response is color-dominated but contains distinct elements of form, even though vague, i.e., blood spot, seaweed, a flower (specifically named flowers may be FC), a finger painting, fireworks. The decision as to whether the response is scored CF or FC is often not easily derived. Careful nondirective questioning remains the rule, of course.

FC: *The Form-Color response.* S's response is form dominated but contains obvious elements of color, i.e., a pretty butterfly, a colorful bow tie, a daffodil, a seahorse. Color coincides with the usual color of the object mentioned in the percept. Some definite inference of the inclusion of the color should be made by S.

NOTE: Beck does not score color naming.

Whenever mention is made by S of the color of the blot, it must be clearly established that he is using the color as a determinant of a percept rather than a mention of the existence of the color on the blot.

Example: This one is pretty.

Example: Oh, I see red and pink and blue.

Example: I don't see how the red things fit into it.

Klopfer Scoring for Color (Chromatic)

C. *The Pure Color response.* Is more restricted in use than Beck's concept of C. Klopfer lists three basic criteria for the scoring of C. (a) It is a totally undifferentiated percept which is (b) without any organizational relationship to any other percept in the card and is (c) repetitive. This last requirement of repetition makes C in the Klopfer scored protocol a distinct rarity. It carries with it the notion that S is responding mechanically.

Example: Red and pink always referred to as blood without organization or integration with other percepts would be scored C. It is a mechanical perseveration.

Example: One or two blood responses in a record *even though without form would not be scored C.*

Klopfer also notes special subdivisions of the Pure-Color responses, all of which are based on the formless concept.

Cn: *The Color Naming response.* S responds to the color by naming hue and sometimes even refers to subtle differences in hues. It is scored provided S indicates Cn as an appropriate method of approaching stimuli. Cn is not scored if S recovers and gives a satisfactory form response.

Example: (Card VIII) Gee, orange and pink and blue and here are two mice. Not scored Cn.

Cdes: *The Color Description response.* S gives descriptions of the color rather than specifying hue, i.e., pretty pastels, water colors. S must intend for his verbalization to be a response.

Csym: *The Color Symbolism response.* S uses color to represent an abstract idea, with no form involved, i.e., anger, evil, youth, pleasantness. If form is involved the symbol F is appropriately indicated, depending upon the degree of involvement of the form, i.e., FCsym, CFsym.

CF: *The Color-Form response.* S defines a response in which color is primary and form is vague or indefinite. The color used must be that of the object in its natural state. Klopfer lists subdivisions of the CF type response in which variations from the basic criteria of the CF scoring occur.

C←→F: Where the color used is not that of the object in its natural state but its use is forced by S.

Example: Blue/blood (Card X).

C/F: Where the color is used in a colorless manner merely to mark off subdivisions of the percept. Usually, these responses are marked by content such as indefinite political maps where specific countries are not mentioned or in anatomical charts or microscopic slides where the color is used descriptively and the parts are vaguely specified.

CF—: Where the basic criteria for the CF scoring exists but there is a notable abuse of the form qualities of the blot.

FC: *The Form-Color response.* S's percept has definite form using color for the object appropriate to its natural state. Special subdivisions of the Form-Color-type response are as follows.

F←→C: Where the color is not that of the object in its natural state but its use is forced by S.

Example: Pink mice (Card VIII).

F/C: Where the color is used in a colorless manner merely to mark off subdivisions of the percept. The use of the color is considered arbitrary such as in colored maps (well specified) or anatomical charts.

FC—: Where the percept includes a colored object of definite form, but where the shape of the blot is inconsistent with the percept.

Beck Scoring for Shading (Variations in Light)

Beck indicates that all responses containing determinants based on the shading or variation in light of the blot can be identified by one or a combination of three basic categories. The category is selected on the basis of whether the determinant is one referring to the flat grey, vista or texture. Each of these three basic categories also includes the use of the symbol F, where appropriate, to designate the influence of the form of the blot area.

Y: *The Flat Grey response.* S refers to the blot area entirely on the basis of the flat grey feature. No form is included. The percept may be of real objects such as fog or may refer to abstractions such as depression.

Example: A strange sky.

Example: Ink.

Example: Evilness.

YF: *The Flat Grey response with vague or indefinite form.* S's percept is primarily based on the light variation, with form being of secondary significance. Often the object cited has vague form in itself, i.e., smoke from a fire, storm clouds, x-rays, a dirty rag.

FY: *The Flat Grey response where form is specific and dominant.* In these types of responses S uses the light variation to add specificity, i.e., a black poodle, transparent wings, a person behind a screen.

NOTE: Beck's concept of the Light-Dark continuum *includes all references to the use of blacks, greys and whites* as colors as well as shading. Thus, whenever S uses achromatic coloring as color itself, i.e., snow (using a white space), the symbol Y is recorded in the appropriate combination with F.

V: *The Vista response.* S uses the variations in shading to represent a three dimensional effect such as something seen in perspective. This category usually includes distant landscapes, some aerial views, heights, some architecture, references to insularity, such as land in water, caves and reflections either in water or mirrors. S's language must refer specifically to the height, depth, distance, reflection or insularity in terms of the differential perspective between the object and its surroundings. The scoring of V without F occurs only when the percept is exclusive of any form; i.e., it reminds me of depth, looking into a cave, the inside of a well.

VF: *The Vista response with vague or indefinite form.* S's percept is determined primarily by the vista but includes some indefinite reference to form or utilizes objects which have highly variable form, i.e., trees off on a hill, a canal dredged out of land, a narrow mountain pass.

FV: *The Form-Vista response.* S's percept emphasizes form with reference to the vista component. The larger portion of vista responses are usually FV. The form of the FV response is reasonably definite and critical to the percept, i.e., a bridge, a skyscraper, a steeple, the entrance to a cave, a path leading up between two big elms.

T: *The Texture response.* S's percept contains an interpretation of the light variation which expresses tactual sensitivity. "It is an experience which the skin feels directly." The pure T response involves form-free percepts; i.e., fuzziness, softness, hardness, oiliness, flesh. The mere perception of a tactual object, i.e., fur coat, does not warrant the scoring of T. Instead, S must verbalize in such a manner to indicate an awareness of the tactual qualities of the object.

TF: *The Texture-Form response.* S's percept is based primarily on the texture component but involves form of a vague or indefinite nature or of obvious secondary importance, i.e., a silky dress or shawl, a shaggy little animal of sorts, a fleecy cloud.

FT: *The Form-Texture response.* S's percept is dominated by form but includes specific reference to the texture indicated by the light variation, i.e., an animal skin jacket, a bear skin rug, a greasy wrench.

Klopfer Scoring for Shading

K: *The Undifferentiated Depth or Diffusion response.* S's percept implies depth or diffusion with no use of form. "Implicit is the feeling of formlessness and flux." In some respects this scoring is similar to Beck's V, but there is also some overlap with Beck's Y. Examples are fog, smoke, mistiness, deepness and some clouds. *K may be scored even though the verbalizations of S do not indicate the use of shading.*

KF: *The Depth or Diffusion response with vague form.* In this response S defines the portion of the blot to indicate some form, i.e., spirals of smoke, a tornado, cumulus clouds. Most KF responses are equivalent to Beck's VF, however, some KF responses are more like Beck's YF responses.

Example: Storm clouds, all black and weary looking — Score KF (Beck score YF).

Example: A fire behind clouds — Score KF (Beck score VF).

FK: *The Differentiated Depth of Vista response.* S's percept refers to vista viewed horizontally where the shading contributes to the depth effect. If the concept is one of three-dimensional landscape or architecture, FK is scored even though S fails to verbalize the use of shading. There is great similarity between FK and Beck's FV.

Example: An elm behind some bushes.

FK is also scored for reflections (similar to Beck's FV), where water is used in the shading and for some vista percepts where the view is horizontal, even though the form is relatively unimportant, i.e., a Canadian forest reflected in a lake in the twilight.

k: *The Undifferentiated Shading response.* "Where the three-dimensional effect is projected on a two-dimensional plane in a way that implies no form at all." This is a very rare scoring. The percept is applied to a heavily shaded area.

kF: *The response in which shape is indefinite and shading is undifferentiated.* The most commonly mentioned examples of kF are unspecified topographical maps and most x-rays wherein there is little or no distinguishing of anatomical parts.

Fk: *The response in which shape is definite but shading undifferentiated* — as in the instance of the kF response. Fk is most commonly scored for topographical maps, where a particular country is defined, or for x-rays, where definite anatomical form is described.

c: *The Undifferentiated Surface or Texture response using no form.* Similar but not identical to Beck's T. S must disregard form completely and, as in the instance of C, offer the response somewhat mechanically in several cards. Klopfer considers this response to be quite rare, being found only in cases of severe pathology.

cF: *The Undifferentiated Surface or Texture response using vague form.* S focuses interest on the surface or texture effect, with form only of secondary importance. Many such responses would be scored T by Beck. Examples cited most commonly by Klopfer are snow, rocks, some shaped pieces of fur, coral.

Fc: *The Differentiated Surface or Texture response in which the object has definite form.* Similar to Beck's FT but requiring less definitiveness to the form so that some Fc responses would be TF in a Beckian System.

Example: A teddy bear, marble statue, bearskin rug — Score Fc (Beck score FT).

Example: Crumpled clay, crushed cellophane, silk cloth — Score Fc (Beck score TF).

Klopfer also uses Fc to denote responses in which the shading is used as chromatic color, i.e., the color spectrum, and for percepts in which the shading is used to specify parts of objects as facial features such as lips, mouths, etc., where the gestalt of the blot is not commonly perceived as creating contour.

Example: A totem pole (top of Card VI) with a face — delineating the eyes and nose according to shading components.

Klopfer Scoring for Achromatic Color

C': *The Pure Achromatic Color response.* Where S designates the blot or a portion thereof as black, grey or white with no use of form.

Example: Black paint, grey dreariness.

C'F: *The Achromatic Color-Form response.* S uses a vague form designating the object as black, grey or white.

Example: A grey hair, a white rag.

FC': *The Achromatic Form-Color response.* S's percept uses a definite form in which the object is designated black, grey or white.

Example: A black bat, a grey goose, a white snowman.

NOTE: The scoring of C', C'F or FC' is also used when certain chromatic areas of low saturation such as brown, green or blue are perceived as grey.

NOTE: As previously indicated, Beck scores responses which refer to the achromatic color under the Flat-Grey category (Y).

MULTIPLE SCORING OF DETERMINANTS

The beginner in Rorschach will quickly discover that many responses include the use of more than one determinant, i.e., both color and movement occurring in a single response. The scoring rationale of Beck and Klopfer differ somewhat significantly on how this situation is to be handled, although each insists that all determinants be included in the score.

Beck Scoring for Multiple Determinants — The Blend

Whenever a multiple determinant response occurs, each determinant used is shown in the scoring, using the appropriate symbols separating each from the next with a dot.

> *Example:* (Card II) Two clowns with hats and dirty overalls clapping hands. They look like clowns because of the colors of the hats and painted faces.
> *Scored:* M.CF. YF+.

Any combination of the determinants M, C, Y, V or T may occur. While Beck does not give the specific order in which they should be listed in the scoring, his examples indicate that he follows the general rule of placing M first in the blend, with C apparently being of next importance. It should be noted, however, that there may be instances in which this suggested order may be modified in light of S's emphasis on given determinants.

Klopfer Scoring for Multiple Determinants — Main and Additional Determinants

Klopfer's scoring method calls for only one determinant to be considered as primary to a response. This is called the *Main Determinant.* In the absence of any other determinants, Form is always the Main Determinant. All other determinants, of a response are called Additional Determinants and are separated from the Main Determinant and from each other by commas.

> *Example:* (Card II) Two clowns with hats and dirty overalls clapping hands. They look like clowns because of the colors of the hats and painted faces.
> *Scored:* M, CF, Fc.

In deciding which of the determinants should be Main and which should be Additional, Klopfer has offered the following rules.

1. The Main Determinant is clearly given more emphasis by S in his elaboration.
2. The Main Determinant will usually emerge earlier in the response, often in the free association but at least early in the inquiry.
3. If two or more determinants occur of seeming equal importance, M determinants are always given preference followed in importance by C determinants followed by c determinants. F is never scored as an additional determinant unless a separate locational score is also used. F is occasionally scored as a Main Determinant with other scores as additional determinants when the additionals are vaguely emphasized or emerge only after considerable inquiry.

NOTE: The concepts of Main and Additional are also applicable to the Location scores; however, the terms are defined somewhat differently than for determinants. For instance, combinations of S with W, D or d may exist, depending upon which carries more importance to the response. When, however, an additional area is mentioned in the inquiry and it is delineated in some manner from the basic or primary area, an entire new score is added below the main scoring which will include Location, Determinant and Content.

> *Example:* (Card VIII) A coat of arms — in the inquiry S states, "and these look like two rats" (not mentioned earlier in the response).
> *Score 1:* W CF Emb.
> *add 2:* D F A.

The student should gain thorough familiarity with Klopfer's elaboration on this point.

CONTENT SCORING

The third basic characteristic of the Rorschach score represents the associational content of the response. As Beck indicates, "Anything may be seen and is seen." The symbols used for the scoring of the associational content represent a method of categorizing S's associations in order to make meaningful comparisons,

Beck Scoring for Content

H: Whole Human, i.e., usual human figures and variations thereof, such as angels, Henry VIII, witch, etc.

NOTE: Some scorers prefer to use (H) when unusual variations of human figures occur; however this is not included in the Beck System.

Hd: Human Detail, i.e., any part of a human but not the whole human such as a headless woman, an arm, fingers, a head of a man, etc.

A: Animal (including animal skins) when the whole animal is used.

Ad: Animal Detail, i.e., any part of an animal.

An: Anatomy pertaining to internal organs or internal body portions (including x rays).

Ab: Abstractions, i.e., moods or emotions.

Al: Alphabet.

Aq: Antiquity, i.e., objects no longer in common existence or use.

Ar: Architecture.

Art: Art, i.e., emblems.

As: Astronomy, i.e., moon, stars.

Ay: Anthropology, i.e., totem pole.

Bt: Botany, i.e., plant life.

Cg: Clothing.

Cl: Clouds.

Dh: Death.

Fi: Fire.

Fd: Food, i.e., prepared food (slaughtered animals are A).

Ge: Geography, i.e., specific places and names for geographic details.

Hh: Household.

Im: Implement, i.e., tools.

Ls: Landscape — includes seascapes, ocean floors, etc., as well as variety of landscapes.

Mn: Mineral.

Mu: Music.

My: Mythology. i.e., dragons, trolls (although many of these may be H).

Na: Nature, i.e., sky, wind, rain (includes seashell).

Pr: Personal, i.e., all objects of personal decorative use.

Rc: Recreational, i.e., games, hobbies.

Rl: Religion.

Ru: Rural, i.e., haystack, barn.

Sc: Science.

Sex: Sex.

Tr: Travel, i.e., all means of travel.

Vo: Vocational, i.e., objects closely associated with a specific vocation.

NOTE: It is not uncommon that a single response denotes more than one associational content. In these cases, both are indicated, the primary content being entered first and separated from additional content by commas.

Klopfer Scoring for Content.

Klopfer's conception of association content is essentially identical to that of Beck; however, some of the symbols are different. Additionals are also indicated.

H: Whole or almost whole human figures.

(H): Human figures portrayed as drawings, sculpture, caricatures and mythological figures, i.e., witches, monsters, ghosts.

Hd: Parts of human figures belonging to a living body.

Hobj: Human parts such as false teeth which are not real parts of the body but closely associated with it.

At: Anatomy.

Sex: Sex.

A: Whole or almost whole animal figures.

(a): Mythological animals, monstrous animals, etc.

Ad: Part of an animal.

(Ad): Part of an animal deprived of reality or humanized.

Aobj: Objects derived from or connected with the body of an animal, i.e., fur, skin, wishbone.

A.At: Animal anatomy.

Food: Prepared food.

N: Nature concepts including landscapes, aerial views, seascapes.

Geo: Geographical concepts, i.e., maps, islands, lakes not seen in vista.

Pl: Plants or parts of plants seen as botanical specimens.
Obj: Object (manmade).
Arch: Architecture.
Art: Art.

Abs: Abstract.
Klopfer calls for other content to be specifically cited such as blood, fire, smoke, slime, explosion, etc.

POPULAR AND ORIGINAL RESPONSES

In addition to the three basic characteristics of the Rorschach score, there are some responses which manifest a fourth characteristic pertaining to the usualness or uniqueness of the percept. When a response is identical to those frequently given by a large "normal" population some scoring indication should be included. Likewise, when the response is exceptionally unique when contrasted with other protocols it should be noted in the scoring.

Beck Scoring for Popular Responses

P: *The Popular response.* This symbol is included in the score, after the content symbol, whenever the response meets the criteria for popularity defined by Beck. Beck includes responses based on a selected statistical frequency. This list includes responses for each of the ten cards which he considers as meeting the criteria for scoring P.

> *Example:* Bat or butterfly for the W Card I is scored P. Other figures such as eagles or birds are not scored P.

The scorer using the Beck method should be cautioned to adhere closely to the list of populars given by Beck rather than over-generalize, since each popular response should meet the criteria specified.

NOTE: Beck does not include a symbol in his scoring system to denote original or highly unique responses.

Klopfer Scoring for Popular and Original Response

P: *The Popular response.* While Klopfer's symbol for popularity is identical to that in the Beck method, the criteria are not the same. Klopfer lists only ten popular responses to eight cards (no populars to Cards VII and IX), while Beck's list is considerably longer. The student familiarizing himself with both methods should give care to the differences.

O: *The Original response.* The scoring of the original should not be undertaken by the beginner since the criterion for scoring O is that the response is one that does not appear more than once in one hundred records.

THE Z SCORE AND THE FORM LEVEL RATING

Both Beck and Klopfer have included in their respective scoring methods rationales for assigning numerical ratings to responses. Both rationales and techniques of the two systems differ considerably. In the Beck system, only certain responses are so scorable, depending on the organizational activity manifest in the response. In the Klopfer system all responses may be rated on the basis of a Form-Level criteria.

Beck Scoring for Organizational Activity

Z: *The Organizational Activity Score.* The fundamental rationale for Z is that S combines two or more percepts, which are not necessarily related, into a new percept, which in turn infers S's meanings for the organized details. All W are Z; adjacent details may be Z; distant details may be Z; the inclusion of space detail in the perceived relationship is Z. Beck has discriminated between the degrees of difficulty in achieving each type of organizational activity in each of the ten cards. These numerical values are listed by Beck in tabular form for easy reference by the scorer, together with a comprehensive discussion of the criteria necessary for scoring Z.

Klopfer Scoring for Form Level Rating

There is no symbol representing the Form Level Rating. It is a score appropriately selected from a scale ranging from −2.0 through 0.0 to +5.0. The rating assigned to the response is estimated, using the combined criteria of accuracy (which apply to the fit of the percept to the outline or form of the blot); specification (the improvement of spoiling of the Accuracy based on S's elaborations or "specifications"); and Organization (organization of the various parts of the blot into a meaningful larger concept). Klopfer offers a comprehensive discussion of the Form-Level Rating which describes the method of arriving at the appropriate score.

QUANTITATIVE SUMMARIES

Once the scoring is completed, the data is then compiled by frequencies, percentages and ratios into a useful summary. The examiner is now concerned with the frequency of each type of scoring which has occurred, the total number of responses, the average first reaction time, total reaction time, as well as important ratios between different scoring categories. Table II shows the important ratios, frequencies and percentages used by Beck.

TABLE II

IMPORTANT RATIOS, FREQUENCIES AND PERCENTAGES USED BY BECK

Z sum: Total number of weighted Z scorings

Z f: Simple frequency of Z scorings

EB (Erlebnistypus): The ratio of color to movement wherein C = 1.5; CF = 1.0; FC = 0.5/all M's = 1.0 each

EA (Experience Actual): Combine values of C + M

$$T/R: \quad \frac{\text{Total Free Association Time}}{R}$$

$$T/1R: \quad \frac{\text{Sum of Time for First R}}{10 \,(\text{or } 10 - \text{no. rej. cards})}$$

$$F + \%: \quad \frac{\text{Total No. F+}}{\text{Total No. F+ + F−}}$$

$$A\%: \quad \frac{\text{A + Ad responses}}{\text{Total R}}$$

P: Actual Number of P responses

$$L \,(Lambda): \quad \frac{(F+ \,+\, F− \,+\, F)}{R − (F+ \,+\, F− \,+\, F)}$$

Table III gives scorings and a summary for a Rorschach Protocol using the Beck System.

TABLE III

SCORINGS AND SUMMARY OF A RORSCHACH TAKEN FROM A TWENTY-TWO-YEAR-OLD MALE

I. 13″	1. W F+ A, P	VI. 27″ 8. D F+ A+
	1.0	VII. 5″ v9. W M.FT+ H, P
	2. D M+ Hd, P	3.0
II. 44″	3. D FC+ A, P	VIII. 20″ 10. Dds F− A
III. 9″	4. D CF− Fd	11. D CF+ Fd
	v5. D M+ Hd	IX. 14″ 12. D F+ Hh
	4.0	X. 10″ 13. D F+ A, P
IV. 80″	6. W Y Cl	14. D FC+ Bt
V. 10″	7. D M+ A	
	2.5	

Total Time: 13′ 15″

W = 3	M = 1	H = 1
D = 10	M.F.T. = 3	Hd = 2
Dd = 0	CF = 1	A = 6
Dds = 1	CF− = 1	Bt = 1
R = 14	FC = 2	Cl = 1
P = 5	Y = 1	Fd = 1
	F+ = 4	Hh = 1
	F− = 1	14
	14	

Z = 10.5	F + % = 80
Zf = 4	A% = 43
EB = 4/3.0	Afr = .55
EA = 7.0	T/1R = 23.2
L = .55	T/R = 56.7

Table IV shows the important ratios, frequencies and percentages commonly used in the Klopfer System. It should be noted that several quantitative relationships not shown in Table IV have been suggested as supplements to the Klopfer System (Klopfer, Ainsworth, Klopfer and Holt, 1954, pp. 240-316). They are not listed here since they do not appear on the Klopfer-Davidson *Individual Record Blank* and because the hypotheses concerning their interpretation are less firmly established at this time.

TABLE IV

IMPORTANT RATIOS, FREQUENCIES AND PERCENTAGES USED BY KLOPFER

$F\%$: $\dfrac{\text{Total F}}{R}$

X *unwgt. FLR*: $\dfrac{\text{Sum of Form Level Ratings}}{R}$

(use only main responses)

$\dfrac{FK + F + Fc}{R}$: $\%$

$A\%$: $\dfrac{A + Ad}{R}$

$(H + A)/Hd + Ad =$

Sum C: $\dfrac{FC + 2CF + 3C}{2}$

EB: $M/\text{Sum C}$

$(FM + m)/(Fc + c + C') =$

W/M

$8 - 9 - 10\%$: $\dfrac{\text{No. R to VIII, IX, X}}{R}$

T (Total Time): measured from beginning to end of Free Association Period

Average Time Per Response: $\dfrac{T}{R}$

Average Reaction Time Cards I, IV, V, VI, VII =

Average Reaction Time Cards II, III, VIII, IX, X =

Table V shows scorings and a summary using the Klopfer System for the same Rorschach Protocol shown in Table III.

TABLE V

SCORINGS AND SUMMARY OF A RORSCHACH TAKEN FROM A TWENTY-TWO-YEAR-OLD MALE

I.	13″	1.	W F A P 1.0
		2.	D M Hd 1.5
II.	44″	3.	D FC A 1.0
III.	9″	4.	D CF− Food −1.0
		v5.	D M Hd 1.0
IV.	80″	6.	W K cloud 0.0
V.	10″	7.	D M A 1.5
VI.	27″	8.	D FM A 2.5
VII.	5″	v9.	W M, Fc H 4.0
VIII.	20″	10.	S F A 1.0
		11.	D CF, Fc Food 0.5
IX.	14″	12.	D F obj. 1.5
X.	10″	13.	D F A P 1.0
		14.	D FC Pl 1.5

Total Time: 13′ 15″

R = 14	M = 4	H = 1
T̄	FM = 1	Hd = 2
R̄ = 56.7	CF = 1	A = 6
T = 13′ 15″	CF− = 1	cloud = 1
W = 3	FC = 2	food = 2
D = 10	K = 1	Pl = 1
S = 1	Fc = 0, 2	Obj. = 1
P = 2	F = 4	

$F\% = 29$

$\bar{x}$ *unwgt.* $FLR = 1.35$

$\dfrac{FK + F + FC}{R} = 29\%$

$A\% = 43$

$H + A/Hd + Ad = 7/2$

Sum C $= 3.0$

$M/\text{Sum C} = 4/3.0$

$(FM + m)/Fc + c + C' = 1/0 \ (1/2)$

$W/M = 3/4$

$8 - 9 - 10\% = 36\%$

$\bar{x}$ *RT I, IV, V, VI, VII* $= 27″$

$\bar{x}$ *RT II, III, VIII, IX, X* $= 19.4″$

References

Beck, S. J., Beck, Anne G., Levitt, E. G., and Molish, H. B.: *Rorschach's Test* (Vol. I, 3rd ed.). New York, Grune and Stratton, 1961.

Beck, S. J.: *Rorschach's Test* (Vol. II). New York, Grune and Stratton, 1949.

Beck, S. J.: *The Rorschach Experiment*. New York, Grune and Stratton, 1960.

Hertz, Marguerite R.: *Rorschach Scoring Symbols with Definitions, Scoring Formulae, and Qualitative Notations*. Dept. of Psychol., Western Reserve University (mimeographed).

Klopfer, B., Ainsworth, Mary D., Klopfer, W. G., and Holt, R. R.: *Developments in the Rorschach Technique* (Vol. I). Yonkers-on-Hudson, New York, World Book, 1954

Klopfer, B., et al.: *Developments in the Rorschach Technique*. (Vol. II). Yonkers-on-Hudson, New York, World Book, 1956.

Klopfer, B., and Davidson, Helen H.: *The Rorschach Technique. An Introductory Manual*. New York, Harcourt, Brace and World, 1962.

Piotrowski, Z. A.: A Rorschach compendium revised and enlarged. In Brussel, J. A., Hitch, R. S., and Piotrowski, Z. A.: *A Rorschach Training Manual*. Utica, New York, State Hospital Press, 1950, pp. 33-86.

Piotrowski, Z. A.: Perceptanalysis. New York, Macmillan, 1957.

Rapaport, D., Schafer, R., and Gill, M.: *Diagnostic Psychological Testing* (Vol. II). Chicago, Year Book Publishers, 1945.

Rickers-Ovsiankina, Maria (ed.): *Rorschach Psychology*. New York, John Wiley and Sons, 1960.

Rorschach, Herman: *Psychodiagnostics* (5th ed.). Berne, Switzerland, Hans Huber, 1951.

Schafer, R.: *Psychoanalytic Interpretation in Rorschach Testing*. New York, Grune and Stratton, 1954.

Sherman, M. H. (ed.): *A Rorschach Reader*. New York, International Universities Press, 1960.

Sundberg, N. D.,: The practice of psychological testing in clinical services in the United States. *Amer. Psychol.*, 16:79-83, 1961.

Chapter III

Responses for Practice Scoring

IN this section of the Workbook there are three hundred responses which have been selected from a much larger number. They are extracted from actual Rorschach protocols which have been administered in guidance centers, community mental health clinics, mental hospitals and by private practitioners.

They have been placed in a hypothetical order of difficulty from easiest to most difficult. They include the various location areas of each of the ten blots rather thoroughly and include a large number that occur frequently in Rorschach protocols as well as some which are considerably rare.

One characteristic of the practice responses which should be noted by the student is the variation in length of verbalization, both in the Free Association and in the Inquiry. The student will no doubt rapidly discover that, frequently, the more extensive the verbalization, the more difficult the scoring. In some instances scoring may seem terribly complex and almost impossible; however, the three hundred responses have been examined by Drs. Beck and Klopfer as well as other accomplished Rorschachers, and all can be categorized in either system. Acceptable scorings for each of the three hundred appear in the Scoring Key in the Appendix to the Workbook.

Card No.	Response No.		Free Association	Inquiry	Scoring
I	1		Well this cld b a moth or s. t.	The entire thing gives me that impression with the wgs and this is the body part. Q. It has feelers & its colored like I would expect one to be colored. Q. Well, its grey like moths are. Q. No.	————
I	2		This lower prt ll a bell.	It has the shape like a bell and this is the ringer. Q. It has a hard look like it was metal. Q. Well its dark like metal would b. Q. No, that's all.	————
I	3	>	This could b a tree.	This part right here (D8) its standing there kind of like an evergreen tree. Q. Its just the way a tree would look to me. Q. No.	————
II	4		It ll 2 dogs playing pattycake.	Well everything here except these top red things, they ll 2 dogs, its just their heads & the upper prts of the body. Q. They have paws together like they were touching sort of like playing a game. Q. No, just the heads and ears and the rest that I already said. Q. No.	————
II	5		This lower red part ll it cld b a flower.	Well it extends out with petals & its red like a rose or s. t. like that. Q. Its not really like a rose but some flower like that. Q. No.	————
III	6		This ll 2 people bending over s. t.	It c. b. 2 men I guess like they were carrying s. t. or getting ready to carry s. t. Q. I dk what this thg in the cntr is or these here red thgs, I don't think they r a prt of it. Q. No. Q. It might b a basket of food. Q. I dk I just thot of that. Q. No.	————
III	7		These thgs up here at the top mite b blood spots.	Well they r red and it ll they r running down on the wall or s. t. Q. Like s. o.: got some blood on the wall & its running down. Q. No.	————

Card No.	Response No.		Free Association	Inquiry	Scoring
IV	8		The W thg ll it c. b. a rug.	Well its like one of those bear rugs or s. t. like that W. The coloring gives the impress. of animal fur to me, fuzzy like. Q. U can c the legs and the body prt but theres no head to it. Q. No.	_____
V	9		A bf coming in for a landing.	It has its wgs stretched out & this is the body prt. Q. These wld b the antennae & these r his legs. Q. No.	_____
VI	10		This top prt ll a totem pole.	Well it has the basic shape of one & these thgs sticking out on either side wld b the way its carved. Q. Like an eskimo totem I think they make them that way. Q. No that's all.	_____
VI	11		This ll a bear skin.	The legs r here & this wld b a head & its stretched out like to dry. Q. The W thg is involved. Q. No that's all. Q. Yes the legs and the ragged edges mostly make it ll that. Q. No that's all.	_____
VII	12		2 little girls talking.	They have pony tails & this is the face & this is the nose & mouth & these wld b the shoulders, u can't c the rest of them. Q. No this lower stuff isn't prt of it. Q. No that's all.	_____
VIII	13		This ll 2 muskrats here.	They have legs & the slinky head. Q. It j ll that to me. Q. No that's all they r shaped like that (D1). Q. No.	_____
X	14		This thg at the top ll 2 A's chewing on a stick or s. t.	Right here (D11) like to little bugs with their antennae up here & these r the legs & they r eating on this other thg. Q. No that's all. Q. No.	_____
X	15		This blue area (DI) ll a crab.	It has a lot of legs like a crab has & the general shape of it ll that to me. Q. No thats all. Q. No.	_____
X	16		These yellow thgs dwn here r eggs.	Well they ll 2 fried eggs to me, this drkr yellow is a yoke & the other is the outer prt of the egg, I can't remember what u call it. Q. I guess the coloring more than a. t., certainly if they were blue I wldn't have thot of eggs. Q. No.	_____
X	17	∨	You know if the W thg is turned this way it ll a pretty flower.	Well its very colorful like a flower & this is the stem & these wld b the petals. Q. All of the stuff outside the pink wldn't be included. Q. I can't think of a name, s. t. like a daffodil but that's not what these r. Q. No thats all.	_____
I	18		The whole thg ll a face of s.s. to me.	Well I'd say a wolfe's face with the eyes & nose & mouth. It ll it has a vicious look to it. Q. Well like I said it looks vicious with the eyes & nose & mouth curled up like that. Q. No that's all. Q. No.	_____
I	19		I get the impression of a dead Bf.	It has a ragged edge, like it wasn't alive anymore, with these holes in it too like that. Q. There r wgs and the body & these cld b the antennae. Q. No. Q. No.	_____
II	20		Gee, that ll 2 dogs.	They have heads & bodies, not the entire body but most of the upper prt of it, I can c the nose & face very clearly, they seem to be sniffing at e. o. Q. They sort of ll terriers to me. Q. No.	_____
III	21		This upper red thg sort of ll a stomach.	Well I d. k. exactly why, I guess this wld b the tube going to the stomach itself. Q. I thk the redness helps too bec. it makes it look more like one but it prob. wld ll one even if it not red. Q. No thats all.	_____
V	22		This ll a Bf.	It has wgs spread out like it was pinned down on a board like in a collection. Q. It has the body & these r the antennae. Q. No thats all.	_____
VI	23		This W side prt ll a face like Cyrano.	It has the long nose here and chin whiskers and a little peaked hat on it. Q. Its just the outline that gives the impression, its quite good in fact. Q. The nose & the location of the eye. Q. Well the shape of the chin prt I suppose. Q. No.	_____
VI	24		This ll prt of a bed post.	(D2) it is just this drkr prt here which ll its s. s. of wood post that has been turned out on a lathe. Q. Well it has distinct shape of it Q. No thats all. Q. No.	_____
VII	25	∨	If U turn it upside down like this it ll an outline of Geo. Washington.	Just this cntr white area. Q. It has the outline like that. Q. Ll he has a hat on like those colonial hats. Q. No thats all I can say about it.	_____
VII	26		Say this ll 2 statues which is balanced.	Well they r statues of people I guess, probably s. s. of Indian heads & it ll they r balanced there. Q. I guess theyr gonna fall backwards, the ft. prt must have just broken off and theyr ready to fall bckward. Q. No thats all I can say.	_____

VIII	27		Id say the W thg ll a coat of arms.	Well its symmetrical and there r As on each side which is often on coats of arms. Q. Its very colorful, I d. think it wld ll one without t coloring, that really gives it the total effect. Q. No thats all.	————
VIII	28		What a mess of colors, pretty tho.	Yes I mean it as a resp. The fact that its pretty colorful. Q. Well there's very nice pastel blue & aqua & bright orange & pink. Q. No I can't say a. t. else it just ll nice color.	————
IX	29		This cntr prt is a bowl.	Not really a bowl but a vase I guess thats what I really meant. Q. Well it has the shape like one & it cld hav water in it. Q. Yes, the light blu ll it cld b wtr to me. Q. Not a. t. else to say. Q. I can't say a. t. else & it. Q. No.	————
IX	30	>	This ll a wm running after a child.	She ll a big fat wm who has just caught this child by the hair. Q. Apparently the child was trying to get away. Q. This W green prt here. Q. No thats all its really just theyr outlines. Q. No.	————
X	31		This ll a dog sitting dwn.	Its a big type of dog like a collie. Q. Well the outline gives the shaggy appearance & he's sitting on his rear legs. Q. No thats all. Q. No.	————
X	32		The thg gives the impression of under the ocean.	Well u can c the crabs here with their long feelers (D1) and this pink stuff is the color of coral. Q. This top part (D8) cld be a lobster with the big claws and these green thgs cld b seahorses I guess. Q. Well I suppose the shapes and colors. Q. I guess if I saw it without the coloring it really wldnt re. me of this. Q. Thats all, the rest cld b different sea creatures. Q. Well I know that the coral wldnt ll that if it werent for the coloring but maybe some of the others might still ll that in fact I think the crabs wld look better if they werent blu. Q. No.	————
X	33		I dont c a.t. at all but colors of ink. Blue, red, green, yellow, pink, and grey.	J a cardboard with colors on it as far as Im concerned. Q. Nothing there to c . . . j as colors, thats all.	————
VIII	34		This prt here ll a skeleton, but none of the rest does. J that very little bit.	Right there bec. of it being open. This is like the backbone and here r ribs like on a skeleton. Q. J ll a piece of a skeleton, not the W thg at all.	————
VIII	35		This ll the pelvic zone like you c in a biology book. S.t. they color them like this.	J re me of pictures Ive seen in biology books. Q. I suppose becuz of the 2 regions u c.	————
X	36		A wishbone.	J the color and shape of a wishbone. I cant tell if its lying dwn or sitting up . . . its sort of floating in space.	————
IV	37		A swans head & neck. Perhaps its dead & dropping & this wld b the tail section.	Here's the head & tail. Q. It lks dead bec. the head is hanging dwn. Q. Ll a fluffy tail bec of the lack of color . . . looks fuzzier than the deeper colored area like s. s. of feathers.	————
V	38		This tiny shape is a silhouette of a bird facing outward.	A duck type thg. A very small bill & a head & this little indication of a tail. Q. J the side of him.	————
IV	39		One of those flat fish.	A sting ray with a tail. Q. Its going away from me. Q. Its thin & u can c thru it & it looks slimy & gooshy . . . the texture makes it ll that.	————
VIII	40		The white prt I can c as a gorilla.	Here is the top notch, eye, nose & mouth. A mean looking A. Q. The eye is set back so far & also the mashed nose. Q. From the side in profile.	————
I	41		Ll the letter M	Its just this edge prt here that ll an M.	————
V	42		Ll a little profile of a mans face . . . J the very edge.	There is his forehead, indentation for the eye, & the long nose. Q. Nothing but the profile.	————
V	43		And there's a worm.	J that little prt right there. Q. It j ll it is crawling on the ground. Q. It j ll a worm to me. Q. No.	————
I	44		A coyotes head.	Heres the big nose & ear. Q. Its gray j like a coyote wld b. Q. Thats all.	————

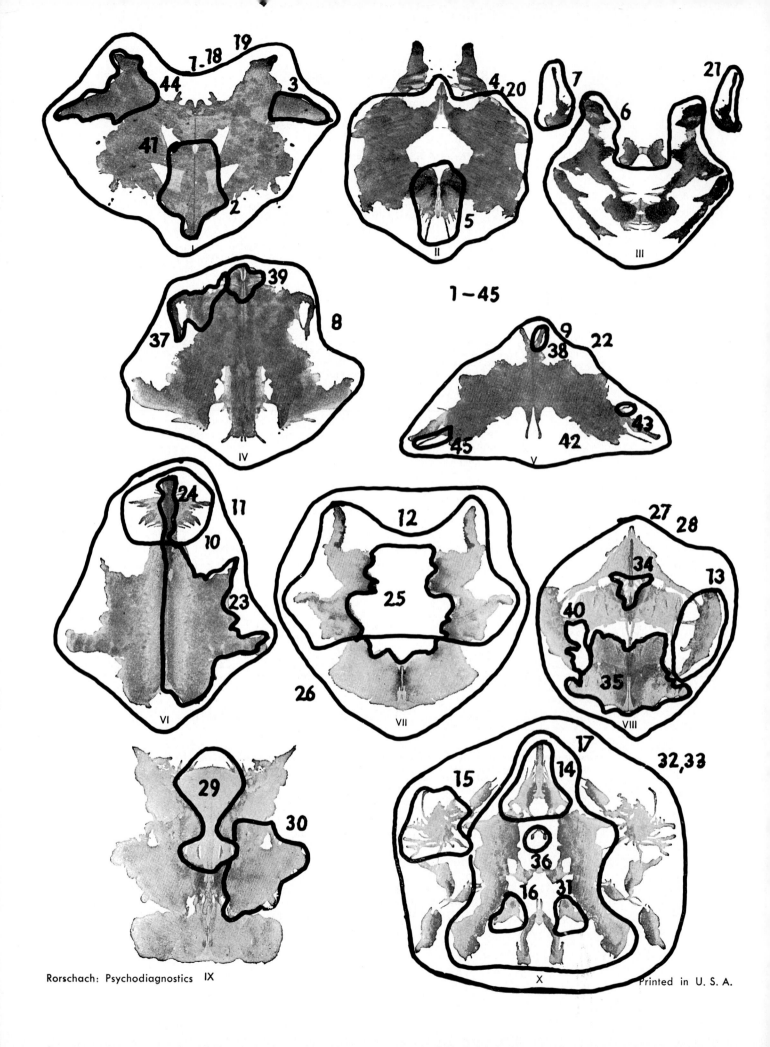

Card No.	Response No.		Free Association	Inquiry	Scoring
V	45		That ll a finger of scorn.	Like something u wld c if s. o. was angry. Like it is pointing sternly. Q. Well if s. o. pointed a finger it wld ll that. Q. Thats all.	_____
V	46		Winston Churchills V for victory.	Like he's holding his hand up for victory. Q. Well, here r the two fingers & this prt is his hand.	_____
I	47		That ll a poodles tail.	Well, it kind of ll a pom pom at the end there. Q. Well, its that little ball of fur the way they clip them. Q. Its fuzzy around the edges. Q. No.	_____
V	48		Shoulder pads.	U kno, lk a football player wld wear. Q. Well, they r big & they r made out of leather. Q. Well, its drk lk leather wld b.	_____
V	49		That ll a nipple.	Well, its kind of shaped lk one. U kno like on a babys bottle. Q. Lk a rubber one on a babys bottle. Q. Nipples r j made out of rubber. Q. It looks rubbery to me. Q. Well I d. k. j s. t. @ it makes it ll that. Q. No.	_____
X	50		Ll one of those paintings where the painter threw blobs of color on the screen.	J the way thgs were blobbed on there. J a sudden impulse reaction. Q. Nothing it was so sudden.	_____
II	51		Footprints.	Here is the arch of the foot like when u come out of the shower or walk on the sand. Q. Its j shaped lk that.	_____
I	52		A crab with its claw spread.	The two bumps r the protruding eyes & its claws r extended. Q. About ready to pinch . . . Its round like one too & this wld b his shell.	_____
II	53		Ts cld b a stomach.	Here. Q. Bec a stomach is shped — Q. No other reason, mayb bec it is red — but a stomach really isn't red unless it is irritiated. Q. No.	_____
VIII	54		Ts cld b some ice.	This being jagged & all. Q. Bec it is jagged & has places where it cld have melted. Q. Bec of different shades of color — dark & light, like it cld hav melted.	_____
I	55		Bf shaped like ones I have seen.	Yes, Ts is tail end. These r wgs. These r some wht spots on back of wg. Q. Yes, black line running down back. Doesn't have everything. Q. Antennae & proboscis. Q. Thats it I guess.	_____
IX	56		Ll a thermometer.	Ll a thermometer in rectum. Q. About the shape of a thermometer. Line gog down center is mercury. Q. J ll it is penetrating anus here. Q. No.	_____
III	57		Ll 2 people bending or trying to lift s.k. of basket.	The legs, body, head, & arms & the basket. Q. Ll girls bec they seem t b wearing high heel shoes & also seem to b "stacked." Skip all the red prt. Q. J holding the basket. Q. From the angle of the legs they seem to b both tugging & not as they both r trying to cooper. Q. No.	_____
II	58		Ll a womans vagina & uterus the ovaries r up there . . . a little narrow. Ll time of menstruation.	Vagina here, this wld b the uterus the hole opening. These wld b the ovaries here. Q. Cut cross-section. Q. The red repres. bl. oozing down from the vagina. Q. No . . the w prt of the body around.	_____
VI	59		A little bird on top.	This has wgs, head like a very colorful bird. Q. Diff. shades re. me of the sorts of colors. Q. Well the liteness wld b liter Cs and dkns wld b drkr Cs. Q. Thats all. Q. No.	_____
VII	60		I c a thermometer.	Mercury is where it is white here. Q. Its sitting in a container & sitting upright, (D6). Q. It is shaped like it. The mercury is light & top drkr. Q. No.	_____
I	61	V	If u turn it upside dwn it looks unhappy.	Looks more ghoulish. There r its eyes & mouth (eyes are Dds 29). Ll it is in some sort of pain. Q. No. Q. Eyes r going down. Mouth is down. Q. No.	_____
VII	62		2 figs. lkng at each other. Mainly heads. Pony tails up in air. Both ll twins.	(Left fig.) Here is pony tail up here. There is outline of face. Here r arms waving goodbye (Dd21).	_____
IV	63		Pot bellied stove.	The legs r extending dwn here. (D1) Q. The design looks precise. Q. It looks like iron. Q. Its the same on both sides.	

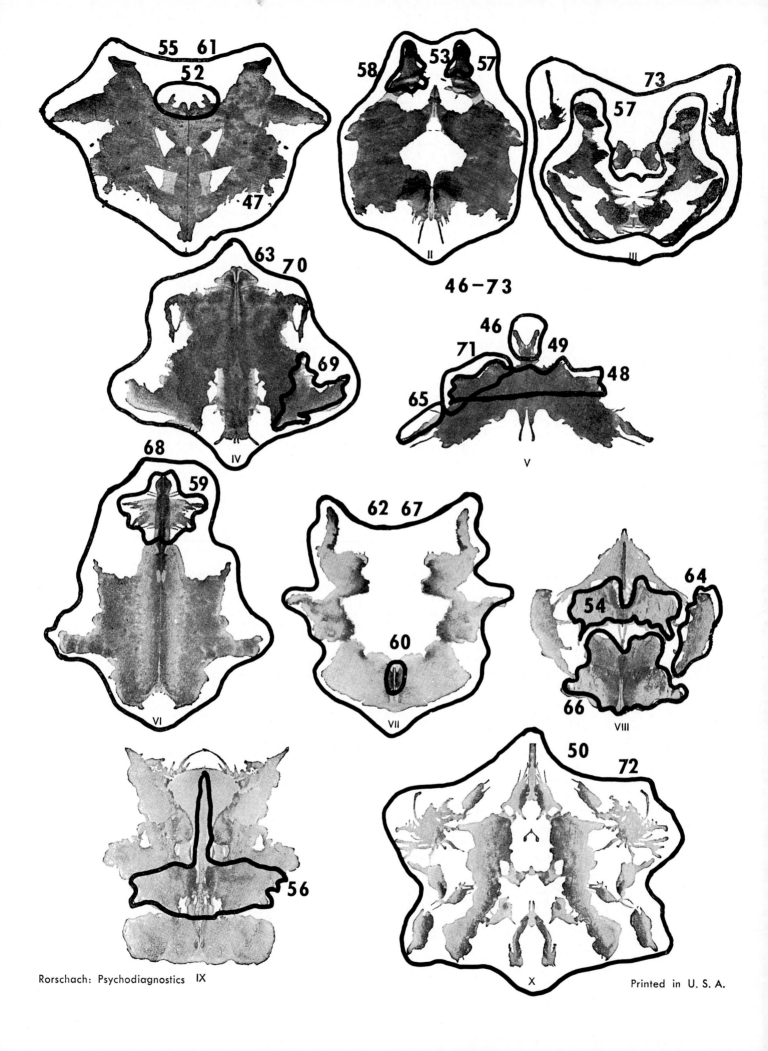

46 – 73

Card No.	Response No.	Free Association	Inquiry	Scoring
			Q. It looks smooth in texture. Q. The lines make it look smooth. Q. No.	
VIII	64	Prt of it ll bld vessels under flesh if s. o. skin were away.	J the pink & the orange (D1, D2). And I was thkg this way . . . when u skin your knee on gravel. Its white then little beads of blood. Its raw w little veins. I wasnt thkg of any shape. Q. This prt where u skinned urself. The liter prt -- its not deep -- not a deep cut. Q. No.	————
V	65	Human limb.	Ll forearm or calf. Excluding hand, or if leg, ex. foot. Just overall shape. Q. No.	————
VIII	66	This upper portion is a Bf.	Ts right here. C had a lot to do with it and overall shape. The way the Cs r blended togthr. Q. Ts is head, and here ı wgs. Q. No.	————
VII	67	Ll a blotch — no—a brooch or pin with 2 dangling objects. 2 dangling objects r scotty dogs.	2 scotty dogs hang by their teeth. Conversational piece. Ts should gold colored, I like gold. A woman looks pretty with gold thgs. Q. Don't know why.	————
VI	68	Sideways I cld c a reflection. The cntr line is the water & this is the foliage. S. k. of bush and a small rock where this liter portion is & it wld reflect in the water. This cld b a weed or wild flowers around the body of water.	The W card. Q. The bushes like clustered — of different sizes or irregular shape — more leaves & stuff. Q. No.	————
IV	69	Ll 2 feet. Thats what I first thot of. 2 boots.	Shaped lk a foot. Here is the heel & its shaped l that. Q. L so was sitting down & had his legs out like that. Q. No.	————
IV	70	Ll a bear skin.	Ll pictures I hv always seen of bear skins tt were hung up to dry. Q. Yes, hung up. Q. The ruffled edges & top part of it looks heavy like fur might b. Head is missing. Q. J kind of looks fluffy. Thats all.	————
V	71	A guys face.	Forehead, nose, mouth open, and beard. Q. Dont know why mouth is open. Q. Hair. Q. Projecting out (D11 & D5).	————
X	72	A bunch of smeared paint — sm kid might have dropped.	Whole tg. Different colors. Blending of Cs. L a splash would make. The blending of blue into red makes it look like it.	————
III	73	This re. me of two African native women & it ll they r preparing s. t. in a pot. Mayb two of them fixing s.t. in a pot.	They seem to b talking & busy. Q. Theyre black & their hair seems very curly & pushed up on their head (points to the edge). That ll a butterfly between the two of them, & that prt cld b the jungle trees (D2).	————
V	74	Cld b a female.	Well the leg; doesnt that ll the leg of a girl to you? Ll it mite be in high heels with the toes pointing dwn but there are no heels. Q. Well, its got the muscles & the general curvature of the leg, if u wanted to go into the study of a womans leg.	————
IX	75 ∨	How about a tree in the Fall.	A pink dogwood, its gotta b pink bec. the color is pink. Q. The shape of it, has a big top & trunk — it doesnt go into anything. Theres no ground for it to go into, its j cut off. The trunk has a suggestion of brown as opposed to the other parts.	————
X	76	Sand crabs.	Lots of arms & 2 big pinchers. Q. It ll hes walking sideways. Q. He also ll hes eating a katydid bec. green here.	————
III	77	2 young men holding s. t. over a fire.	The pink between them might hav been the blaze. Q. Well the fact that they were slender, chests extended, and waist line lks smaller. Q. The other red doesnt count.	————

Card No.	Response No.	Free Association	Inquiry	Scoring
I	78	Ll a halloween cat's face, its black.	J the shape of it, here are eyes and the mouth. Q. Hes leering at me, it lks frightening. Q. Like a mask of one.	————
IV	79	A man sitting on a stool.	Long feet, legs, small arms. Q. He has a heavy wool suit on — or flannel. Q. The colors here. Q. Theyre different in here. Q. Thats all I guess.	————
II	80	Blood veins.	Ll blood cell — veins. Q. Red like blood cells & veins. L when I fell dwn stairs & fell & cut myself. Q. Its all bloody like that. Q. No.	————
X	81	A sex symbol at the top.	That isnt very good — j the shape of the thg. Q. Its basically the same shape as a male organ. Q. It has the testes too. Q. No thats all.	————
I	82	It cld b an eagle.	J the wgs & the head. Q. It j ll a tatoo I saw one that resembled this. Q. It j resembles an eagle in flight.	————
I	83	The rear prts of a monkey.	The prts here ll a monkey when he holds on to wire with his rear end turned in. Q. Thats all.	————
I	84	The resemblance of a face.	Here is the eye, nose, & hair. The chin wld b kind of chopped off. Q. It wld j be a face — not speaking, j one in thot or meditation. Q. Its a man. Q. No.	————
I	85	Head of a dog.	This is the eye, the nose, neck & forehead. Q. Hes looking for s. t. — like affection or a reward. Q. Like a flat faced dog — pekinese or s. t. like that. Q. No.	————
VII	86	Cloud formation.	The ragged edges & the diff in the colors of the clouds. Q. Different shades of the same color. Q. It ll a storm cld to me. Q. Well parts are real dark. Q. No.	————
VIII	87	Ll a bunch of umbrellas standing on top of each other opened up.	Ll u cld get under it & it wld protect u from getting wet. Q. Well I dk why I said bunch cause I dk. Q. I suppose bec. it looks thick-like. Q. Thats all.	————
II	88	Two dog heads.	Ears & side view of heads & they ll their noses r pushed together. Q. Like s. t. knocked their heads together.	————
VIII	89	Color chart like in the navy . . . to see if u r color blind.	In the navy, they ask u what color that is & that is, to see if u r color blind. Q. Well its all those colors like one of those. Q. No.	————
III	90	X-ray pictures of the ribs & upper torso.	Well, the shape of neck & these thgs. ll ribs bec. of the shape of them. Q. Also bec. of this dark spot which wld b the spinal column.	————
VII	91 ∨	It cld represent the ace of spades.	The ace of spades is shaped l this & re. me of it. Q. It just was was that pointed shape like spades have. Q. No.	————
I	92	Ll a teddy bear.	This cld b the ears, head, body, & this is the tail. Q. He cld b standing up. Q. Bec. his tail is down. Q. Thats all.	————
VI	93	This way going dwn like a step, like a couple of steps.	The shape, the outside of it. Q. It ll 2 steps. Q. I dk a. t. else.	————
V	94	Saddle on a horse.	Top prt here is where the fellow sits. Q. The shape of it here. Q. No, just the shape. Q. Thats all.	————
VI	95	This prt here, this black cld b the leg of a table.	Usually on the dining room buffet chairs. Q. (black?) The darker prt, the form of it. Q. Its the form like a table leg. Q. No.	————
IV	96	This prt cld b a backbone.	Well, you see skeletons & you notice the bone. Q. The form of it there, thats all. Q. Its like an x-ray of a bk bone I guess. Q. Black.	————
VII	97	Top of this cld b a squirrel.	Head, Body, tail. Q. He cld b either on the ground or up in a tree standing out on a limb. Q. No.	————
VIII	98	This cld b a twig of a tree.	This cntr prt, this dark prt. Q. If it were the same color as this, it wouldnt b no form to it. Q. Thats all just ll one.	————
II	99	Lipstick or blood.	Looks more like lipstick bec blood is a darker color. Q. J the color, it doesnt ll lips or anything.	————
III	100	A monkey swinging by his tail.	Long tail, legs are here. Q. J the over-all shape of it & its hanging dwn like that.	————

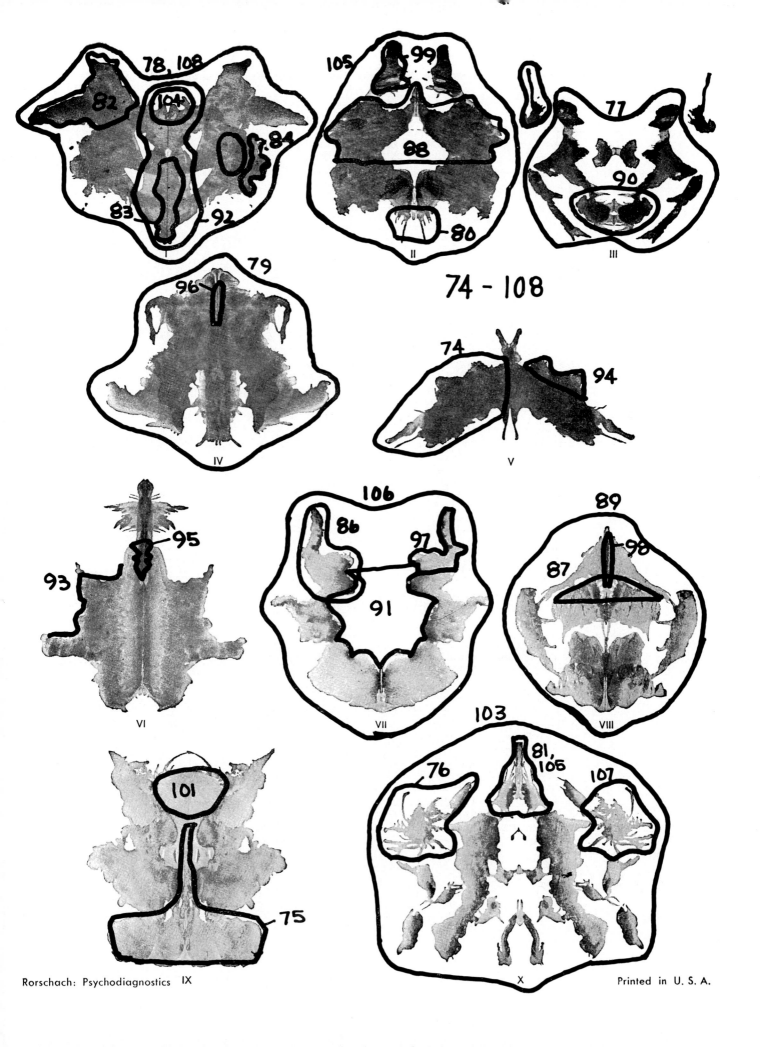

74 - 108

Card No.	Response No.	Free Association	Inquiry	Scoring
IX	101	Mist.	Sort of like for or mist. Q. It ll that thats all — nothingness j the mist. Q. No. Q. Like s. t. u look into but cant see a. t.	————
X	102	That cld b the base for those iron trimmings, on fireplaces.	Usually one on each side. Q. Usually cast iron & this is colored like one. Q. Its gray. Q. Just shaped like one.	————
X	103	That ll a garden of flowers.	I like flowers. Q. All the diff cs re. me of flowers. Q. Dont carry distinct flowers as such, only colorful arrangement lk a flower garden.	————
I	104	This cld b a spider or a . . .	For a spider — 2 hands there — front of it. Not a spider — a crawdad — called it a spider.	————
II	105	Cld b elephants.	2 elephants — one here & one here (both sides). These are eyes, ears, feet, tail, & the what-you-call-it up in front. Q. Standing up.	————
VII	106	Ll 2 mexican girls dancing.	Mexican girls — skirt, hands, heads. Have pigtails. (Dancing?) Their shape. I remember it from TV. Q. Legs, arms, head, like theyre twirling. Q. No.	————
X	107	These ll 2 clams.	Round lk clams. Q. Just ll that to me. Q. Well I can't say a. t. else it just re. me of clams.	————
I	108	Ll a crocheting. design.	All of the dots at side ll prts of material that wld stick out. Q. All of this is open work for the table cloth to show through.	————
II	109	The serrated edge of a knife.	J the edge, thats all. Doesnt ll a knife otherwise. Q. Its just jagged along the edge like that.	————
IV	110	X-ray of a chickens neck.	No head or body — like chopped o. Q. The dark & light areas. Q. The dkness re. me of an x-ray. Q. No.	————
I	111	Cld b a person tied to a stake with other people dancing around.	The wm is in the cntr with her hands up. These thgs r people dressed up in costumes dancing about her. Q. I cant tell what they rep. bec it all ll smoke about her. Q. Yes, it ll smoke bec its all dark & hazy but I dont see any fire.	————
V	112	Right there it ll a match stick.	Well, it j does. Q. Y can c that its black as though it has burned dwn to the bottom & only the charcoal is left. Q. No.	————
VI	113	Theres a fist…like someones going to get poked in the mouth.	Well, u can c it right there like a fist looks. Q. J the way it looks when you make your hand like that. Q. Knocking s. b. out like in a boxing match . . . pow.	————
X	114	The 2 yellow thgs is a couple of pups.	Sitting up like Spitz dogs. Quite a bit of fur on them. Q. (Feels cards J sort of ll u cld feel the fur.	————
II	115	2 elephants facing e. o. w trunk together forming an arch.	1st thg that caught my eye r the 2 trunks facing e. o. w trunks in an arc. 2 heads, trunks coming off the nose. Q. J ll they might b in a circus right now bec thats the only place Ive seen them forming such a pattern.	————
VI	116	Ts ll pituitary gland in the brain.	Except its not bobed, is it? The shape & size in proportion to the mass around it. Q. The pituitary gland, as I re. it, is about the same color as this is. Q. Brain is light grey area.	————
V	117 ∨	A very small portion of it ll a profile of a mans head.	Forehead, nose, mouth, jaw. Q. The forehead, nose, — jaw — ll s. t. Id draw. Q. Cause I cant draw.	————
I	118	Ll a bat thats in the rain.	The shape. Q. From above. Q. Bec. of the wet speckles on it & coming off of it (points to dark spots). Q. J in its flight, theyre falling right off.	————
IV	119	Different depths of water.	The shading — all over — the light to darker shades in the ink itself. Q. L when I flew to Cuba once.	————
IX	120	Rt there it ll 2 fists doubled.	Ll a thumb here, doubled up, & a fist there. Q. A mans fist. Q. No reason — no, j that outline, that prt there ll a thumb.	————
X	121	Ll 2 tomato worms.	Theyre green -- thats what re. me of a tomato worm, its long. Body of it shaped l a tomato worm. Q. Ll its j crawling—thats all.	————
IV	122	This prt c. b. the head of a caterpillar.	J this lower prt (D1) ll that w the feelers sticking out. Q. It ll its crawling out from under a leaf the rest of this blob c b a leaf I guess it has kind of a ragged form like one wld hav. Q. Oh u can c the middle vein of the leaf but I really didnt think of it as one until I got to talking about the caterpillar. Q. No.	————

Card No.	Response No.	Free Association	Inquiry	Scoring
IX	123 ∨	It cld b an atomic explosion if u turn it upside dwn.	The pink stuff wld b the fire cld, u kno the mushroom effect & all ths other stuff wld b the smoke & fire, especially the orange ll fire to me. Q. Well the green is real billowy & the diff. colors of green make it ll smoke to me & the W thg is pushing upward to make the mushroom cld. Q. No.	————
II	124	Ths lwr prt, no not j the lwr prt but ths cntr too, it ll the organs of a wm, its sort of weird.	I d. k. how to describe it very well, I guess it has the outline of it with the bottom prt repres. hair — the midl prt being the actual opening. Q. Well the way that its painted dwn here gives the impress. of some hair, this is sort of vulgar to me, but it ll hair & here I c the, uh, well u kno the opening kind of lk it was waiting or no, even begging for it. Q. I cant say anymore. Q. It j looks spread out like it was waiting. Q. No.	————
II	125	This top prt ll a pagoda.	L the top of a temple made of s. k. of shiny metal, l gold or platinum. Q. The way that it stands off in the distance really made me thk of it. Q. I dont kno exec. it has a shiny appearance of it like some precious metal wld hav. Q. I d. k. I guess I thot of it being in the distance bec. its small. Q. No.	————
IV	126	Id say it ll a monster of s. s.	Hes sitting on a stump the way it lks. to me. Q. Well its lk I c him in perspective lk I was laying dwn & lkg up at him. Q. Hes all furry lk s. k. of mysterious monster u c in books about the beginnings of man. Q. Thats all, I can c his arms & huge feet & body but Im not sure about the head, it must b back there but I dont see it. Q. No.	————
IV	127	A dirty boot (D6).	It has the gen. outline of a boot thats all worn out & prob. real muddy. Q. The way it is shaped there resem. a boot real well, actually theres 2 of them but I was really ref. to this one (on left. Q. O its all drk & wrinkled up lk a boot. Q. No thats all. Q. I guess the smudgy coloring of it makes it lk that way. Q. No.	————
VI	128	This cntr prt (D5) ll a deep pit.	Its a cutaway view of lk a mine shaft or s. t. lk that. Q. U can c the diff. types of coal repres. by the changes in coloring. Q. The whitish prt wld b like the elevator shaft I guess. Q. No thats all. Q. No.	————
VIII	129	It ll s. k. of drawing of s. b. insides.	I guess lk u mite c inside s. o. if u opened them up. Q. Its all diff colors lk the liver here I guess (D5) & ths wld b s. bones (D3) & ths m b lungs here on sides. Q. Suppose that the W thg cld b s. o. insides, lks gory. Q. No.	————
IV	130	The w thg is j black on a piece of crdbrd.	Thats all I can say ab it. Lk at it & youll c that it j ll black ink w shades of gray in it. Q. Thats all.	————
VIII	131	That ll a confection — a soda jerks dream.	Its com. with marshmallow, raspberry, blueberry. Q. Heres orange & lemon sherbet & all the various syrups. Q. All the colors mk it ll that & the diff. shades with those little lines in it mk it ll that grainy, icy look.	————
IV	132	The top ll a mold or fungus that grows on trees.	The texture & shading eff. mks it ll the type that grows on trees. Q. Its sticking out of the paper, three dimensional lk. Q. J the shading & the way Im used to seeing it on trees, sticking out.	————
IX	133	A crab — the liter portions wld b shell & the appendages here wld b the claws.	The white area wld b the shell. The claws r open s. w. but Im lkng dwn on it lk it was on a table, lying there.	————
I	134	Theres a map there of s. p. w islands off the coast.	J that prt there w the islands off in the watr. Q. I d. k. — no place Ive ever seen, but the diff. shades mk it ll one of those maps in school where the diff. colors show the heights of mts & stuff.	————
II	135	Ths cld b one of those prehistoric shell thgs.	Here. Q. Hrd shelled. Q. Bec its the way they were. Q. J the shape. Q. D. k. Q. Well those kind r hard shelled I guess. Q. No.	————
III	136	Ths cld b a nice splatter of blood here.	Right here. Q. Its red, ll it hs thickness. Q. The drkns of it. Bec. of the thickness of blood, it has stayed the way it was splattered. Q. Nope.	————
IX	137	A dressed up teddy bear.	These ll his ears & here is jacket. Ths wld b zipper dwn front & these wld b his pants (D3). Q. They r round ab the shape of	

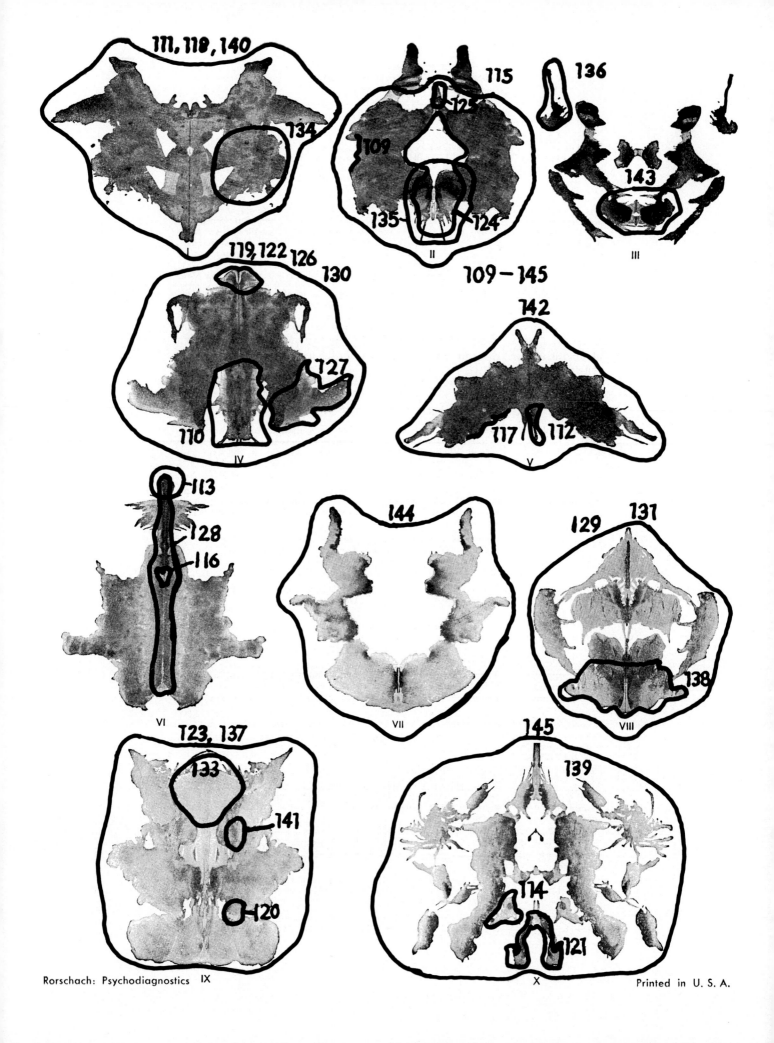

Card No.	Response No.	Free Association	Inquiry	Scoring
			the one u c in story bk. Q. L1 his arm comin out here. Q. J the pants dwn to thighs. Q. Thats it. Q. Color to some extent I suppose, makes it look fuzzy. Q. No.	————
VIII	138	Mushrooms growing.	Here they r. Q. Theyre an off color yellow & pale. Q. Shape. Q. No.	————
X	139	2 little gray men at top. Sm to b arguing over s. t.	Here r 2 lit gray men. (D8) Standing on 2 legs & hv an arm or leg out at side. Q. Dont l very happy at each other — sort of unhappy. Q. J the fact tt they hv their mouths open & r talking.	————
I	140	Face of a devil.	His horns & his nose r shiny cause hes not (D3). Litl white spot mks u think its shiny. Q. The horns mk me think of the devil. Q. Eyes r slanted, he lks mean.	————
IX	141 <	A dinosaur skeleton head.	Right here (D2). Q. He lks old cause of the color. Q. The color ll a skeleton. Q. No, it ll its brownish l a dried skel. wld b. Q. No.	————
V	142	The W thg gives me the impress. of a ballet leap.	Mainly bec. of the 2 projections w heads together & toes pointing out. The curve here makes me thk of that. Q. J from the feet. Hav square toes & all. Q. I c it sort of as an abstract j lk a graceful leap. Q. No.	————
III	143	Taffy being pulled apart.	This prt (D7) & when you pull taffy its stringy lk that. Q. Lk these r the 2 big balls of taffy & where the liter shadows r it comes out in points that mks it ll strings. The middle prt is stronger & that stays together longer. Q. No.	————
VII	144	Mayb the rough edges ll an ice sculpture.	The W thg ll snow or frosty. Q. I d. k. why it ll snow. Q. Thr must b lite s. p. bec it is reflected from the side. Q. J has that feeling of snow. Q. J ll snow, but I d. k. why.	————
X	145	Re me of a movie — 20,000 Leagues the Sea — the caves whr the colors were (W).	In a cave & the crystalization made e. t. reflect its own lite. I was only thkng of the color w no shape at all. It was a pretty effect. Q. J the color. I didnt c any shape. I d. k. why I thot of that. Q. No.	————
VI	146	It ll s. s. of large container that had a plant in it that is dead.	All of it. Q. The plant lks shriveled & these streaks here appear stiff l a dead plant is. Q. Theyre sticking out strait. Q. Its the shape. Q. No.	————
V	147	Ll a jet plane.	Its flying thru the cloud. Q. Its hazy & cloudy around the wngs. Q. Its drk & u cant c thru it.	————
II	148	Ll an x-ray of pelvic region.	Yes, 2 sides r stronger prt of pelvis. Cntr is prob. visceral prt — genitals. U hv these little liter areas u wld c in an x-ray. Prts in between r bones. (Cntr line.) Is extension of spinal cord. Q. Ovaries of woman or gonads of man. If I wanted t b a sexual pervert. Q. Besides its wht they ll.	————
VI	149	Re. me of an amoeba or s.t. that one sees thru a microscope. C a rippling movement.	His movement is forward — as an — in hs ripples. Up at the top is his mouth. Q. Ths thgs at the side help amoeba to move. Q. These lite & drk areas mk it ll ripples.	————
IX	150	Ts ll a ref. in water. Ts ll the line, u dont very often c clouds lk that.	Hr is line (thru cntr of card) — kind of brown. Ths ll trees. Ths mst b clouds reflected in wtr. Q. (What mks them ll trees?) The C & shape. Q. (Why do they ll clouds?) Cannot think of a. t. else tt wld b up there & catch reflection in wtr. (D2, in prt is trees & D3 & 1 & 9 r clouds).	————
VIII	151	When u lk from one end up it re me of the opening of West Side Story — changing colors & all.	Lkng up its lk at a spectrum. When they change colors, they change the names. The changing of the colors as u lk up. Q. If u lk up quick or dwn. J the change in color re me of the change in color — the opening. Q. No.	————
II	152	Ll a crow in flight. mayb it ll s. b. hs shot him. H lks kind of bloody.	Hr is his head & here r his wgs. He is flying. Q. Hr is blood. (Head is D4) Q. The red — the black re me of a crow.	————
V	153	A cloud formation. A thunder storm.	W thg. Is a bl cloud. Heres trails behind it. Q. Usually r a liter C than rest of cloud ordinarily. Caused by wind.	————

Card No.	Response No.	Free Association	Inquiry	Scoring
VII	154	A chain of lakes.	Ll small connec. channels. Shore line. Q. Rough coves. Sm sandy beaches. Q. Liter C than rest of them. Q. Land is white . . . & drk is water.	————
VIII	155	Couple of Bfs.	Hr is one & hr is other. Hr is split tail. Q. Hr is head. Q. Going towards e other. Q. The variations of C make them ll Bfs. Q. No.	————
II	156	It ll it cld b coming out of Aladdins lamp.	2 genies, but the lamp isnt hr. Q. Right hr 2 feet r coming together out of the lamp, & their head r right hr, ths r arms & that the head. Q. No, they r vague & drk blk that ll a cloud.	————
II	157	Ts cld b s. s. of face, on it eyes, 2 eyes & a mouth (Ws.)	Ths ll eyes (Dds 30), ths is the nose, mouth (Ds5, D3). 1st thot it had s. s. of beard, & mustache there. Q. Ths prt in here ll eyes, sorta liter in there makes it ll the eyes sorta bulge out, lk sorta sad bec. they r slanted dwn & if they were eyes they r not wide open, sorta slanted shut. Really cant c the w mouth, ll a mustache. Q. Bec. of the fringed prt there (edge).	————
II	158	Praying hands.	Rite hr & on top (D4): they seem t b pointed up, seem t b a distinction thr between the fingers & wrists: of course there arent any fingers clearly distinct. Q. Fin. wld b the liter prt & wrists wld blge out whr the drkr prt is.	————
II	159	Blood stains.	They r right in hr on both sides. They ll finger prints that hav touched blood & then pressed against s. e. Ll the size of a fingertip & the lines going across seem to give the texture of skin. Q. I mentioned the color & then the fact that they ll not fresh blood but blood thats been dry. Q. The color.	————
III	160	Ll 2 butlers or waiters in real formal dress, picking up lrg kettles or s. t. It ll a sloppy kitchen where soup or whatever they got in the kettle is slopping all over.	Q. Mainly bec. they r holding their heads sort of alert & straight. They r always trying t b very formal. Ll they are leaning over this which cld b a kettle of s. t. They ll theyr wearing stiff straight collars of s. s. bec. this section here lks very straight. Q. Actually I said it ll a sloppy kitchen, stuff splashed around, Q. I was thkng of soup, mayb bec. of the color, tomato.	————
III	161 V	A battered stork.	Ths 2 thg dwn here (D2). They lk the worse for wear, the feathers r all battered, disheveled (points to edge). Q. Ll 1st a bird bec. of the feather type of effect & 2nd a stork bec. of long legs. Q. The lgs lk a little bowed in sense that theyr carrying little too much weight, the heads drooped & implies a forelorn feeling: it doesnt seem to hav too much stamina. Q. No.	————
III	162	Hr r 2 foetal dogs hanging by umbilical cords, hanging upsd dwn (D2).	Hr: Q. The shape of the head, the rest of the body is not too def. except for the paws that hav been pulled behind them: very sadistic. Q. U get the impres that eyes r still closed, & thr is no hair on them. Q. Eyes arent open bec thr is no indentation thr. Q. The shade of red, lks to me almost beige, the color of skin & not hair: thats the way I wld picture . . . the impres that I got from the picture.	————
V	163	If u were lkng at the white prt dwn here, it ll people huddling around a flame, or it ll they cld b lkng into it or s. t.	Ts wht prt dwn hr (all white space across the bottom of the blot) ll 2 people. I suppose just bec thr is prt that ll a head & ths cld b a flame bec of the shape pointing upwrd (Dds27). Its a bit too symmetrical but it cld b. Q. Bec. of the rough outline: they cld b peering into it as if they were just trying to get warm or they wldnt b so close lkng into it.	————
VII	164 <	It cld b a cloud formation reflected in water.	If ths were the horizon hr (W, cntr line) ts wld hav to b lkng at a body of watr that went clear out to the horizon. Ths wld b the clouds (D8). Q. They hav a sort of blurry, hazy lk: they dont lk like anythg extremely solid, like sorta hazy. Q. The fact that there is two.	————
VII	165	Ll girls w pony tails lkng at e. o.: theyre pony tails r sticking up in mid-air . . . By the way, the girls hav dirty faces from eating chocolate.	Ths r the pony tails & u know where girls usually hav bangs, thrfr these ll bangs to me. The rest of hair, if it was pulled up, wld ll that. Thr is no suggestion of strands of a. t. lk that, j silhouetted. Q. Its black, dirty, drkr: its choc. bec its the drkst of the candies. Besides little girls lk choc. candy: besides I lk. choc. candy.	————

Card No.	Response No.	Free Association	Inquiry	Scoring
VII	166	Mayb somebodys mouth.	That wld b if you disre. any of the ink prt. If u j lk at the wht. prt: ths ll it wld be nostrils & ths wld b the prt in a big smile, w mouth open. Q. No. Q. No.	————
VII	167 ∨	Stalactites.	Ths simply seem t b hanging & appear rough & sharp bec of the coloring. (D5) Q. The accent, the drk hr on the lite. Q. They seem conn. only on 1 side, at the top hr & suspending.	————
VIII	168	From the texture, not from the shape or a. t., ll diff. kinds of ice cream or sherbert—straw-berry, orange, lime.	The texture ll its grainy might b sherbert or ice cream. Q. Bec of the colors orange, raspberry, strawberry.	————
VIII	169	Mayb a volcano.	(W) In this respect, ths drk area ll it mayb ready to burst Re me of a geography bk or s. t. whr they show u all the diff. layers & show u whats causing it to burst away out at the top. Q. Except for that sloppy prt whr lava flowed dwn over sides, mainly the color, the diff. colors. Q. No.	————
VIII	170	Here we go — we hav the rocket ship taking off: its tak-ing off bec its got red flames shooting out from the bottom.	This is very indefinite, from here to the top there is some sug-gestion of a ship but what caught me was red flames shooting out like this. Q. Its traveling out back: 1st it comes out in a stream & then flames out. Ths dwn hr wld b flames & smoke: all the red & pink. Q. No.	————
IX	171	Well, this mite b a couple of spread thighs here, w the vagina there. (D6)	The contours r round & it seems to hav a human glow, a pinkish glow of flesh. Q. No.	————
X	172	This up here ll a couple of roosters, I thk or parrots. Sm kind of birds having a serious disc. over s. t.	These 2 litl thgs (D8) hr. They ll they mite hav beaks, eyes, & s. t. sticking up on top of their heads lk the combs of a rooster & that ll a tail. Q. From the expression on their faces if u can call them that: they lk kinda serious. The mouths appear to b open & talking.	————
IX	173	Ths r male faces, eyebrows, eyes. Ths projections r not arms, but a picture of thr speech between them.	The projections ll speech, not physical contact. Q. Almost as if they r spitting fire towards one another, s. t. fierce or heated. Q. I thk the color suggested it.	————
II	174 <	A rabbit ice sliding on a pond.	No snow on this pond tho, bec. this is his reflec. Q. The line hr. Q. He cld b sliding across it running away from some dog or hunter. Q. No.	————
I	175	Ll a heart: Dads heart.	Heart in cntr. Inside on sides hr & Dads tail bone dwn hr. Q. Wait & Ill show u clothes off. Q. Dk. Q. Dk. Q. C tail bone & heart, hr. Q. Prt of my Dad. J body. Q. Dk. Q. Hip bone on side. Q. Dk.	————
II	176	Mans penis.	Here — j a slight resemblance to one, thats all. Q. Well, in an erection, I guess. Q. No.	————
VI	177	A canal.	Straight thru the cntr. Q. The prt hr is wider & it ll the forma-tion of a river. Q. Im lkng dwn lk a map or s. t.	————
II	178	Ll an x-ray of a stomach & be-tween the ribs.	These ribs hr lk in an x-ray. Q. I cant say j why it ll an x-ray, it has hole in it. Q. Its drk lk an x-ray.	————
X	179	This ll a pen point.	The line dwn the middle & the discoloration of the pen point. From the midl dwn is the iron or silver point. Q. The color makes it lk diff. between the upper & lower prt. Q. Its shaped lk a pen point.	————
VI	180	A cat.	Well ths 2 thgs sticking out hr r the whiskers lk on a cat, so ths wld b the rest of him. Q. Thats all.	————
I	181	Ths lks. s. t. lk an x-ray but I d. k. what of. Its drk & lite lk one wld b.	There is nothing I can tell u about it except that it is s. t. lk bones showing thru hr.	————

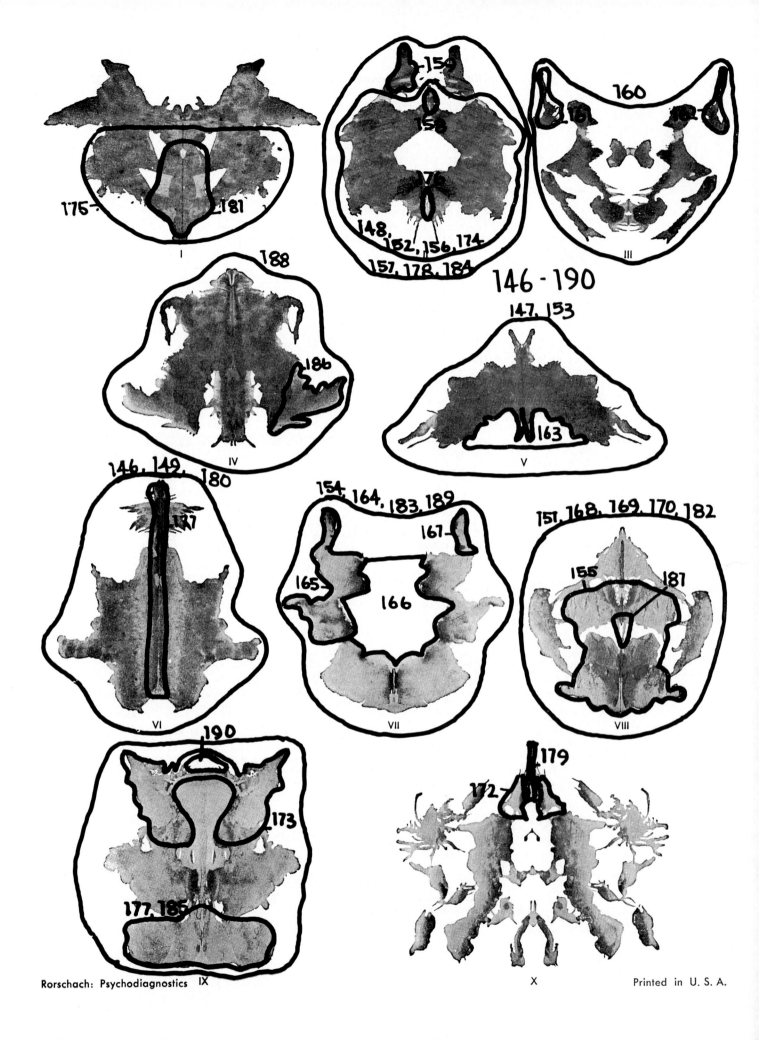

Card No.	Response No.	Free Association	Inquiry	Scoring
VIII	182	Ll some type of — lk the inside of s. t. wld u say?	Thats what it ll to me. Hr it ll lungs & bronchial tubes & this ll prt of the diaphragm. Ths is similar to the intestine & extending straight dwn is the spinal column. Q. Ive dissected a few As — but it really re me of a biology book. Q. Its colored lk it.	_____
VII	183	A coral atoll the South Pacific or a lagoon.	Atoll — a build up of a coral deposit until it reaches the surface of the ocean. However, it is too much alike to b an atoll. Q. J the irregularity of the shore line & a lagoon hr w the water. Q. As viewed from above lkng straight dwn lk from an aircraft.	_____
II	184	A lion with mouth open, bloody eyes & bloody mouth.	The rest of his head. Q. Hes alive & hungry. Q. Hes going to jump at u. Q. His eyes & mouth r dripping blood out of them. Q. Well, its all red at his mouth. Q. No.	_____
IX	185	Pink candy cotton.	Pink. Thats ab the only thg, & the cotton texture. Q. Thats all. Q. Well it ll its fuzzy.	_____
IV	186	Gray stuff re me of snow.	Ll snow that has thawed at one time or a. o. bec. of its irreg. Q. The shape of it, too. Q. Color is import. but it wld b dirty for snow.	_____
VIII	187	A milk bottle.	Well, its white lk one wld b & its shaped lk it too. Q. J on a doorstep in the morning.	_____
IV	188	Cld represent a piece of skinned fur from a bear. Badly skinned job.	Badly skinned fur piece. Q. Well the drk prts here — thats black — & it even lks furry.	_____
VII	189	A string of clouds.	Diff. patterns of clouds that r a smoky lkng color — kind of grayish. Q. Mostly the coloring.	_____
IX	190	Snow.	Its white — thats all. Q. Its such a pure white that all I cld thk of was snow.	_____
V	191	A Bf.	The way the wngs r spread & the shape. Q. J the shape. Q. If the wngs werent spread lk that it wldnt ll a Bf. Q. Its j there — I guess I c it from above.	_____
III	192	A bird.	Heads, white collars, black feathers. Q. Doesnt ll feathers but it is black. Q. Sitting on a limb.	_____
VI	193	Lungs.	The shape of it. Q. Its liter color brought it out more. Q. If it were drkr it wldnt hav shown, its lk an x-ray of lungs really. Q. No.	_____
IX	194	An attractive vase	Its a very pretty blue, hazy. Q. No. Just the blueness of it made me thk of a vase. Q. It has a vase shape too. Q. No.	_____
IX	195	This ll fall, color of orange.	J the orange prt. Ive seen so many flowers that color. Q. No object, j the color — its j fall.	_____
VIII	196	The colors in this r blue, orange, pink, gray.	Its kind of pretty w all those colors.	_____
II	197	A cross up here.	A cross, an emblem in the shape of a cross. Q. No j an emblem, its vague but thr in this litl prt. Q. No.	_____
VIII	198	Mountains.	This resemb. mts as seen on a map. Q. Drk & lite places in there — theyre pictured. Q. The drkr prt is used to rep. mits lk they do on maps.	_____
VII	199	Some statues facing e. o.	Head, neck, arm sticking out hr. Q. They kind of lk grainy l a statue wld lk. Q. Bec. of the coloring in here. Q. Lks as tho theyre not real. Q. No.	_____
V	200	A huge man w a cape dragging 2 bodies. Its walking away from me.	Its a strange H of s. k. Q. Legs, arms, head, & body. Q. A rabbits head on a bats body. Q. What an imagination. Q. Bodies r people — I cant tell too well tho. Q. It ll it is in bk of them, Q. No.	_____
VI	201	A bird getting ready to take off.	This top prt. Q. Wngs, head — these ll feathers. Q. Its white & gray in here. Q. He hasnt taken off yet, but hes ready.	_____
X	202	A flower j starting to bloom.	This yellow prt here. Q. It ll its opening up. Q The shape made it ll that. Q. Probably a rose.	_____
VIII	203	Easter.	All the diff colors cld b eggs in a basket. Not really that but I thk of Easter. Q. It cld b shaped lk an easter basket. Q. Pink, orange, blue, general shape of a basket. Q. It rep. Easter.	_____
III	204	2 people being pulled apart.	By the way theyre stooped over it ll s. t. is pulling them bkwrds. Q. Legs, arms, bodies, heads. Q. They arent doing a. t. but being pulled bkwrds. by s. t. I d. k. what.	_____

Card No.	Response No.	Free Association	Inquiry	Scoring
X	205 ∨	E. t. is flying off in diff. directions.	These colors r j flying apart. Q. Mayb a lite being broken into its component colors. Q. Nothing else — its j flying apart in blobs.	————
II	206	Red ll s. t. burning.	J the fact that it was red. Q. I cant c what is burning thru, mayb a fire, yeah a bonfire. Q. No.	————
VI	207	This ll a violin.	J the cntr from top to btm. Q. J came to mind bec of shape & drk prts — lk highly polished wood. The black prt at top ll the black handle of a violin.	————
VII	208	The head of a cobra.	J c arched head & prt of neck. Poised, ready to strike. Q. J the head up like to strike. Q. No.	————
IX	209	Its awful — I c 2 eyes there.	They r looking at me. Q. Only c eyes. Q. They ll it — monster — not human but certainly no A.	————
IV	210	Pr. of boots.	Heel, toe prt — cowboy boots. Hrs buckle to put them on w. Q. The tall type of black boots hanging up on sm sort of object. Q. Theres a post in bk of them	————
II	211	The cntr ll a temple of worship w a tower of silver or platinum.	This white prt ll the temple & this thg hr ll the tower & its colored. Q. I cant tell u a. t. else except mayb that the metal prt is what really attracts people to the temple.	————
IV	212	Ll s. big monster out of science fic. sitting on a stump & Im lkng up at him.	The W ll that, ths is the stump & the rest is the mons. Q. Well its a grotesque shape & it lks furry all over. Q. Yes its lk I was sitting or lying on the ground lkng up at him. Q. J some science fic. kind of indefinite thg w a pair of boots on. The boots r drkr & the top is liter.	————
VIII	213	That blue in the middle cld b a rectangular patch lk on pant legs.	It ll its being torn apart now. It re me of the kind of patch kids wld hav on their dungarees. Q. Well its blue & its tearing & its rectangular.	————
I	214 ∨	Well, Ill be — theres a penis.	Its right there. Q. Well j the shape of it — erect I guess u cld say. Q. No thats all.	————
II	215	Blood.	The color red. Q. Lk u cut your thumb. Q. This is chicken bld bec of the liter & drkr colors. If it were your own bld, it wldnt hav these streaks in there.	————
VIII	216 <	2 mountain sheep.	Walking across rocks. Q. The gen. shape & the rest of it mk up the mt. or rocks. Its by a lake & this is the reflection in wtr. Q. J the reflection.	————
VII	217	Ll clouds.	Bec. they lk fluffy & theyre sound — they hav kind of a floaty lk — edges r kind of feathered. Q. Theres diff. shadings in them — this litl liter spot in middle mks it lk kind of round.	————
X	218	A human body cut open.	Not complete, but its cut & laid open. Q. J the lower prt of a person. Q. The diff colors suggested it. There r no definite prts — I guess j made me thk of the insides of a person.	————
I	219	A question mark.	Its j these litl thgs here, they ar formed lk a ?. Q. They j ll that to me. Q. Thats all.	————
VI	220	I like the feel of this one.	Feels fuzzy (rubs card). Q. Also like pretty lite & dark gradations — mks it lk fuzzy. Q. No, doesnt ll a fur or anything.	————
I	221 ∨	A crown.	It j has the outline of a crown the way I c it. Q. The pointed prt in cntr & curled prts on the edges. Q. No its j this white prt here. Q. No that.	————
II	222	The indian on the nickel.	He has the protruding jaw lk that indian has & his gen profile is lk that. Q. No thats all.	————
III	223	It ll a martini glass.	Its mostly this white prt but this drkr area is included too, it must hav a clouded stem or s. t. Q. It j has that shape to me. Q. No.	————
III	224	A finger pointing.	It cld ll a whole hand in fact w the thumb & this wld b the finger pointing out toward s. t. Q. It j has that lk to me. Q. No.	————
IV	225	Gee that ll a tooth.	It must hav some decay in it the way its shaded there. Q. I sup. I mean this prt here j the tooth & the drk cntr ll decay. Q. It ll one of those big black teeth I dont know the name. Q. No.	————
V	226	A fellow from the Ku Klux Klan.	It j ll one of those guys dressed up in a sheet with the big pointed hat affair. Q. It j re. me of that. Q. No.	————

191 - 230

Card No.	Response No.	Free Association	Inquiry	Scoring
V	227	A straight pin.	Right dwn the cntr, this drk line & up at the top it is a litl larger where the head of the pin is. Q. In fact as I lk at the top it is more lk an needle cause u can c the place where the thread wld b, the eye of the needle. Q. No thats all.	____
X	228	Lungs.	They j ll that to me — thats what I first thot of when I looked. Q. I suppose the way they r shaped there. Q. No thats all.	____
VI	229	A motor boat tearing thru water.	Well this lite prt here is the motorboat — speed boat I should say & this line is the wake of it aftr it has sped thru the wtr. Q. Oh no this outer prt isnt included j the cntr prt rite hr & the boat itself. Q. It doesnt ll a boat real well but I j guessed it was. Q. I d. k. a. t. else	____
VII	230	2 people standing holding hands.	It ll a man & wm j standing there holding hands w e. o. Q. Well they r gen. shaped lk 2 people & one lks a little more lk a man than the other. Q. The shape I guess. Q. No.	____
VII	231 V	Geo. Washington's head.	I cant really say its him but its the type of hat that he wore & u hav to imag. a face hr. Q. U can even imagine the round cheeks. Q. J this white prt hr. Q. No thats all.	____
VII	232	A unicorn.	Well its j this litl prt. Q. It has the horn sticking out & u can c most of the body prt too. Q. Its j shaped lk one to me don't u c it? Q. No thats all I can say.	____
VIII	233 V	A milk bottle.	It j has the shape of one if u ask me. Q. Its white too indicating that theres milk in it. Q. Thats all.	____
VIII	234	A pig.	It has the shape of a pig. Q. J this white prt hr. Q. I cant think of a. t. else to say about it. Q. No.	____
IX	235	Claws.	Well it ll claws u mite c on a hawk to me. Q. They j ll claws. Q. I cant tell a. more about them, they j ll that. Q. No.	____
IX	236 V	A bell.	It j has the shape of a bell to me. Q. Well if u lk at it this way it has the shape of one of those bells u mite hang on a Xmas tree. Q. No.	____
X	237	A paddle.	Well the gray prt up hr (D11) is the handle & this white prt is the paddle prt. Q. It j re me of a fraternity paddle or a canoe paddle of s. s. Q. No thats all I can thk of. Q. No.	____
IV	238	An animal.	An insect animal. Q. Here r the feelers. Q. Dont c rest of it. Q. This whole thg is an insect bec I c the antennae here OK.	____
X	239	Wow. Purdy Cs. Here is brown, blue — my favorite C — green, red, mm, yellow . . .	J c the nice colors.	____
X	240	Ll one of those cartoon insects u c in funny papers.	Doesnt really ll any A I have ever seen — sort of a green blob. Q. Has a funny lk on his face as if he is yelling at s. o. Green colored as in Sunday funny papers.	
I	241	The little boy in the tire ad.	I cant re which tire co. but he is all in white & is shown carrying a candle I thk. Q. It has the shape of that lk he was in a white nightgown walking along w a candle in his hand. Q. No, thats all I can say. Q. No.	____
I	242	A belt & buckle.	Right here in the cntr prt. Q. The buckle prt is shiny lk & the belt itself is drk, it re me of a cowboy belt w the big buckle. Q. Thats all I can say about it. Q. No its j laid out lk in a display case. Q. No. Q. Thats all.	____
II	243	Stalagmites.	Ths thgs here ll those permanent icicles, I thk thats what u call them. Q. Well they r shaped lk that I guess. It sort of ll some of them r broken off. Q. No thats all. Q. No.	____
II	244	A spinning top.	It has that shape to it & the way its balanced so well means that it must b spinning. Q. Thats all. Q. No.	____
IV	245 V	A meat cleaver.	This is the handle & here is the blade prt. Q. It j ll one to me. Q. No.	____
IV	246	A Bf.	J this prt in here. Its sort of vague but u can c the wgs & the indented V prt at the top where they spread out. Q. its j a sort of vague shape to me I guess. Q. No.	____
V	247	A spear.	It j ll the top prt of a spear to me. Q. Its pointed lk one. Q. Its long & thin. Q. No.	____

Card No.	Response No.	Free Association	Inquiry	Scoring
VI	248	A bedpost.	This litl thg here ll the end of a bedpost lk u mite c on a maple bedsted. Q. Oh it has the type of design that a bedpost end on a maple bed often has. Q. No.	————
VIII	249	A javanese dancer.	Well it ll a dancer, lk they hav in Java, u kno those wiggly kind, it ll she has her hands up over her head. Q. Shes all dressed in one of those gold dresses lk they wear. Q. Well its colored lk a gold dress. Q. Thats all.	————
X	250	A Buddah.	It has the shape of a Buddah squatting lk those statues of Buddah do. Q. Ths brwn isnt included here. Q. Its j the form of it I guess thats what I thot. Q. No.	————
I	251 >	A bridge w people walking across.	It ll a rock bridge w some people wlkng across it. Q. Well the color of it ll rock & u can make out some people wlkng across it. Q. No thas all I can say. Q. Oh yes u can tell its a bridge bec the way u can c under it as well as over it. Q. Well theres air on both sides.	————
I	252	Owls eyes.	These drk spots r the eyes & the places around them ll the bigger area that u can c around owls eyes. U know what I mean? Q. Well they hav little pupils but bigger prts to their eyes. Q. Thats all.	————
II	253	A forest fire on a mt.	Well the red prt in the fire & it ll its along way off & u can c most of the mt. isnt burning yet. Q. The red is hazy too lk there was a lot of smoke. Q. Thats all.	————
III	254 ∨	2 trees way up on a hill w a path going up there.	This red cntr thg is the gate to the path & then the white is sort of lk the path & then these r the 2 trees, they ll oaks bec theyre big & bulky. Q. No thats all. Q. The red thg doesnt lk much lk a gate but u can imag. it as one.	————
IV	255 ∨	Frankenstein's head.	Right here in the white, the outline of his head as I rem. it. Q. The big forehead & the monkey lk nose I guess. Q. Thats all.	————
IV	256	Tonsils.	These thgs here ll tonsils to me. Q. J the way they r they ll tonsils. Q. I d. k. they j ll that to me. Q. No.	————
VI	257	The head of a goose.	It ll hes traveling at hi speed the way the head is stretched out lk that. Q. J the head & neck, the head is shaped lk the head of a goose. Q. No.	————
VI	258	Ice tongs.	The tong ends r here at the end & the handle is here in the middle in fact u can c the knuckles of s. o. who is holding on to them. Q. Well the two round bumps in the cntr here ll knuckles as if s. o. were holding on to the tongs. Q. The pointed ends r really what mks the tongs ll tongs. Q. No.	————
IX	259 >	It ll s. o. is hanging on to a dead tree in the wind or s. t.	Well it ll a person grabbing onto a tree but the tree its dead or at least it doesnt have any leaves on it. Q. Its j the outline of a person so u cant tell if its man or wm. Q. No thats all except the way they r hanging on it must b a strong wind. Q. No.	————
X	260	Walnuts.	It ll a walnut to me bec its colored lk they r brown, & theyre round what else? Q. Thats all I can say about them.	————
IX	261 ∨	You can call this prt fire & this smoke.	Its yellow lk fire & its lk a fires smoke, its lite lk this. It starts lk this & goes up. Q. Its hazy too thats the smoke. Q. No.	————
III	262	2 monkeys falling.	Q. This is their tail & theyre bkwrds. They prob. fell off their bar on to the mat. Theyre in the zoo.	————
VIII	263	A mt.	Q. Its green & its lk a hill, it goes straight up. Ll its a volcano hill, the drk green ll its coming out the hole & running down.	
IX	264 ∨	Inside a human being — the chest prt.	Its k of rough on the outside lungs hr (edge). This wld b the good or the air. This wld b the muscles. Leave the orange prt out. Q. Lungs? Ll its shaped lk it & ll filled w s. t. bec of the shading. Q. No, the tubes that go dwn, I took the idea from the lungs. Q. Muscles? First of all, c the outline, lk the muscle prt or the arm & chest.	————
I	265 <	S. t. lk a dog, lks kind of ragged (edge), cld b reflection, dog & his reflect.	Q. No, ear, leg, theres 2 of 'em. Q. He cld b barking at his reflection in the water.	————
VII	266	Ll piece of cloth thats moth eaten.	Ll s. t. been eating at it bec of the ragged edges on the inside. Q. In a way it cld b leather or s. t. else, it ll wld b fibrous bec. it isnt a distinct outline — sort of lk fibre coming out.	————

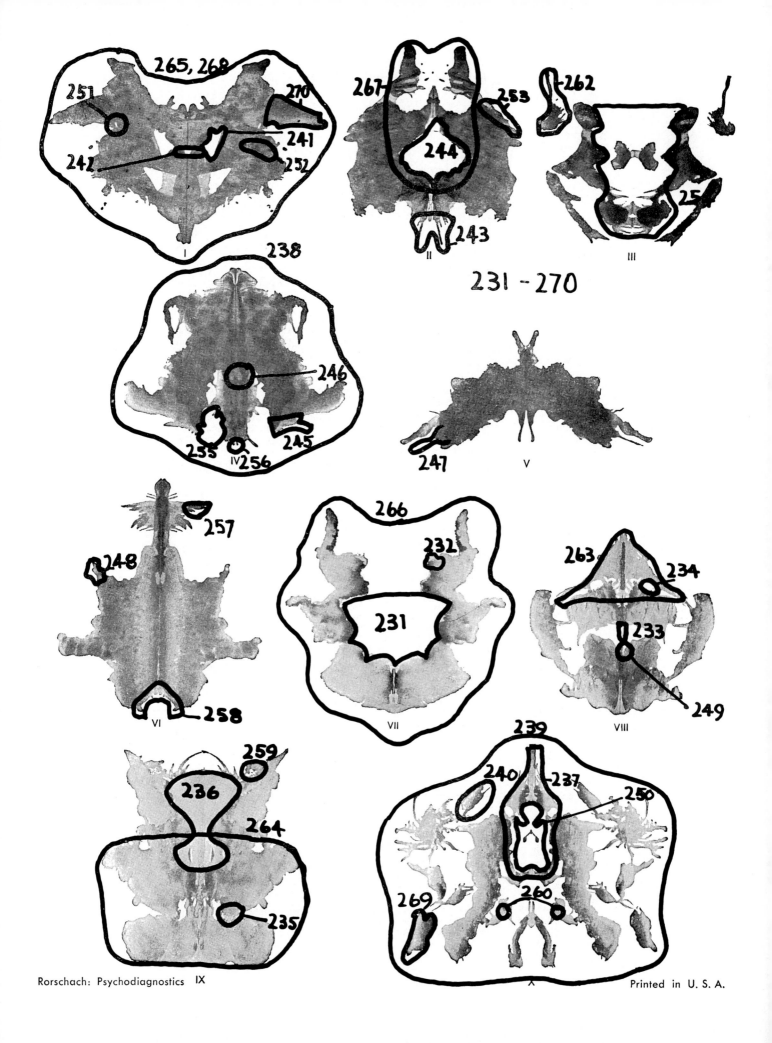

265, 268

251

270

242

241

252

I

238

267

253

262

244

243

II

25

III

231 - 270

246

235

IV 256

245

247

V

257

248

266

232

263

234

258

231

233

VI

VII

249

VIII

259

236

264

235

239

240

237

250

269

260

IX

X

Card No.	Response No.	Free Association	Inquiry	Scoring
II	267	A mask of tragedy.	The drk reds in hr r eyebrows & eyes. Nose hr. While prt is mth. Q. The eyes lk sad & white under the eyes wld b tears. Q. No.	———
I	268	A shadow of s. t. The midl prt ll a woman.	R here, r there. Q. Ll mayb a woman there & I dont kno mayb trees or s. t. beside her. Q. 2 men beside her right there. Q. They cld b dancing w her. Q. The men ll theyre standing behind or dancing beside her & mayb shes singing. Q. Mayb thrs a spotlite & youre lkng at them on the white curtain. Q. Its drk & its kind of rickety — its not its real shape. Thats the same woman.	———
X	269	Orange sheep jumping across fences — imag. fences.	J lks sort of fluffy & wooly & u can c the front legs, hind legs, body & head. Q. The texture & outline is sort of rounded. Q. Well, the orange sheep r imag., but they r orange there on the card.	———
I	270 >	It ll an icicle.	Its long & pointed . . . & its cold lkng. Q. Its kind of gray & its dripping. Q. Lk its melting.	———
II	271	A scene where s. o. was left wounded.	This is j the spot where it happened, where s. o. was shot & later picked up. Q. Hr is trampley ground or grass & hr is the blood. Q. The diff shading mks it ll its trampled with a scattering of red smudges throughout.	———
III	272	2 cannibals over a big boiling pot.	The blk made me say cannibals, the grayer portion ll a pot & the drkr portion ll smoke. There is a head, neck, & body. Q. J the blk. Q. Theyre female. Q. The breast. Q. J standing at opposite ends of the pot lkng at e. o. Q. No.	———
IX	273	The grn ll sea foam or sea mist.	J the grn prt. Q. J the color & the c lks kind of greenish & misty. Q. Bec its more pastel. Ths prt hr the liter prt & I picture the c — ll grn wtr & the mist comes over it. Q. No shape oi a. t. j the color re me of it. Q. No.	———
VIII	274 <	Sideways, it ll a chameleon climbing over colored rocks & reflec. in a pond or lake. It ll hes going from a place where its sunlit to a cave where its shadowy.	Ll sunlite bec the orange wld b brite to progressively duller colors toward the left. Q. They ll rocks bec I was j trying to thk of what a chameleon wld b climbing over. Q. No.	———
IX	275	Mayb a candle of s. k.	The candle is ths prt hr. That wld b the candle & at the top wld b the flame in the liter prt. All around the top of it it is liter, lk the glow & dwn hr it gets rougher lk wax dripped dwn.	———
IX	276	This way it lks lk possibly a fountain w watr shooting up w diff levels, w diff colors of lite shining on 'em.	This prt is the fountain; that must b watr bec. wtr wld b easiest to shoot up & wld ref. the lite easier. There r diff colored lites shining at diff levels. This prt in here ll it mite b the fountain bec. it is in the cntr section. Q. No.	———
IX	277	Possibly diff smokes from a chemical reaction.	The diff colors of gasses. Q. The fact that its there & they dont lk very solid, theyre hazy, indefinite. I suppose they mite b floating in air, theyre not resting on a. t. Q. No.	———
I	278	This cntr prt ll a wm w her hands raised lk she was appealing to the sun god or s. t.	She has her hands raised in a fashion lk adoration or s. t. Q. Well u only c her outline, she seems hidden by this veil, its very drk & shrouded lk a veil is. Q. She has her back to me & the veil ll s. s. of that sort. Q. It ll if I cld touch it it wld b soft & smooth. Q. Yes thats the way it lks. Q. No.	———
IV	279	The thg ll ice to me.	It j ll a piece of ice, its all drk & cld lkng a piece of ice wld b. Q. Well I mean its dirty & gray lkng, lk it was real cold. Q. If u touched it it wld feel cold. Q. No.	———
VII	280	Grayish smoke.	All of it ll gray smoke. Q. The diff in the liter or drkr areas & its gray lk smoke is.	———
IV	281	Ll a skinned raccoon.	Ll a head & the black mask & quite a lrg tail & the front paws. Q. On a tanning device tacked up on a barn to dry out. Q. The fur is up — it j ll fur bec that is the way they usually put them w the fur on the outside. It ll its tightening up. Theres pull to it. Q. No.	———

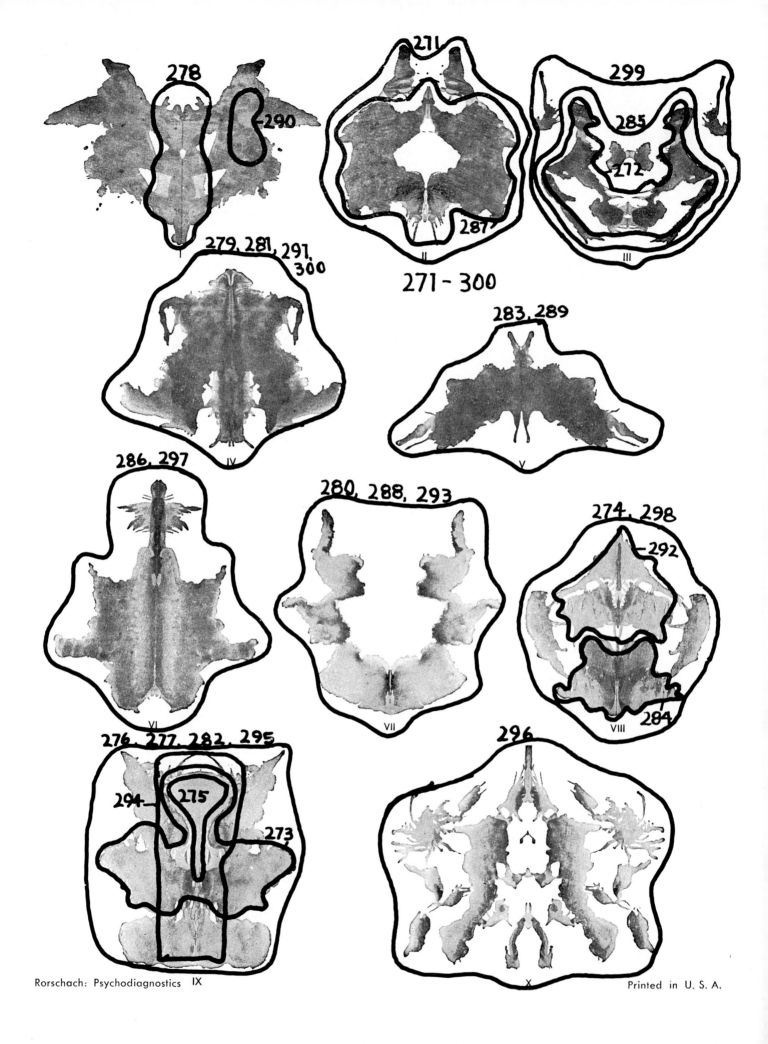

Card No.	Response No.	Free Association	Inquiry	Scoring
IX	282	Oh...three dimensional color. Refracted lite in a cave — subterranean.	Had to b refracted to b pink — pink & purple not quite going to the mauve. Q. I wld b lkng dwn into the cave lk in Carlsbad Caverns.	————
V	283	There is a beautiful Bf in the negative of a photograph.	Its orange & drk blu w a few dots of diff colors. Q. Well the colors dont come out bec its negative but they r there. In fact it cld b an x-ray of a Bf even tho u wld never c an x-ray of such a thg.	————
VIII	284	A translucent gem that is uncut.	The color formation of it . . . being pink & orange. It seems to emit lite. Q. It seems transparent yet it seems to reflect lit bec the rays seem to b bouncing off of it. Q. No definite shape bec its uncut.	————
III	285	A shadow of people roasting s. t. over a pit or fire.	The side red doesnt count. Q. It cld b a shadow of 2 men cooking . . . the red prt is the fire. Q. The black is the same color as a shadow wld b thats all.	————
VI	286	Ll wool.	The W thg lks soft. Q. I d. k. I guess the white & black colors . . . it j ll s. t. purry. Q. Thats all.	————
II	287	This has the color of orange in it. Its s. t. lk a butterfly.	Prts r drk & prts r brite. Q. All but the top red. Q. Its in flight. Q. Bec of the shape & the diff colors too.	————
VII	288	Clouds on a dark windy day.	When its windy after a rain the clouds divide lk these r doing. Q. Well there arent clouds lk this on a brite day — these arent white they r drk gray.	————
V	289	2 objects pushing against one another.	Each side is an object & they r pushing toward the cntr. Q. I d. k. what they r, j two thgs pushing against e. o. Q. Mayb stones or s. t. leaning against e. o.	————
I	290	I c s. t. indistinct, lk in a mystery movie.	This area in here. Ll a special trick film effect. Lite shines on lense & blocks view of object behind it. Q. The black spots & the lite & drk areas.	————
IV	291	A symbolic repre. of depression.	The W. thg. Q. U get a feeling of nothingness. Q. Its j all blkness & gloom. Q. No thats all.	————
VIII	292	Tree.	Ll a forest. Theyre all grn, ll a real deep woods. Q. Its real drk grn & ll trees r real high from grd. Q. They got a lot of leaves & it covers the woods up. Q. The dots ll the trees hav been cut dwn & r layg on the grd. Q. Trucks r hauling them away. Q. The l dots ll trucks. Q. No.	————
VII	293	Ll 4 t pots balanced on s. b. 2 hands.	Q. Theye shaped lk 4 pots & it ll s. b. holding them lk this (dem w hand out, palm up). Q. No.	————
IX	294	It ll a w'fall.	Q. Rite here in the midl, it ll wtr is falling dwn thru the cntr of it. These r rocks around it. Q. The c falls dwn & its all at l angle. Its blue-green.	————
IX	295	Cripes. I guess it ll sx inters right at the climax.	Well, everythg is involved hr. Hrs the guys penis & this is her organ & it ll a burst lk they were both having a climax, even her rump muscles r tight. Q. The color re. the feeling, hot & wild. Q. I cant say anymore about it.	————
X	296	Well, this ll its raining on a wtr painting.	U kno a wtr color, the rain is hitting it now & the colors r running dwn lk. Q. The blue is splashing & the pink has already run dwn. Q. Its all so c'ful it must b a kids painting. Q. No.	————
VI	297 <	This is a battleship stuck in the ice & the men on it r frozen.	It ll the wind is blowing hard & has caused the wtr to fly up over it & its so cold it is freezing. Q. Well, I really dont c any men but they must b there & theyre frozen. Q. No. Q. It ll its icy. Q. No.	————
VIII	298	It ll s. b. being torn apart by some force.	It ll they r ripping apart w all their insides being scattered all over. Q. Some strange force I d. k. what. Q. J bld & guts. Q. The forms of these & theyre all C'd that way. Q. I'd say its a H but d. k. whether M or F. Q. No.	————
III	299	Well, here r 2 people.	They r 2 great people lkng dwn at their stomachs & their heart is in the midl & their livers r up here (upper red). Q. They r ghosts, all drk & spooky lk ghosts & they r lkng at the prts of them that they dont hav anymore. Q. Its all blk & fuzzy lk a ghost. Q. (Fuzzy) Well fuzzy u kno lk a ghost, shaded funny. Q. The livers & the heart r still bleeding. Q. No.	————
IV	300	This is a depressed man.	Hes sitting on a stool & hes hiding his head. Q. The blkness of it repre. his feeling. Q. It ll he mite b wearing boots & a skin or lk that. Q. Well, its all blk so it must b depression.	————

Annotated Bibliography

THE WHOLE

ABRAMS, ELIOS, N. Prediction of intelligence from certain Rorschach factors. *J. Clin. Psychol.*, 1955, *11*, 81-83.

F plus %, M, W and R scores were correlated with the WB on 400 V.A. mental hygiene clinic patients. The multiple correlation between these determinants and the WB Full Scale IQ was .53. A formula for estimating IQ was given.

BASCH, K. W. Ganzeigenschaften als Determinantenlrager im Rorschach-Versuch mit besonderer Beruchsichtigung der Farbantworten. (Whole qualities as Rorschach determinants with consideration of color responses. *Schweiz. Z. Psychol.*, 1957, *16*, 121-126.

This study shows that certain qualities of wholes (essentially their physiognomy) are embodied in certain Rorschach determinants (especially color) and that the psychological sign of the determinants is derived therefrom. English and French summaries are included.

BECK, S. J. The Rorschach Test as applied to a feebleminded group. *Arch. Psychol.*, 1932, *136*, 84.

The article correlates results on the Rorschach with intelligence of eighty-seven children in the New York City Children's School for the feebleminded as reported by the Stanford-Binet test. W is one of the five indices of intellectual functioning.

BECK, S. J. Configurational tendencies in Rorschach responses. *Amer. J. Psychol.*, 1933, *45*, 433-443.

Beck attempted to determine whether the W response is the most significant score or whether other scores indicate a higher organizing ability. It was found that the organizational value varies from card to card. The significance of the analysis to Gestalt psychology was discussed.

EICHLER, R. M. Experimental stress and alleged Rorschach indices of anxiety. *J. Abnorm. Soc. Psychol.*, 1951, *46*, 344-355.

In an investigation of the influence of a stress-produced anxiety on the occurrence of fifteen Rorschach factors related to anxiety, it was found that one of these (W) decreased as anxiety increased in a stress-producing situation.

GARRISON, M., JR. Relationships between Rorschach scores and clinical changes in mental patients. *J. Personality*, 1948, *17*, 146-152.

Eight Rorschach scores (W, D, F, M, C, IRT, Mean IRT/C and R) were intercorrelated with seventy-three scores from thirty-eight other psychological tests for thirty-two patients. The results, based on concomitant variations, show some validity for the method, and further research is encouraged.

GUIRDHAM, A. The diagnosis of depression by the Rorschach Test. *Brit. J. Med. Psychol.*, 1936, *16*, 130-145.

The Rorschach Test, in reflecting the underlying mood of the subject, indicates that depressive states are manifested by an accentuation of whole and small detail responses.

KAVAYANJIAN, T., AND GURVITY, M. S. The W% on the Rorschach as a measure of orality. *J. Hillside Hosp.*, *(Glen Oaks)*, 1953, *2*, 213-218.

The hypothesis tested was that all oral individuals would "devour each inkblot . . . in its entirety," eliciting a high W%. Tests of sixty-nine alcoholic addicts, admittedly suffering from oral regression, were compared with one hundred controls. Results and further investigation needed are enumerated.

KEYES, E. J. An experimental investigation of some sources of variance in the whole response to the Rorschach Ink Blots. *J. Clin. Psychol.*, 1954, *10*, 155-160.

The effect on W by two variables — presence or absence of training in perceptual organization and usual instructions or instructions to perceive wholes only — was studied through analysis of variance using four treatment groups. Training contributed to the variance in W and W+ at a significant level. W reflects both training in perceptual organization and an additional tendency or set to organize. These two factors interact to present together an increase in the number of W and W+.

LEVENTHAL, H. The effects of perceptual training on the Rorschach W and Z scores. *J. Consult. Psychol.*, 1956, *20*, 93-97.

Forty-nine male college students were divided into three groups with two groups receiving training on perceptual tasks (Mooney Closure Figures or Gottschaldt Figures) and a control group which was given the Shipley-Institute of Living Scale. It was found that the group trained on the Gottschaldt Figures had significantly lower W and Z scores than the other two groups. Thus, the author concludes that caution should be used in interpreting Rorschach W and Z scores.

MARINESCO, G., KREINDLER, A., AND COPELMANN, L. Le test de Rorschach et la dynamique de l'ecorce cerebrale d'apres les lois des reflexes conditionnel de Pavlov (The Rorschach Test and the dynamics of the cerebral cortex according to Pavlov's laws of the conditioned reflex.) *Ann. Medicopsychol. (Paris)*, 1935, *93* (Part 1), 614-623.

Interpretation of the Rorschach figures as a whole is due to irradiation in the cerebral cortex. A proper ratio of whole to detailed responses is due to a proper balance of irradiation and concentration in the cerebral cortex. Manics tend to give mainly W interpretations with kinesthetic elements.

McCANDLESS, B. R. The Rorschach as a differential predictor of academic success for matched groups of highly Two matched groups of highly superior men enrolled in superior men. *Amer. Psychol.* (abstract), 1947, *2*, 414-415. a Maritime Service Officers School were given the Rorschach. The group with low grade-point averages showed more fluidity and strength of emotion and less anxiety in some areas than the high grade-point average men. The high grade-point men paid slightly less attention to the blocks as a whole and more to the large, common and small, uncommon details, and had more popular responses.

RANZONI, JANE H., GRANT, MARGUERITE Q., AND IVES, VIRGINIA. Rorschach "card-pull" in a normal adolescent population. *J. Project Techn.*, 1950, *14*, 107-133.

Adolescent Ss of an eighteen year longitudinal study were given Rorschachs which were evaluated on the basis of "card-pull." The authors found a marked W pull to the first six cards, breaking down at VII with a D upswing. The authors feel that their study gives norms for a randomly selected population.

STOPOL, M. S. Rorschach performance in relation to two types of stress. *J. Consult. Psychol.*, 1954, *18*, 11-15.

The purpose of this experiment was to determine the ability of persons to understand two types of stress conditions designated as "failure stress" and "task-induced" stress as determined by the Rorschach. Low W% and high D% and a greater number of form-dominant over form-subordinate responses were correlated with the two criteria when failure stress was followed by task-induced stress, it was found.

WISHNER, J. Rorschach intellectual indicators in neurotics. *Amer. J. Orthopsychiat.*, 1948, *18*, 265-279.

Neurotic patients were tested with the Rorschach and WB test, from which it was determined that, of the seventeen reputed intelligence indicators, R, W% and Z were the most significant.

WITTENBORN, J. R. Certain Rorschach response categories and mental abilities. *J. Appl. Psychol.*, 1949, *33*, 330-338.

Sixty-eight Yale testees were given the Rorschach, which was then scored by Klopfer-trained examiners. There was no evidence that certain types of W responses are correlated with certain types of abilities.

WITTENBORN, J. R. A factor analysis of Rorschach scoring categories. *J. Consult. Psychol.*, 1950, *14*, 261-267.

The author found that a new scoring system should be set up, based upon a weighted combination of the whole, color-form, pure color and pure texture response categories.

WITTENBORN, J. R., AND METTLER, F. A. A lack of perceptual control for the Rorschach Test. *J. Clin. Psychol.*, 1951, *7*, 331-334.

The author has developed a lack-of-perceptual-control formula consisting of total R of all those in which the form determinant is lacking as well as those in which the area determinant is W. On a group of forty schizophrenic patients, low negative correlations were found with all symptom clusters except conversion hysteria, where a low positive correlation was found. Only the symptom clusters of Depression and Hebephrenia were significant at the 5 per cent level.

ZUBIN, J. A. A quantitative approach to measuring regularity of succession in the Rorschach experiment. *Character and Personality*, 1941, *10*, 67-78.

To determine the preference for either a progressive (D to W) or a regressive shift (W to D), the author used the mean contingency coefficient technique and the null hypothesis. His results relate somewhat to diagnostic categories.

THE WHITE SPACE

BANDURA, A. The Rorschach white space response and "oppositional" behavior. *J. Consult. Psychol.*, 1954, *18*, 17-21.

The following conclusions were made from data gathered from eighty-one high school Ss: The use of the experience type as a differential factor in interpretation of white space should be discontinued until better evidence is found; white space does seem to reflect oppositional tendencies; and no evidence was found that white space reflects inadequacy or self-distrust feelings.

BANDURA, A. The Rorschach white space response and perceptual reversal. *J. Exp. Psychol.*, 1954, *48*, 114-118.

The number and temporal sequence of the occurrence of space responses on the Rorschach and the rate of perceptual reversal on the Necker Cube were obtained. A moderate degree of significant positive relationship was found between rate of reversal and primary space responses on the Rorschach. The number of primary space responses increased with the increasing of exposure time of the Rorschach cards.

DIERKENS-DOPCHIE, N., AND DIRKENS, JEAN. Correlation entre les donnees cliniques et certains facteurs du test de Rorschach. (Correlations between clinical data and certain factors of the Rorschach Test.) *Rev. Psychol. Appl.*, 1953, *3*, 314-319.

From a sample of hundred-fifty-two children with behavior disorders, it was found that white space has no clear correlation with social aggressivity, but that white details seen as "holes" correspond to aggressive tendencies.

FONDA, C. P. The nature and meaning of the Rorschach white space response. *J. Abnorm. Soc. Psychol.*, 1951, *46*, 367-374.

Two personality questionnaires and two inkblot tests were given to one hundred-fifty college students. Relatively consistent sets were then observed in some Ss. These sets were: (a) in the inkblot test to give responses to the white space; and (b) in the questionnaires to make frequent use of the (?) response. The tendency for these to appear in the same individual was prevalent. This partially supports Rorschach's hypothesis that white space responses indicate some sort of opposition tendency.

HAMMES, J. A., and OSBORNE, R. T. Discrimination of manifest anxiety by the Structured-Objective Rorschach Test. *Percept. Motor Skills.*, 1962, *15*(1), 59-62.

Thirty-eight low-anxious and thirty-one high-anxious Ss choosen by scores obtained on a manifest anxiety scale were given the Structured-Objective Rorschach Test. Of twenty-six Rorschach factors, only Dd and S gave measures of anxiety.

INGRAM, WINIFRED. Prediction of aggression from the Rorschach. *J. Consult. Psychol.*, 1954, *18*, 23-28.

Ingram tried to determine whether white space responses were a valid interpretation of aggression. It was found that: (a) high S subjects were more aggressive in the interview than low S; (b) high S group was no more aggressive than low S group in a situation of intellectual challenge where social interaction was held to a minimum; (c) judges' impressions of aggression based on the total Rorschach record were slightly related to aggression measured experimentally.

LORD, EDITH. Experimentally induced variations in Rorschach performance. *Psychol. Monogr.*, 1950, *64*, Whole No. 316.

It was found that white space responses occur most frequently when they are concomitant with reaction to inked areas of the plates. The total use of white space varies with the type of administration and administrator. That is, negative administrations provoked more white space responses, but the positive administrations evoked even more than negative or neutral administrations. The number of whole responses varied once at the 5 per cent level with successive testing, but remained stable through variation of administrator and administration.

MINKOWSKA, F. Le Rorschach: son aspect, clinique, formel, humain. (The Rorschach: its clinical, formal, human aspect.) *Ann. Med. Psychol.*, 1950, *2*, 145-189.

The schizoid component as reflected in the Rorschach expresses itself in the predominance of W at the expense of detail. Often there is in this pronounced opposition an urge for S to seek forms in the white, especially the perimocular white.

MURRAY, D. C. An investigation of the Rorschach white space response in an extratensive experience balance as a measure of outwardly directed opposition. *J. Project. Techn.*, 1957, *21*, 40-46.

Six assumed measures of oppositional tendencies were given to 101 college students of both sexes along with individual administrations of the Rorschach. The criterion hypothesis was to measure a variety of different types of opposition. It was found that white space is not an outwardly direct oppositional tendency measure as compared with the six criterion measures.

MURRAY, D. C. White space on the Rorschach: interpretation and validity. *J. Project. Techn.*, 1957, *21*, 47-53.

A review of the theoretical and research literature pertaining to the interpretation of Rorschach white space as it applies to research and different diagnostic categories was made. The conclusion was that the studies have weaknesses which prevent their being definitive. Many suggested interpretations have not been tested.

NELSON, W. D. An evaluation of the white space response on the Rorschach as figure-ground reversal and intellectual opposition. *Diss. Abstr.*, 1955, *15*, 459.

This study was concerned with whether the perception of white space on the Rorschach Test is related to a tendency to reverse figure ground, whether the perception of primary white space is qualitatively different from the perception of secondary white space and whether the use of white space reflects intellectual opposition. The results, while supporting the first hypothesis, failed to support the second and third. An alternative hypothesis was suggested: that the perception of white space is indicative of flexibility.

ROSEN, E. MMPI and Rorschach correlates of the Rorschach white space response. *J. Clin. Psychol.*, 1952, *8*, 283-288.

This study dealt with the investigation of the relationship between Rorschach white space and MMPI Pd score using 109 psychiatric patients. It was found that white space responses were less frequent in psychopaths than in other patients. White space responses were not related to Multiphasic Pd scores of psychopaths, but the use of the white space was an associated sign with higher Pd scores of patients not diagnosed as psychopathic deviates.

SCHAEMANN, T. Die Zwischenraumdeutungen im Rorschach-test. Versuch einer gestaltpsychologischen Erklarung. (White space responses on the Rorschach Test. An attempted gestalt psychological explanation.) *Beih. Schweiz. Z. Psychol.*, 1950, *19*, 64-72.

White space responses resulting from reversal of figure ground are considered a phenomena of perception and intelligence and not necessarily indicative of hostility. Of fifty-five tests administered to brain-injured and lesioned Ss, twenty-four had from one to five "S" responses and showed greater intellectual and appreceptive flexibility than the thirty-one protocols devoid of "S."

VIOLET-CONIL, N. Le test de Rorschach et le diagnostic de l'angoisse. (The Rorschach Test and the diagnosis of anxiety.) *Rorschachiana*, 1952, *1*, 78-127.

Anxiety creates a protective system and liberates psychic energy and thus may be connected with life instincts or aggressive instincts. Among others, anxiety may be reflected in the Rorschach Test by few W and S. Anxiety is the cause of psychological regression.

WERNER, H. Rorschach method applied to two clinical groups of mental defectives. *Amer. J. Ment. Defic.*, 1945, *49*, 303-306.

Two groups of mentally deficient children, brain-injured and non-brain-injured cases, matched as to chronological and mental age, were observed for the characteristic responses on the Rorschach inkblot test. Brain-injured children gave significantly more responses to white instead of to colored and black spaces, it was found.

WERNER, H. Perceptual behavior of brain-injured, mentally defective children: an experimental study by means of the Rorschach technique. *Genet. Psychol. Monogr.*, 1945, *31*, 51-110.

On a comparison made between two mentally defective groups, one group was deficient due to brain injury while the other was not. It was found that the brain injury cases gave fewer responses, more whole responses and a higher percentage of white space responses.

THE DETAIL

ABBOT, W. D., DUE, F. O., and NOSIK, W. A. Subdural hematoma and effusion as a result of blast injuries. *JAMA*, 1943, *121*, 739-741.

The Rorschach responses of subjects having subdural hematoma showed lowered productivity, popular "easy" whole responses, little attention to detail and no particular color shock.

ARBITMAN, H. D. Rorschach determinants in mentally defective and normal subjects. *Train. Sch. Bull. (Vineland)*, 1953, *50*, 143-151.

Lower R, D, M, higher FM seem typical for fifty subjects with mean MA of 7-4. Do is so infrequent a response with mentally deficient persons that it should be abandoned as a so-called oligophrenic response.

BASH, K. W. On the definition and significance of small detail responses (Dd) on the Rorschach Test. *Beih. Schweiz. Z. Psychol.*, 1950, *19*, 73-78.

The varied definitions offered for the scoring of Dd responses in introductory Rorschach manuals are surveyed. Small size, relative infrequency and obscureness of responses are usually emphasized. The significance and interpretation of Dd responses are discussed in terms of Gestalt principles.

BECK, S. J. Problems of further research in the Rorschach Test. *Amer. J. Orthopsychiat.*, 1935, *5*, 100-115.

General practice suggests that further research with the Rorschach is needed to find constant, experimentally tested criteria for the rare detail.

BLEULER, M., and BLEULER, R. Rorschach's inkblot test and racial psychology: mental peculiarities of Moroccans. *Character and Personality*, 1935, *4*, 97-114.

Moroccans show a marked preference for small detail responses and lose the whole perspective while becoming engrossed in some minor pattern. These differences seem to be due to peculiarities in their racial history and not to mental inferiority.

BUTTON, A. D. A Rorschach study of 67 alcoholics. *Quart. J. Stud. Alcohol.*, 1956, *17*, 35-52.

Results from the hospitalized patients are compared with normals and other alcoholics from the literature. All studies agree on certain features, such as poor M, high C, high W% and low D%.

CARUSO, I. A. Intelligence and affectively-toned Do responses in Rorschach Test. *Wien. Z. Prakt. Psychol.*, 1949, *1*, 17-20.

The sudden appearance of a detail response in the midst of intellectually superior responses signifies an unconscious fear of the whole configuration which may be rooted in a neurotic complex. Do (oligophrenic detail) occur as the result of an emotional disruption of the intellectual function.

DEFRANCO, F. The interpretative process in the Rorschach Test. *Arch. Psicol. Neurol.*, 1951, *12*, 53-69.

The problem of the classification of usual and unusual details in responses to the Rorschach Test is analyzed. A list of types of details distinguished by various Rorschach workers is given. The author considers that not only structural characteristics of the inkblot determine the normal or unusual details, but also differences in race, age, sex, culture and socioeconomic status.

deRENZI, E., ISOTTI, M., AND SAROVOLD, D. The influence of sex and age on the Rorschach in the normal adult Italian. *Arch. Psicol. Neurol.*, 1958, *19*, 497-507.

Three hundred Ss had less variation in responses than anticipated. Men have more of a tendency to give dr responses, while women give more d and D.

DIMMICK, G. B. An application of the Rorschach Inkblot Test to three clinical types of dementia praecox. *J. Psychol.*, 1935-1936, *1*, 61-74.

The Rorschach Inkblot Test was administered to eighty-five patients — hebephrenic, paranoid and simple. The writer concludes that the present method of scoring involves too large a subjective factor for the Do category as well as others.

EICHLER, R. M. Experimental stress and alleged Rorschach indices of anxiety. *J. Abnorm. Soc. Psychol.*, 1951, *46*, 344-355.

An investigation of the influence of a stress-produced anxiety on the occurrence of fifteen Rorschach factors alleged to be signs of anxiety revealed increased weighted shading responses, increased number of oligophrenic details and others at a moderate level of statistical reliability.

GAIR, MOLLIE, Rorschach characteristics of a group of very superior 7 year old children. *Rorschach Res. Exch.*, 1944, *8*, 31-37.

Subjects were twenty-one girls and eight boys. Analysis of the protocols revealed the following trends (Stanford-Binet used): More W and fewer D responses than for the average child of equal and somewhat higher ages and IQ's.

GANZ, E., AND LOOSLI-USTERI, M. The Rorschach Test applied to 43 abnormal boys. *Arch. Psychol. Geneve.*, 1934, *24*, 245-255.

It was found that small details are more numerous with the retarded children (ten to 14 years), while the oligophrenic details that Rorschach believes more characteristic of abnormals were found more numerous in the normals. The authors propose the term "inhibiting details" for the above.

GARDNER, G. E. Rorschach Test replies and results in 100 normal adults of average IQ. *Amer. J. Orthopsychiat.*, 1936, *6*, 32-60.

The Rorschach responses given by one hundred normal adults of average IQ are tabulated and classified, with total percentages and the average number of different responses (including the detail responses) to be expected with normal adults given in the summaries.

GUSTAV, A. Estimations of Rorschach scoring categories by means of an objective inventory. *J. Psychol.*, 1946, 22, 253-260.

One hundred-thirty female college students were tested in an attempt to discover a technique of estimating individual Rorschach scoring categories by means of an objective inventory. Scores on the objective personality inventory significantly estimated the following Rorschach scoring categories for female college students — W%, D%, FC, H, FM and C.

HALLOWELL, A. J. The Rorschach Test as a tool for investigating cultural variables and individual differences in the study of personality in primitive cultures. *Rorschach Res. Exch.*, 1941, 5, 31-34.

Attention to details, awareness to color and so forth may be group variables related to cultural tradition.

HERTZ, M. R. The normal details in the Rorschach Inkblot Test. *Rorschach Res. Exch.*, 1936-37, 1, 104-121.

Normal details for the Rorschach Test were statistically determined in this investigation, on the basis of a frequency distribution of all the details selected for interpretations and the number of times such selections were made. The normal details so determined coincide with many of the first grade normal details described by Klopfer and Rickers.

HERTZ, M. R. Scoring the Rorschach Test with specific reference to "normal detail" category. *Amer. J. Orthopsychiat.*, 1938, 8, 100-121.

Comparison of three lists of normal details for use in scoring Rorschach showed the highest percentage of agreement between Hertz and Beck. The lists were the Hertz list, statistically determined, the Beck, list, empirically based, and the Klopfer-Rickers list, qualitatively determined.

HERTZ, M. R. The scoring of the Rorschach inkblot method as developed by the Brush Foundation. *Rorschach Res. Exch.*, 1942, 6, 16-27.

Results of a decade of study with adolescent groups by the Brush Foundation are presented in table form. The scoring differs little from that of Beck and Klopfer. No differentiation is made between first and second degree normal and rare details.

HERTZMAN, M., AND MARGULIES, H. Developmental changes as reflected in Rorschach Test responses. *J. Genet. Psychol.*, 1943, 62, 189-215.

The Rorschach was given to a group of sixty junior high school boys and a group of sixty-two male college students. The older group gave more responses and patterned them differently, making more use of rare details, among other trends.

KADINSKY, D. Significance of depth psychology of apperceptive tendencies in the Rorschach Test. *Rorschach-iana*, 1952, 1, 36-37.

The relation between Dd and external adjustment was

found to be negative; between Dd and internal adjustment, it was positive. A Do tendency is revealed by Q (Ad + Hd) : (A + Ad). Dd is related to mother archetype. A Do tendency is a special case of Dd. These findings were tested against the development of the child and against findings among boys and girls where Do emerged as the most fundamental difference.

KAGAN, W. Shifts in Rorschach patterns during a critical period in the institutional experience of a group of delinquent boys. *Rorschach Res. Exch.*, 1940, 4, 131-133.

Rorschach Tests were administered to six institutionalized delinquent boys twice, at an interval of approximately one month. The protocols were analyzed for shifts during this period. A secondary shift was a decrease in W responses, increase in D and d responses.

KELLEY, D. McG., MARGULIES, H., AND BARRERA, S. The stability of the Rorschach method as demonstrated in electric convulsive therapy cases. *Rorschach Res. Exch.*, 1941, 5, 44-48.

Protocols of twelve individuals showing various clinical syndromes were obtained just before and after one shock treatment. The subjects showed no changes in the fundamental Rorschach patterns. Some changes did occur in the number of responses of D, F% and E.B.

KIKUCHI, T., KITAMURA, S., SATO, L., AND OYAMA, M. Rorschach performance in alcoholic intoxication. Part II. *Tohoku Psychol. Folia.*, 1962-63, 21 (1-2-3), 19-46.

Both alcoholic intoxication and the effects of retesting were measured in two administrations of the Rorschach. One of the results was increased D.

KLEBANOFF, S. G. The Rorschach Test in an analysis of personality in general paresis. *J. Personality.*, 1949, 17, 261-272.

The subjects were a homogeneous group of twenty-six paretic males and twenty-six normals carefully matched as to age and education. Fisher and Snedecor statistics were employed, and one of the findings was a significant difference at the 10 per cent level for R, W% and Dd%.

KLOPFER, B. Discussion of M. R. Hertz's "The Normal Details in the Rorschach Ink-blot Test. *Rorschach Res.*

Hertz's statistics have verified thirteen second grade normal details. Future statistics have to prove how many of the other d's now chosen on qualitative criteria will be verified as normal ones.

McFATE, MARGUERITE, Q., AND ORR, FRANCES G. Through adolescence with the Rorschach. *Rorschach Res. Exch.*, 1949, 13, 302-319.

This longitudinal study of a group of children analyzes their Rorschach protocols at four different age levels during adolescent period. Among the findings, the per cent of adolescents using d and Dd increases through the four ages.

MAJUMDAR, A. K., AND ROY, A. B. Latent personality content on juvenile delinquents. *J. Psychol. Res. Madras*, 1962, 6(1), 4-8.

Exch., 1937, 1, 119-120.

The common Rorschach characteristic in the delinquent personality were found to be high F%, decrease in W responses and increases in d, Dd and odd responses.

MARINESCO, G., KREINDLER, A., AND COPELMANN, L. The Rorschach Test and the dynamics of the cerebral cortex according to Pavlov's law of conditioned reflex. *Ann. Medicopsychol. (Paris)*, 1935, 93, Part 614-23.

The detailed interpretations are due to a concentration in the cortex. A proper proportion of whole and detailed interpretations suggests a proper balance of irradiation and concentration in the cerebral cortex. Melancholics give predominantly detailed interpretations with practically no movement.

MELTZER, H. Personality differences between stuttering and nonstuttering children as indicated by the Rorschach Test. *J. Psychol.*, 1944, 17, 39-59.

Fifty stuttering and fifty control children aged eight to seventeen, equated as to age, sex, grade, school and intelligence, were given the Rorschach. Stutterers made significantly higher scores on Z, W, Ds (white space details) and F(C), while the control group scored significantly higher on F+.

MINKOWSKA, F. The Rorschach: its clinical, formal human aspect. *Ann. Medicopsychol. (Paris)*, 1950, 2, 145-189.
The Test is characterized by the association of two components — the rational-schizoid and the sensori-epileptoid. The schizoid is reflected in the predominance of global responses at the expense of great detail; on the other hand, the epileptoid component reflects itself in impulsiveness, in explosiveness, in the concrete and in very great detail.

MOLISH, H. B., MOLISH, ELLEN E., AND THOMAS, CAROLINE B. A Rorschach study of a group of medical students. *Psychiat. Quart.*, 1950, 744-774.

Sixty fourth year medical students were similar to other superior adults on such areas as intellectual drive and so forth. They differed from other superior adults in the use of rare detail responses.

OHKURA, K. Rorschach study with delinquents. *Jap. Fam. Court. Mon.*, 1957, 9(5), 1-37.

One hundred delinquents (40 per cent thieves) aged fourteen to nineteen were tested on the whole as compared to other studies on normals. There are no differences in W:D:Dd, W:M and A%.

PAGE, H. A. Studies in fantasy-daydreaming frequency and Rorschach categories. *J. Consult. Psychol.*, 1947, 21, 111-114

A fantasy scale was used which dealt with the experience of daydreaming and the Rorschach Test. There are qualitative indications suggestive of a tendency for the frequent daydreamer to perceive movement in partial human figures in unusual locations.

PEISTER, O. Results of the Rorschach Test with oligophrenics. *Allg. Z. Psychiat.*, 1925, 82, 198-223.

PESCOR, M. J. A further study of the Rorschach Test applied to delinquents. *Public Health Rep.*, 1941, 56, 381-395.
The Rorschach was applied to 476 prisoners in a Federal penitentiary. Correlation was found — namely between educational grade status *versus* the total detail responses, mental age *versus* analysis of card — by the general to detail and detail to general methods.

PRADOS, M. Rorschach studies on artists-painters. I. Quantitative analysis. *Rorschach Res. Exch.*, 1944, 8, 178-183.
Rorschach Tests were administered to twenty professional creative artists. Analysis of results showed overemphasis on W, with underproduction of D, high F% with signs of refined control and so forth. Author offers interpretation of these signs.

RABIN, A., PAPNIA, N., AND MCMICHAEL, A. Some effects of alcohol on Rorschach performance. *J. Clin. Psychol.*, 1954, 10, 252-255.
To determine if alcohol would act as a depressant on Rorschach responses, fifty-three normals were tested 3½ hours after ingesting nine to fifteen ounces of alcohol. It was found that F%, A% and W% increased, where as Dd% and F+% decreased significantly on the retest.

RAZONI, JUNE H., GRANT, MARGUERITE, Q., AND IVES, VIRGINIA. Rorschach card pull in a normal adolescent population. *J. Project Techn.*, 1950, 14, 107-133.
Adolescents of an eighteen year longitudinal study were given Rorschachs which were analyzed on the basis of the properties of the inkblots which predispose the S to the use of certain aspects of the blot. The authors find a marked W pull to the first card, breaking down at Card VII, where D begins an upswing. Other findings are cited.

RICKERS-OVSIANKINA, MARIA. The Rorschach Test as applied to normal and schizophrenic subjects. *Brit. J. Med. Psychol.*, 1938, 17, 227-257.
The test was given to thirty-seven schizophrenics and to twenty normal subjects. The schizophrenics showed more responses to the whole card, lacking normal details, as well as other responses.

ROE, ANNE. Analysis of group Rorschachs of biologists. *Rorschach Res. Exch.*, 1949, 13, 25-43.
Group Rorschachs were obtained and scored from 188 biologists. Findings based on subgroups indicated relatively high number of entries for above-average use of unusual details, a very high incidence of shading and color shock, etc.

SALY, ROSAS, F., JERI, R., CUNZA, J., AND SANCHEZ, G. Classification of responses on the Rorschach Test. *Rev. Neuropsiquiat.*, 1950, 13, 567-588.
With the view to establishing norms for Peruvians on the Rorschach Test, the responses of eight hundred and fifty protocols of normal persons are classified as to frequency of type and localization of reponse. The proportion of response to small detail is high as compared with that of European investigators.

SARBIN, T. R., AND MADOW, L. W. Predicting the depth of hypnosis by means of the Rorschach Test. *Amer. J. Orthopsychiat.*, 1942, 12, 268-271.
Sixteen subjects with high, and eight with low, hypnotic indices were compared on the Rorschach Test. The only item which successfully differentiated the two groups was the W/D ratio. The hypnotizable subjects gave more whole than detailed responses.

SCHACHTER, W., AND COTTE, S. Prostitution and the Rorschach Test. *Arch. Int. Neurol.*, 1948, 67, 123-138
Some of the findings on the Rorschach on one hundred

female prostitutes after arrest were: the average number of D's was 12.48, which is lower than normal; the average Dd was 4.7, which is higher than normal; the mean Dbl is .77; the mean Do is .13.

SENDER, SADIE. Discussion of M. R. Hertz's "The normal details in the Rorschach Inkblot Test." *Rorschach Res. Exch.*, 1937, *1*, 118-119.

She points out that the differences in agreement between the Klopfer-Rickers and Hertz's lists of normal, large and small details may be due in part to the fact that her group consisted of adolescent children.

SENDER, SADIE, KLOPFER, B., AND RICKERS-OVSIANKINA, MARIA. Description of the first grade normal details for the ten test plates. *Rorschach Res. Exch.*, 1936, *1*, 1-17.

A discussion of detail answers to the ten Rorschach cards is presented. They conclude that the fundamental patterns of the D's are that they emerge almost spontaneously at the moment one attempts to break up the whole blot into its most natural divisions. The second grade normal details are found in a peninsular-like position, rather than insular. The remaining details fall in the dd, di, de, dr categories.

SINNETT, E., AND ROBERTS, RUTH. Rorschach approach type and the organization of cognitive material. *J. Consult. Psychol.*, 1956, *20*, 109-113.

There is no support for the hypothesis relating Rorschach approach and thinking in terms of generalizations or details using either a structured or unstructured cognitive task.

STAINBROOK, E. The Rorschach description of immediate post-convulsive mental function. *Character and Personality*, 1944, *12*, 302-322

Fifty psychiatric patients undergoing electroshock treatment served as the subjects. Changes in frequency and quality of various Rorschach indices, such as low number of responses, poorly conceptualized form and whole concepts confabulated from part of the blot, were characteristic of various stages of recovery.

STAINBROOK, E., AND SIEGEL, P. S. A comparative group Rorschach study of Southern Negro and white high school and college students. *J. Psychol.*, 1944, *17*, 107-115.

Forty white high school students and forty-five white college students were compared with corresponding numbers of Negro students. It was found that Negro secondary students were lower than white in R, D, S, m, K, CF and higher in FC. Negro college students were higher in Fm/M, lower in R, D, S, etc.

STANCAK, A. S., AND FRAENKEL, E. Factor analysis of Rorschach findings regarding neurosis before and after the application of ethylalcohol. *Cesk. Psychol.*, 1961, *5*, 263-372.

Rorschach experiment with forty-five neurotics aged eighteen to fifty immediately following and four days after consumption of .5 grams pure alcohol. The factors in the experiment found to be increased were Do, O (original response) and W.

STOPOL, M. S. Rorschach performance in relation to two types of stress. *J. Consult. Psychol.*, 1954, *18*, 11-15

Two distinct types of stress conditioning were designated as failure stress and task-induced stress. It was found that low W%, high Dd% and a great number of form-dominant over form-subordinate responses were correlated with the two criteria when failure stress was followed by task-induced stress.

STOTSKY, B. A. Factor analysis of Rorschach scores of schizophrenics. *J. Clin. Psychol.*, 1957, *13*, 275-278.

Common and rare detail scores cluster together on one, while whole responses tended to load on the other factor. Separate factor analyses were performed for F, D and P. They were found to have a common loading on one factor, especially F and D.

STRAVIRIANOS, B. An investigation of sex differences in children as revealed by the Rorschach method. *Rorschach Res. Exch.*, 1943, *6*, 168.

Study of 131 children from five to eleven years. It was found in the case of D responses, the sex difference is −1 per cent indicating that the boys' score falls below the group mean by one per cent, while the girls' score exceeds the mean by one per cent. Taking all age groups (three) together, 66 per cent of the boys underemphasized the D location, while only 36 per cent of the girls did.

SWIFT, J. W. Rorschach responses of 82 pre-school children. *Rorschach Res. Exch.*, 1945, *9*, 74-84

The purpose was to provide normative data for children of preschool age. Significant sex differences were found with respect to frequency of FC, A+, Ad, rejections, average D% and per cent of responses to Cards VIII, IX, and X.

VAN KRENELEN, D. A. The Rorschach list in childhood. *Beih. Schweiz. Z. Psychol.*, 1948, No. *13*, 87-94.

Twenty children from four to six years of age were given the Stanford-Binet and the Rorschach and divided into three levels of intelligence for analyses. Developmental stages were apparent in perception from vague to disorganizd whole. More intelligent children showed an excess of large details, more F+ and a number of movement responses.

VERNON, P. E. The Rorschach Inkblot Test. *Brit. J. Med. Psychol.*, 1933, *13*, 271-295.

A summary of three papers, which includes Rorschach's symbols for classifying response to the inkblots with criticisms of the test.

VIOLET, C. The Rorschach Test and the diagnosis of anxiety. *Rorschachiana*, 1952, *1*, 78-127.

Anxiety may be disclosed in Rorschach terms: Bohm's signs; few W, a special sort of Dd, Do and S; few M, often M−, pure C, many shadings, shocks and special features in the contents.

VORHAUS, P. G. Rorschach reactions in early childhood. Part III. Content and details in preschool records. *Rorschach Res. Exch.*, 1944, *8*, 71-91.

An analysis was made of the Rorschach protocols of 138 children of both sexes aged two to seven years. The results of a detailed examination of the Rorschach categories are given, in terms of details, content originals, forms of perseveration and responses to Cards III and VIII.

WALD, LILLIAN, AND VORHAUS, PAULINE. Rorschach reactions in early childhood. Part II. Intellectual aspects of personality development. *Rorschach Res. Exch.*, 1943, 7, 71-78.

Purpose was to ascertain the development of certain cognitive factors of preschool children by examining their Rorschach records. Among the results, it was found that the number of W and D+d responses tend to increase with age. The D populars are fewer at each level than the W populars.

WELLICH, E. Auditory, olfactory, gustatory and thermic Rorschach responses. *J. Ment. Sci.,* 1949, 95, 667-672.

Records of eighty children, CA 8 to 14, and of adults were analyzed for responses. It was found that thermic, olfactory-gustatory responses are very rare, the lower D of Card III being the most common thermic response.

WITTENBORN, J. R. Statistical tests of certain Rorschach assumptions: The internal consistency of scoring categories. *J. Consult. Psychol.,* 1950, 14, 1-9.

The present data are in no sense a justification for the common practice of ascribing important personality differences between individuals as a result of small differences of the frequency with which occur movement, whole or large detail responses in the protocols of the individual.

THE ERLEBNISTYPUS (EXPERIENCE BALANCE, EXPERIENCE TYPE, M:ΣC)

ALLEN, ROBERT M. The M determinant and color in Rorschach Test. *J. Clin. Psychol.,* 1953, 9, 198-199.

The production of M responses appeared independent of the presence or absence of color.

ALLIEZ, J., AND JAUR, J. M. Test de Rorschach et orientation professionnelle. (The Rorschach Test and vocational orientation.) *Ann. Medicopsychol.* (Paris), 1945, 103, 416-423.

There was found considerable diversity as to types of reactivity (Erlebnistypus) with adolescent boys showing a rare predominance of the ambi-equal type and a conspicuous intravertiveness and girls showing a dominance of intravertiveness.

AMES, LOUISE B. Longitudinal survey of child Rorschach responses: Younger subjects 2 to 10 years. *Genet. Psychol. Monogr.,* 1960, 61, 229-289.

Results showed that Ss do follow the changes predicted by group means in number, movement, color, form, correct form, content and experience balance.

AMES, LOUISE B., LEARNED, J., AND METRAUX, R. W. *Rorschach Responses in Old Age.* New York: Harper & Brothers, 1954.

The nature of the E. B. response is discussed as seen in normals, preseniles and in seniles.

BARISON, F. Studi sul retlivo di Rorschach II Attivazione ed inattivazione dell Erlebnistypus. (Activation and inactivation of the Erlebnistypus.) *Arch. Psicol. Neurol.,* 1949, 10, 157-173.

The interpretation of the Erlebnistypus facilitates a better understanding of temperamental elements that are at the disposal of the individual, even though he may not be using them.

BASH, K. W. Erlebnisfeld und Erlebnistrpusumkehr im Rorschach-Verfahren. (The field of experience and reversal of experience type in the Rorschach method.) *Rorschachiana,* 1952, 1, 158-162.

Manipulation of testing conditions showed extratensive to become more introversive, and introversives become more extratensive. This seemed to show a compensatory relationship between reaction types.

BASH, K. W. Einstellungstypus and Erlebnistypus. *J. Project Techn.,* 1955, 19, 236-243.

The author discusses both Jung's and Rorschach's concepts of introversion and extroversion as representing psychological types. It was concluded contrary to common conception, that Jung's and Rorschach's ideas about introversion-extroversion are essentially identical.

BASH, K. W. Uber die Bestimmung und statistische Verteilung der Introversion und Extratension um Rorschach-Versuch. (The determination and statistical distribution of introversion and extratension on the Rorschach Test.) *Rorschachiana,* 1953, 1, 333-343

Analysis of test protocols of "normal" subjects reflects relatively extratensive trends among men and introversion trends among women.

BECK, S. J. *The Rorschach Experiment: Ventures in Blind Diagnosis.* New York: Grune & Stratton, 1960.

The Experience Balance is considered prior to the discussion of representative case illustrations.

BECK, S. J. Rorschach's Erlebnistypus: An empiric datum. cussion of representative case illustrations.

BEHN, E. H. *Psychische Schuleruntersuchungen mit dem Formdeutversuch Ernst Bircher Verlag.* Bern u. Leipzig, 1931.

Summarizes the Rorschach results of 209 children, ages thirteen to fifteen, with emphasis on the changes taking place in the "Erlebnistypus" during adolescence.

BELL, J. E. *Projective Techniques.* New York: Mantauk Bk. Mfg. Co., Inc., 1948.

The EB is briefly explained along with the detailed meaning of introtensive and extratensive interpretations. Hertz's classification of these terms by degrees of intensity is used.

BIERI, J., AND BLACHER, E. External and internal stimulus factors in Rorschach performance. *J. Consult. Psychol.,* 1956, 20, 1-7.

Using modified Rorschach cards, it was found that Ss in the M>Sum C group generally had significantly longer reaction times to the blots than did Ss in the Sum C>M group. It was also found the M:shading ratio proved to differentiate Ss' total reaction time behavior as well as the M:Sum C ratio.

BINDER, H. Die Helldunkeldeutungen im psychodiagnostischen Experiment von Rorschach. *Schweiz. Arch.*

Neurol. Psychiat., 1932-33, *30*, 1-67.

Binder shows that the Erlebnistypus depends upon the distribution and the quality of the M and C responses and upon the content of their respective interpretations.

BLEULER, M., AND BLEULER, R. Rorschach's Inkblot Test and racial psychology: Mental peculiarities of Moroccans. *Character Personality*, 1935, *4*, 97-114

Excess M appeared in people who are independent of the environment, who are gudied by their thoughts rather than their feelings, which tend to be repressed. When C predominates, subjects are prone to react to external stimuli quickly in an emotional way.

BURT, C. The Rorschach Test. Laboratory notes, 1945, University of London.

Burt points out the difference between the terms *extra-tension* used by Rorschach and *extraversion* as used by Jung. He does not accept Rorschach's M/C concept of EB.

CARVALKAL, REBAS J. Psico-diagnostico de Rorschach. (The Rorschach Test.) *Rev. Clin. S. Paulo*, 1942, *11*, 31-34.

The part played by movement responses in relation to color responses is discussed as an important indicator of personality.

CHENG, FA-YU, CHEN CHU-CHANG, AND RIN, HSIEN. A personality analysis of the Ami and its three subgroups by the Rorschach Test. *Acta Psychol. Jaiwanica*, 1958, *1*, 131-134.

Administration of the Rorschach to 249 Ss of the Ami tribe showed them to have imaginative and introversive tendencies reflecting a dominance of M to C.

DELAY, J., PICHAT, P., LEMPERIERE, T., AND PERSE, J. *The Rorschach and the Epileptic Personality*. New York: Logos Press, 1958.

The experience balance is discussed as it manifests itself in athletic epileptics, in children and in idiopathics, temporal and traumatic epilepsy.

ENKE, W. Die Konstitutionstypen im Rorschachschen Experiment. *Neurol. Psychiat.*, 1927, *108*, 645-674.

Reports the test records of patients suggest a correspondence between manic tendencies and extratension, and schizoid tendencies and introversion, to some extent validating the claim of the M and C factors.

FONDA, C. The nature and meaning of the Rorschach white space response. *J. Abnorm. Soc. Psychol.*, 1951, *46*, 367-377.

The EB classification by formula M/M and Sum C appeared to have limited reliability. In this study, 57 per cent of the subjects were identically classified on the Rorschach Inkblot Test and a parallel series of inkblots by Harrower.

GUIRDHAM, A. The diagnosis of depression by the Rorschach Test. *Brit. J. Med. Psychol.*, 1936, *16*, 130-145.

In depression states the appreciation of color and movement is reduced, and thus the EB is constricted.

HALVORSEN, H. Eine korrelation zwischen Rorschach test und graphologie. *Arch. Angew. Psychol.*, 1931, *40*, 34-39.

Correlations between slope of handwriting and ratio M/Sum C are satisfactorily high, averaging .60, showing that traits accorded these different angles of script cor-

respond to introversive and extratensive types.

HARRIMAN, P. L. The Rorschach Test applied to a group of college students. *Amer. J. Orthopsychiat.*, 1935, *5*, 116-120.

Reporting on a group of college men and women, movement was found to be slightly but significantly more numerous than color responses, showing a control over the more introversive tendencies and more control over the emotional life.

HARROWER-ERICKSON, M. R. *Psychodiagnostic Inkblots, a Series Parallel to the Rorschach Inkblots*. New York: Grune & Stratton, 1945.

In comparison with the Rorschach Test, it was reported that the M/Sum C ratio was unchanged in 88 per cent of the cases retested with the parallel series of inkblots.

HAYS, W. Age and sex differences on the Rorschach experience balance. *J. Abnorm. Soc. Psychol.*, 1952, *47*, 390-393.

The experience balance seems to vary with both sex and age. Analysis shows a constriction of EB in subjects over fifty, especially females, and an introversive trend in male subjects over fifty.

HAYS, W., GELLERMAN, S., AND SLOAN, W. A study of the relationships between the verb-adjective quotient and the Rorschach EB. *J. Clin. Psychol.*, 1951, *7*, 224-227.

Verb-adjective ratios were compared with three different estimates of the Rorschach EB. The authors concluded that speech involves a definite relation to the nature of the Rorschach record of the EB.

HERMAN, J. L. Ideational and motor correlates of the Rorschach experience type. *Diss. Abstr.*, 1960, *20*, 3831-3832.

It was found that Rorschach introversives showed greater motor inhibition and ideational productivity and less gestural motor expression and need for motor activity than Rorschach extratensives.

HERTZ, M. R. The reliability of the Rorschach Inkblot Test. *J. Appl. Psychol.*, 1934, *18*, 461-477.

A 73 per cent correspondence between the EB types was found in comparing half of the test.

HERTZ, M. R. The Rorschach Inkblot Test: Historical summary. *Psychol. Bull.*, 1935, *32*, 33-66.

Broad summary of earlier findings with regard to the "Erlebnistypen." It was concluded that a preponderance of M over C is suggestive of submission, lack of aggression, inability to control and persuade others, introversion. A preponderance of C over M reflects ascendency, aggressiveness and ability to control others.

HERTZ, M. R. Personality patterns in adolescence as portrayed by the Rorschach method: IV the "Erlebnistypus." *J. Gen. Psychol.*, 1943, *29*, 3-45.

Age and sex of adolescents were studied in terms of the changes in the movement and color factors which go to make up the EB. The data indicates changes frequently taking place, and these shifts were attributed to being associated with maturity.

HUNTER, M. Responses of comparable white and Negro adults to the Rorschach Test. *J. Psychol.*, 1937, *3*, 173-182.

From equated groups of white and Negro subjects, it was found that the white group showed more introversion, while conversely the Negro group showed more extratension.

KADINSKY, D. Human whole and detail responses in the Rorschach Test. *Rorschach Res. Exch.*, 1946, *10*, 140-144.

Responses with human content have introversive value and show the importance of consciousness and morality. H% and EB are interrelated. H% in a coaretated record is a clue to the true EB. Low H% in introverted records shows mental maturity.

KARNETSKY, C., AND GERARD, D. Effect of increasing the number of Rorschach responses on Sum C and M. *J. Abnorm. Soc. Psychol.*, 1954, *49*, 592-593.

The results suggest that the frequency of color and human movement-determined responses is probably due to the influence of the number of responses as an independent variable.

KIMBLE, G. A. Social influence on Rorschach records. *J. Abnorm. Soc. Psychol.*, 1945, *40*, 89-93.

Rorschachs administered to students, first in the lab and then in the social atmosphere of a cafeteria, showed a striking increase in color and a decrease in the ratio between the number of movement responses and the color sum (EB).

KLUVER, H. An analysis of recent work on problem of types. *J. Nerv. Ment. Dis.*, 1925, *62*, 560-596.

A theoretical discussion on the similarity of the Rorschach types with other systems such as Jung's and Kretschmer's.

KOHLMANN, T. Psychologische untersuchungen an psychosen in der elektroschock-behandlung. (Psychological tests in psychoses in electro shock therapy.) *Wien. Klin. Wschr.*, 1947, *59*, 140.

Following electroshock therapy, a narrowing of the Erlebnistype occurred in schizophrenics.

LEVY, D., AND BECK, S. J. *The Rorschach Test in Manic-depressive Psychosis.* XI. Research publications of the Association for Research in Nervous and Mental Diseases. Baltimore: Williams & Wilkins, 1931, 167-181.

Differing psychograms are reported for manic and pressive subjects, validating in part claims for color and movement.

LOOSLI-USTERI, M. Le test de Rorschach applique a differents groupes des enfants de 10-13 ans. (Application of the Rorschach Test to different groups of children from 10-13 years of age.) *Arch. Psychol.*, 1929, *22*, 51-106.

Comparison of Geneva primary school children with asylum children found the asylum group to be more frequently introversive in character. The Rorschach EB types are also discussed.

LOOSLI-USTERI, M. Les interpretations dons, le test de Rorschach. Interpretations kinesthesiques et interpretation-couleur. (Interpretations of the Rorschach test. Kinesthetic and color interpretations.) *Arch. Psychol.*, 1932, *23*, 349-365.

While it was found that color response interpretations were basically the same for adults and children, the kinesthetic response interpretations were not normal for ages nine to fourteen.

LOPFE, A. Uber Rorschachsche formdeutversuche mit 10-13 jahrigen knaben. *Exp. Angew. Psychol.*, 1925, *26*, 202-253.

Norms for different age groups showed little change with age. Individual differences were greater than any age differences noted.

MANN, L. The relation of Rorschach indices of extraversion-introversion to certain dream dimensions. *J. Clin. Psychol.*, 1955, *11*, 80-81.

A study was made of the relationship between Rorschach E.I. indices and certain dream dimensions. None of the relationships yielded significant results.

MELTZER, H. Talkativeness in stuttering and non-stuttering children. *J. Genet. Psychol.*, 1935, *46*, 371-379.

The analysis of Rorschach protocols of a group of stuttering children showed 54.7 per cent to be extratensive and 21.9 per cent to be constrictive or ambi-equal.

MEYERNOFF, H. Das syndrom der traumatischen hirnleistungschwache im Rorschachtest. (The syndrome of traumatic brain function weakness in the Rorschach Test.) *Psychiat. Neurol. Med. Psychol.*, (Leipzig), 1950, *2*, 176-182.

In performance of two hundred brain-injured patients on the Rorschach test, three fourths of the cases presented a characteristic syndrome including altered Erlebnistypes.

MIRY LOPEZ, E., MEYER-GINSBERG, A., ABREV-PAIVA, G., AND DE OLIVETRA, A. Comparison entre le type de caractere (Erlebnistypus) selon le test de Rorschach et le type somatique selon la classification de Sheldon. (Comparison of the type of character according to the Rorschach and the somatic type according to the classification of Sheldon.) In Baumgarten, Franziska. *La Psychotechnique dans le Monde Moderne.* Paris: Presses Universitaire de France, 1952, pp. 148-152.

The relationship between the two types is positive, but the material at hand is insufficient for categorical conclusions.

MONS, W. *Principles and Practice of the Rorschach Personality Test.* London: J. B. Lippincott Co., 1950.

A brief definition of EB with a broad general explanation of its meaning.

MUNZ, E. Die reaktion des pycknickes im Rorschach'schen psychodiagnostischen Versuch. *Z. Neurol. Psychiat.*, 1924, *91*, 26-92.

Munz's results show the pyknic type corresponding to the extratensive type and the "schizaffin" to the introversive.

MURRAY, D. C. An investigation of the Rorschach white space response in an extratensive experience balance as a measure of outwardly directed opposition. *J. Project. Techn.*, 1957, *21*, 40-46.

Extratensive EB and outwardly directed oppositional tendencies were found not to be related. The use of S in an extratensive EB was also found as not being indicative of outwardly directed oppositional tendencies.

OESER, O. A. Some experiments on abstraction of form and color. Pt. II. Rorschach Test. *Brit. J. Psychol.*, 1932, *22*, 287-323.

Oeser confirms Rorschach's conjecture that women are more extratensive than men.

PALMER, J. O. Rorschach's experience balance: The concept, general popular characteristics, and intellectual correlates. *J. Project. Techn.*, 1955, *19*, 138-145.

EB was determined for large groups of white and Negro patients of both sexes and of normal adolescents and adults. In all samples, EB was normally distributed, and there was an absence of age, sex and racial differences. An ambi-equal EB appears to be positively related to intelligence as measured by WB intelligence scale.

PALMER, J. O. Attitudinal correlates of Rorschach's experience balance. *J. Project. Techn.*, 1956, *20*, 207-211.

Each of the four EB types were selected from a psychiatric population and administered the MMPI and Drake's IE (Social Introversion)) scale. Few, if any, of the specific traits attributed to the EB groups in the current literature appeared.

PALMER, J. O. Some relationships between Rorschach's experience balance and Rosenzweig's Frustration-Aggression patterns. *J. Project. Techn.*, 1957, *21*, 137-141.

Extratensives were found to show more obstacle dominance and less extrapunitive need persistence; the intratensives showed higher extrapunitive need persistence. Coarctate and ambi-equal groups showed less defensiveness than either of the introextratensive extremes.

PALMER, J. O. Alterations in Rorschach's experience balance under conditions of food and sleep deprivation: A construct validation study. *J. Project. Techn.*, 1963, *27*, 208-214.

The food-deprived Ss showed a marked increase in extratensive responses, while the sleep-deprived group showed a marked intratensive shift. The results of the study were interpreted as lending support to the EB construct.

PALMER, J. O., AND LUSTGARTEN, B. J. The prediction of TAT structure as a test of Rorschach's experience balance. *J. Project. Techn.*, 1962, *26*(2), 212-220.

Rorschach intratensives tend to emphasize internal feelings of their heroes on TAT stories; but extratensives do not stress external personality characteristics or environmental presures. The coarctate group bore the highest ratings for "violence." Ambi-equals mentioned both external and internal characteristics of their TAT heroes.

PHILLIPS, L., AND SMITH, J. G. *Rorschach Interpretation: Advanced Technique.* New York: Grune & Stratton, 1953.
Presents the general interpretive significance of M to Sum C in addition to a table which presents characteristic ratios for fifteen nosological groups. Current use of the ratio is criticized.

PIOTROWSKI, Z. A. The reliability of the Rorschach's Erlebnistypus. *J. Abnorm. Soc. Psychol.*, 1937, *32*, 439-445.
The author points out that the measure of reliability of the EB by split-half method cannot be justified by the Rorschach method; consequently, these measures are inadequate. The confusion concerning the meaning of the EB is also discussed.

PIOTROWSKI, Z. A. Blind analysis of a case of compulsion neurosis. *Rorschach Res. Exch.*, 1937-38, *2*, 89-111.

Piotrowski views the EB as one of the most important aspects of personality.

POPPINGA, O. Die teilinhaltliche Beachtung von form und farbe bei Erwachsenen in ihrer Beziehung zur struckturpsychologischen typenlehre. *Z. Psychol.*, 1931, *121*, 137-177.

In this study, form-color types were compared with the Erlebnistypen. No similarity was observed between form-color types and Rorschach intro-extraversive types.

PRADOS, M. Rorschach studies on artists-painters. I. Quantitative analysis. *Rorschach Res. Exch.*, 1944, *8*, 178-183.
Analysis of the results of the administration of the Rorschach to twenty professional creative artists revealed a large number M outnumbering FM and high CF:FC ratio, resulting in a dilated Erlebnistype tending to extratensiveness or ambi-equality.

RABIN, A. I., AND BECK, S. J. Genetic aspects of some Rorschach factors. *Amer. J. Orthopsychiat.*, 1950, *20*, 595-599.
At onset of adolescence, a marked decline in the extratensive experience balance was noted in a school population, ages six to fourteen.

RAPAPORT, D., GILL, M., AND SCHAFER, R. *Diagnostic Psychological Testing* (Vol. II). Yearbook Publishers, 1946.
Rationale and significance of M to Sum C ratio, as related to a fairly complete list of clinical diagnostic categories.

ROSENTHAL, M. Some behavior correlates of the Rorschach experience balance. *J. Project. Techn.*, 1962, *26*, 442-446.
Comparison of EB to matchstick test showed M group to be significantly more deliberate and cautious in its approach, while the C group was characterized by more motor activity and less response delay.

SCHACHTER, M. Le facteur "sexe" et le test de Rorschach. (The sex factor and the Rorschach Test.) *Acta Neurol. Belg.*, 1950, *50*, 157-158
The salient sex difference was the effect that men were predominantly coarctated and the women were predominantly extratensive.

SCHENCK, H. Experimentell-strukturpsychologische Untersuchungen uber den "dynamischen typus." *Z. Psychol.*, 1929, *113*, 91-208
Comparing Erlebnistypen with eidetic types, Schenck finds that J-1 corresponds to a tendency toward extratension, while the J-2 type tends toward introversion.

SINGER, J. L., AND SPOHN, H. E. Some behavioral correlates of Rorschach's experience type. *J. Consult. Psychol.*, 1954, *18*, 1-10.
In a study of spontaneous and inhibited motor activity using a schizophrenic population, it was found that introtensives, M>C, showed longer inhibition times and less motor activity during a waiting period. Extratensives, C>M, showed the opposite response with a greater tendency toward environmental responsiveness.

SUARES, N. D. Personality development in adolescence. *Rorschach Res. Exch.*, 1938, *3*, 2-12.
In a longitudinal study attempting to show changes in EB, analysis of Rorschach protocols of adolescent youth

show an increased introversiveness for boys, while the girls showed an increase in extratensiveness. While boys show a strong M increase, for girls C becomes more likely.

THORNTON, G. R., AND GUILFORD, J. P. The reliability and meaning of Erlebnistypus scores in the Rorschach Test. *J. Abnorm. Soc. Psychol.*, 1936, *31*, 324-330.

M/C scores were found not to be correlated with any of the five factors scored by the Nebraska personality inventory: a scale of introversion-extraversion.

VAN DEN BROEK, R. De relatie tussen het begrip "belevingstype" von Rorschach en de "instellings" typologie von Jung. (The relation between the concept "experience type" or Rorschach and the attitude types of Jung.) *Neder. Psychol.*, 1954, *9*, 517-525.

The concept of EB and Jung's introextroversion are found to be strongly similar. The Jungian concept of attitude is believed to be mirrored in the experience type of the Rorschach Test.

VAUGHN, J., AND KRUG, O. The analytic character of the Rorschach Inkblot Test. *Amer. J. Orthopsychiat.*, 1938, *8*, 220-229.

The M/C ratio was compared with Bernreuter ratings. Sum C correlated .52 with the Bernreuter measure of

neurotic tendency and M correlated .178 with the measure of introversion.

VERNON, P. E. The Rorschach Inkblot Test. II. *Brit. J. Med. Psychol.*, 1933, *13*, 179-200.

Using the split-half technique for obtaining a correlation coefficient for the M-Sum C/R index, a reliability of .55 was found.

VERNON, P. E. Recent work on the Rorschach Test. *J. Ment. Sci.*, 1935, *81*, 894-920.

The author reviews the research on the Rorschach since his last review article in 1933. Erlenistypus is discussed under a main heading.

WYSOCKI, B. A. Differentiation between introvert-extrovert types by Rorschach method as compared with other methods. *J. Psychol.*, 1957, *43*, 41-46.

Ratio between form and color assesses of intro-extrovert types by Rorschach method as compared with other methods. *J. Psychol.*, 1957, *43*, 41-46.

WYSOCKI, B. A. A factorial study of Rorschach protocols. *Percept. Motor. Skills*, 1960, *10*, 105-106.

Factorial analysis of Rorschach protocols indicated that color to form rather than color to movement is the primary index of experience balance.

FORM

ABRAMS, E. N. Prediction of intelligence from certain Rorschach factors. *J. Clin. Psychol.*, 1955, *11*, 81-83.

The F% was correlated with the WB full scale IQ and a formula for estimating IQ from the Rorschach is given.

ARLUCK, E. W. A study of some personality differences between epileptics and normals. *Rorschach Res. Exch.*, 1940, *4*, 154-156.

One of the chief differences is in the per cent of F responses. The epileptics as a group give a more unfavorable picture.

BECK, S. J. The Rorschach Test as applied to a feebleminded group. *Arch. Psychol.*, 1932, *136*, p. 84.

Sharp form is one of the Rorschach indices to intellectual functioning. A correlation between F and mental age was found to be .64.

BECK, S. J. Problems of further research in the Rorschach Test. *Amer. J. Orthopsychiat.*, 1935, *5*, 100-115.

On the basis of the author's experience with the Rorschach, several suggestions are made. One is to standardize statistically the response representing good form and bad form.

BECK, S. J. Psychological processes in Rorschach findings. *J. Abnorm. Soc. Psychol.*, 1937, *31*, 482-488.

Good or clearly perceived forms occur with high frequency in healthy adults and infrequently in the feebleminded.

BECK, S. J. Trends on orthopsychiatric therapy: Rorschach F plus and the Ego in treatment. *Amer. J. Orthopsychiat.*, 1948, *18*, 395-401.

Beck identifies the F+ with the work of the ego, upon the maturation of which the therapist bases his hope of constructive therapy.

BERKOWITZ, M., AND LEVINE, J. Rorschach scoring categories as diagnostic signs. *J. Consult. Psychol.*, 1953, *17*, 110-112.

F + % was significantly different for each group in a comparison of a group of neurotics and a group of psychotics.

BOSQUET, K. T., AND STANLEY, W. C. Discriminative powers of Rorschach determinants in children referred to a child guidance clinic. *J. Consult. Psychol.*, 1956, *20*, 17-21.

P, F% and A% increased significantly with age in a group of boys seven to thirteen years of age.

BUHLER, CHARLOTTE, AND LEFEVER, D. W. A Rorschach study on the psychological characteristics of alcoholics. *Quart. J. Stud. Alcohol.*, 1947, *8*, 197-260.

It was found that the alcoholic differs from the psychopath in better functioning rationality (good F%).

COOK, P. G. The application of the Rorschach Test to a Samoan group. *Rorschach Res. Exch.*, 1942, *6*, 51-60.

Among the differences compared to protocols in our culture was an extremely high percentage of F responses. Criteria established in our culture do not apply to Samoa.

CURNUTT, R. H., AND LEWIS, W. B. The relationship between Z scores on the Bender Gestalt and F plus % on the Rorschach. *J. Clin. Psychol.*, 1954, *10*, 96-97.

These two reputed measures of ego strength were correlated, and no significant relationship was found.

DELAY, J., AND PICHOT, P. On the psychopathology of vision in the Rorschach. *Encephale*, 1957, *46*, 547-563.

F + % equals 70 is an index of organicity. It is a measurement of perceptual acuity which is more sensitive to the organic syndrome than is the IQ.

DIMMICK, G. B. An application of the Rorschach Ink Blot Test to three clinical types of Dementia Praecox. *J. Psychol.*, 1935, *1*, 61-74.

The author states that the present method of scoring involves too large a subjective factor for the F+ and F−.

DUBITSCHER, F. Rorschach's form-interpretation experiment with adult psychopaths and psychopathic and dull children. *Z. Ges. Neurol. Psychiat.*, 1932, *142*, 129-158.

F responses were fewer in psychopaths than in normal persons. He concludes that there is essentially a reduction in all intelligence factors quantitatively in psychopaths, and they show heightened affective and impulsive tendencies.

FELDMAN, M. J., GURSSLIN, CAROLYN, KAPLAN, M. L., AND SHARLOCK, NIDIA. A preliminary study to develop a more discriminating F plus ratio. *J. Clin. Psychol.*, 1954, *10*, 47-51.

The authors offer Feldman's F + % to evaluate ego strength from the Rorschach.

FIELDING, B., AND BROWN, F. Prediction of intelligence from certain Rorschach factors. *J. Clin. Psychol.*, 1956, *12*, 196-197.

Abrams formula for obtaining an IQ from Rorschach determinants M, F+, W and R was tested, and the results indicated that the formula is satisfactory for those groups whose WB IQ falls between 90 and 110, and for those protocols in which M is greater than three.

GIBBY, R. G. The stability of certain Rorschach variables under conditions of experimentally induced sets: the intellectual variables. *J. Project. Techn.*, 1951, *15*, 3-25.

It was found that not all intellectual variables are equally stable. F + % is one of the most stable.

HAFNER, A. J. Response time and Rorschach behavior. *J. Clin. Psychol.*, 1958, *14*, 154-155.

Subjects who were instructed to respond as quickly as possible to each card and were told to limit themselves to two responses obtained significantly lower F + % than the control group which was given the test under standard conditions.

HENRY, EDITH M., AND ROTTER, J. B. Situational influences on Rorschach responses. *J. Consult. Psychol.*, 1956, *20*, 457-462.

Knowledge of test purpose resulted in significantly more form responses and more good form-level.

KAMMERER, T., SINGER, L., AND DURAND DE BOUSINGEN, R. The prognostic value of comparative Rorschach Tests before and after psychosurgery. *Evolut. Psychiat. (Paris)*, 1956, *1*, 207-224.

Unfavorable prognosis is indicated by a diminuation in perception of good forms and animal responses.

KELLY, D., MARGULIES, H., AND BARRERA, S. The stability of the Rorschach method as demonstrated in electric convulsive therapy cases. *Rorschach Res. Exch.*, 1941, *5*, 44-48.

After one shock treatment, changes did occur in F%. It was suggested, therefore, that this determinant is less

important from a quantitative point of view than some of the other determinants.

KIMBAL, ALICE J. Evaluation of form level in the Rorschach. *J. Project. Techn.*, 1950, *14*, 219-244.

The results of this appraisal indicate the need for objective and clearly defined criteria for scoring form-level in the Rorschach.

KIMBAL, ALICE J. History of form-level appraisal in the Rorschach. *J. Project. Techn.*, 1950, *14*, 134-152.

The author cites the present disagreement among Rorschach experts, and the need for a reliable and standard form-level scoring technique is pointed out.

KLEIN, G. S., AND SCHLESINGER, H. J. Perceptual attitudes of 'form-boundedness' and 'form-lability' in Rorschach responses. *Amer. Psychol.*, 1950, *5*, 321.

It was found that form-boundedness and form-lability could be experimentally defined by use of the flicker fusion and the phi-phenomenon techniques.

KLOPFER, B., AND DAVIDSON, H. H. Form level rating: A preliminary proposal for appraising mode and level of thinking as expressed in Rorschach records. *Rorschach Res. Exch.*, 1944, *8*, 164-177.

A method is proposed whereby the form level of Rorschach responses may be objectified with provision made for both plus and minus scores.

KUMAR, P. The Rorschach Test in psychoneurotic and normal groups. *Indian J. Psychol.*, 1951, *46*(4), 169-172.

Only the F+ scores had a significant chi square value in differentiating the two groups.

LEVI, J. Rorschach patterns predicting success or failure in the rehabilitation of the physically handicapped. *J. Abnorm. Soc. Psychol.*, 1951, *46*, 240-244.

Records giving a neurotic personality pattern and characterized by a very high F + % and responses of aggressive animals seem to be indicative of a good prognosis.

LINE, W., AND GRIFFIN, J. D. M. Some results obtained with the Rorschach Test, objectively scored. *Amer. J. Psychiat.*, 1935, *92*, 109-114.

Twenty advanced graduate students in psychology and twenty-three patients representing a variety of psychoses were tested. There were no differences between the groups in the scores for form, whole responses, movement and color.

LUCENA, J. Modifications of Rorschach Test findings during phases of insulin shock. *Rev. Psychol. Appl.*, 1958, *8*, 25-35.

It was found that changes in Rorschach indices of personality organization, such as F% and F + %, changed significantly more often from the preinjection test to favorable than for the unfavorable cases.

McREYNOLDS, P. Perception of Rorschach concepts as related to personality deviations. *J. Abnorm. Soc. Psychol.*, 1951, *46*, 131-141.

The overall differences in means of F + % in several varied psychiatric groups were significant at the .01 level or better.

MELTZER, H. Personality differences between stuttering and non-stuttering children as indicated by the Rorschach Test. *J. Psychol.*, 1944, *17*, 39-59.

MONNIER, M. The Rorschach Psychological Test. *Encephale*, 1934, *29*, 189-201, 247-270.

The author presents the history of the test and discusses the origins of form.

MONTALTO, F. D. An application of the group Rorschach technique to the problem of achievement in college. *J. Clin. Psychol.*, 1946, *2*, 254-260.

One of the conclusions of this study is that academic achievement is most closely related to several factors, including F%.

MOTOAKI, H., TOMITA, M., AND YUMOTO, Y. A study of form-level rating in the Rorschach Test. *Jap. J. Psychol.*, 1957, *28*, 86-93.

Average form levels, both weighted and unweighted, are given for all scoring categories of the Rorschach protocols obtained from 125 students.

OHKURA, K. Rorschach study with delinquents. *Jap. Fam. Court Monogr.*, 1957, *9*(5), 1-37.

F% was found to be significantly higher in delinquents than in normals.

PAULSEN, A. Rorschachs of school beginners. *Rorschach Res. Exch.*, 1941, *5*, 24-29.

F% and F + % were among the factors most closely associated with the Binet Test results in children five to seven years of age.

PEMBERTON, W. H. General semantics and the Rorschach Test. *Pap. Amer. Congr. Gen. Semant.*, 1943, *2*, 251-260.

The author sketches the psychological significance of the predominance or absence of form and other determinants.

PRADOS, M. Rorschach studies on artists-painters. *Rorschach Res. Exch.*, 1944, *8*, 178-183.

An analysis of the protocols of artists revealed a high F% with signs of refined control.

RABIN, A., PAPANIA, N., AND MCMICHAEL, A. Some effects of alcohol on Rorschach performance. *J. Clin. Psychol.*, 1954, *10*, 252-255.

F% increased, but F + % decreased significantly on retest after ingestion of nine to fifteen ounces of alcohol.

ROBAYE, FRANCINE, AND VAN NYPELSEER, J. L. Essay on the validation of the Rorschach indices, particularly F black response, W and experience balance with levels of aspiration and expectation. *Bull. CERP*, 1955, *4*, 3-19.

Those who have negative level of expectation and high level of aspiration gave more F black responses. F% was higher in groups with high levels of expectation.

SHERESHEVSKI-SHERE, EUGENIA, LASSER, L. M., AND GOTTESFELD, B. H. An evaluation of anatomy content and F plus % in the Rorschachs of alcoholics, schizophrenics, and normals. *J. Proj. Techn.*, 1953, *17*, 229-233.

It was found that alcoholics had a marked tendency to fall below the minimum F + % range of 65 per cent.

SIEGMAN, A. W. A culture and personality study based on a comparison of Rorschach performance. *J. Soc. Psychol.*, 1956, *44*, 173-178.

In comparing the protocols of a group of college students and a group of Yeshiva students, a significant difference was found in F% which suggests that personality differences are culturally conditioned in these two groups.

SMITH, S., AND GEORGE, C. E. Rorschach factors related to experimental stress. *J. Consult. Psychol.*, 1951, *15*, 190-195.

It was found that there is a curvilinear relationship between F% and alterations in behavior caused by stress. Also, the F factor does not predict behavior under stress for older subjects studied (over twenty-nine years).

SPIEGELMAN, M. Rorschach form-level, intellectual functioning and potential. *J. Proj. Techn.*, 1956, *20*, 335-343.

A correlation of .55 was found between average form-level and IQ.

SWIFT, J. W. Rorschach responses of 82 preschool children. *Rorschach Res. Exch.*, 1945, *9*, 74-84.

It was found that F% was one of the factors related to mental age.

TAMKIN, A. S. An evaluation of the construct validity of Barron's ego-strength scale. *J. Clin. Psychol.*, 1957, *13*, 156-158.

Ego-strength score was not significantly correlated with F + %. As expected, F and critical item scores were highly correlated, and both were significantly negatively correlated with ego-strength. F also differentiated significantly between psychotics and nonpsychotics.

WALKER, R. G. An approach to standardization of Rorschach form-level. *J. Proj. Techn.*, 1953, *17*, 426-436.

The form-level of each of 299 Rorschach W responses taken from Beck's form-level tables was judged by one hundred normal adults. The form-levels thus obtained were more effective in differentiating between normal and paranoid adults than Beck's tables.

WILLIAMS, M. An experimental study of intellectual control under stress and associated Rorschach factors. *J. Consult. Psychol.*, 1947, *11*, 21-29.

This study attempts to validate the Rorschach factors which are said to have relation to intellectual control. The results confirm the assumed relationship.

WISHNER, J. Rorschach intellectual indicators in neurotics. *Amer. J. Orthopsychiat.*, 1948, *18*, 265-279.

F + % did not correlate significantly with any Wechsler-Bellevue score.

WOOD, A., ARLUCK, E., AND MARGULIES, H. Report of a group discussion of the Rorschach method. *Rorschach Res. Exch.*, 1941, *5*, 154-165.

Koffka suggested that the F response be investigated with relation to continuity, balance and Pragnanz.

MOVEMENT

ABEL, T. M., PIOTROWSKI, Z. A., AND STONE, G. Responses of Negro and white morons to the Rorschach Test. *Amer. J. Ment. Defic.*, 1944, *48*, 253-257.

Found that the Negroes as a group gave a greater number of human movement responses than did the whites as a group, but that this difference was not significant.

ABRAMS, E. N. Prediction of intelligence from certain Rorschach factors. *J. Clin. Psychol.*, 1955, *11*, 81-83.

Found the multiple r between Rorschach determinants F + %, M, W and R with the WB Full Scale IQ to be .53.

ALLEN, R. M. The M determinant and color in Rorschach Test. *J. Clin. Psychol.*, 1953, *9*, 198-199.

Found that the production of M responses appeared to be independent of the presence or absence of color.

ALLEN, R. M., AND DORSEY, R. N. The effect of suggestion on human movement productivity in Rorschach's Test. *Z. diagnostic Psychol.*, 1954, *2*, 137-142.

Test-retest situation. In retest situation, S was told to "see a person or persons doing something." Total productivity decreased 50 per cent and human movement percepts increased significantly.

ALLEN, R. M., RAY, C. D., AND POOLE, R. C. The Lesy Movement Test: Suggestions for scoring and relationship to Rorschach movement responses. *J. Consult. Psychol.*, 1953, *17*, 195-198.

On the basis of findings in this study, the hypothesis that the Lesy Movement Cards Test can be employed as a check on the Rorschach movement responses of a subject is rejected.

ALLISON, H. W., AND ALLISON, SARAH, G. Personality change following transorbital lobotomy. *Proc. Okla. Acad. Sci.*, 1952, *33*, 265-271.

Following a transorbital lobotomy, there was a significant decrease of m% and FK% and a significant increase in W% and reaction time.

ALTUS, W. D. Some correlates of the group Rorschach and the schizophrenia scale of the MMPI among two groups of "normal" college students. *J. Consult. Psychol.*, 1948, *12*, 375-378.

Found a "high" correlation. The three most valid items in the group Rorschach in terms of the Sc scale criterion are P%, four or more FM, and total responses divided by number of content categories, 3.0 or higher.

ALTUS, W. D. Group Rorschach and Q-L discrepancies on the ACE. *Psychol. Rep.*, 1958, *4*, 469.

Concludes that the verbalist (high-L person) tends to produce more human movement responses than the quantitatively orientated (high-Q) person produces.

ALTUS, W. D., AND ALTUS, GRACE T. Rorschach movement variables and verbal intelligence. *J. Abnorm. Soc. Psychol.*, 1952, *47*, 531-533.

Found that the curvilinear regression of M on intelligence is, apparently, a function of the unstereotyped M. Popular M, FM and m, while correlating positively with intelligence, do so to a low degree.

AMES, LOUISE B. Age changes in the Rorschach of individual elderly subjects. *J. Genet. Psychol.*, 1960, *97*, 289-315.

Studied six elderly people, ages 70 to 102 years. Many showed increasingly high F%, increasingly low F + %, lower M and FM and higher A%. There were exceptions, however.

AMES, LOUISE B. Age changes in the Rorschach responses

of a group of elderly individuals. *J. Genet. Psychol.*, 1960, *97*, 257-285.

Found a general trend of people over seventy to exhibit an increasing restriction of Rorschach responses. However, a few of the better endowed showed with increasing age a lower F%, higher F + % and increased M, usually impersonal M.

AMES, LOUISE B. Longitudinal survey of child Rorschach responses: Younger subjects two to ten years. *Genet. Psychol. Monogr.*, 1960, *61*, 229-289.

Found R, M, C, etc., to increase during this age period.

ANSBACHER, H. L. Social interest, an Adlerian rationale for the Rorschach human movement response. *J. Project. Techn.*, 1956, *20*, 363-365.

Author interprets M as a function of social interest.

BARROB, F. Threshold for the perception of human movement in inkblots. *J. Consult. Psychol.*, 1955, *19*, 33-38.

Found that the threshold for human movement perception was uncorrelated with intelligence, originality and associative fluency. Concludes that the M tendency is a stylistic variable and relates to a perference for intrapsychic living.

BAUGHMAN, E. E. A reply on Stein's "Note on a comparative analysis of Rorschach forms with altered stimulus characteristics." *J. Project. Techn.*, 1955, *19*, 466-567.

Defends position that there is an identity in the psychological processes underlying M and FM responses.

BECK, S. J. Problems of the further research in the Rorschach Test. *Amer. J. Orthopsychiat.*, 1935, *5*, 100-115.

Author summarizes his reactions to use of the test. Among these is a calling for an experimental identification of the true movement response.

BECK, S. J. Psychological processes in Rorschach findings. *J. Abnorm. Soc. Psychol.*, 1937, *31*, 482-488.

"Movement" could validly be interpreted as an introversive trend in the sense of an inner creative activity in the healthy adult of superior intelligence. Concludes that it is not possible at all times to interpret the same Rorschach factor as having the same personality value.

BERRYMAN, EILEEN. Poets' responses to the Rorschach. *J. Gen. Psychol.*, 1961, *64*, 349-358.

Found FM to be indicative of the productive artist.

BIERI, J., AND BLACHER, E. External and internal stimulus factors in Rorschach performance. *J. Consult. Psychol.*, 1956, *20*, 1-7.

Study used modified Rorschach, one detail being eliminated from each card. Found that Ss in the M>ΣC group had longer reaction times to the cards than Ss in the ΣC>M group. Also found that the M:Sh (shading responses) ratio proved to differentiate Ss' total reaction time behavior.

BOSZORMENYI, G., AND MEREI, F. Zum Problem von Konstitution und Prozess in der Schyoprenie auf Grund der Rorschachversuches. (The problem of constitutional and process in schizophrenia on the basis of the Rorschach Test.) *Schweiz. Arch. Neurol. Psychiat.*, 1940, *45*, 276-295.

BRICKLIN, B., AND GOTTLIEB, S. G. The prediction of some aspects of marital compatibility by means of the Rorschach Test. *Psychiat. Quart.* [*Suppl.*], 1961, *35*(2), 281-303.

The smaller the difference in numbers of M responses between husband and wife, the fewer the nonconcordances in M qualities. The fewer distorted M, the greater the compatibility with communication.

BRUDO, C. S. The alpha index in the EEG and M response on the Rorschach and PMS Tests. *Diss. Abstr.*, 1954, *14*, 393.

M correlated .37 with occipital alpha index. FM correlated − .34 with occipital alpha index. Both were concerned theoretically with kinesthesis.

BUTTON, A. D. A Rorschach study of 67 alcoholics. *Quart. J. Stud. Alcohol.*, 1956, *17*, 35-52.

Alcoholics show a more constricted protocol in general than do normals; also, poor M, high C, high W% and low D%. Content was not valuable as an index for alcoholics.

CATTONARO, E. Le interpretazioni kinestetiche nel Rorschach di fancuilli deboli mentali. (Kinesthetic interpretations in the Rorschach of mentally defective children.) *Arch. Psicol. Neurol.*, 1959, *20*, 309-343.

Relates lack of movement responses to the failed development of body image and lack of kinesthetic sensations.

CHAMBERS, G. S., AND HAMBLIN, R. M. Rorschach "inner life" capacity of imbeciles under varied conditions. *Amer. J. Ment. Defic.*, 1957, *62*, 88-95.

Found that imbeciles have some capacity for M responses, that repetition of the Rorschach steadily increases the number of M and H, that putting imbeciles in a new living situation may increase M and that glutomis acid does not have any significant effect on M.

CONSALN, C., AND CANTER, A. Rorschach scores as a function of four factors. *J. Consult. Psychol.*, 1957, *21*, 47-51. Found that M was loaded on the intelligence factor while FM was not.

COPELMAN, L. S. La conception actuelle sur la schizophrenie dans la lumiere du psychodiagnostic de Rorschach d'apres les lois des reflexes conditionnels. (Present conception of schizophrenia in light of the Rorschach Test according to the laws of conditional response.) *Ann. Medicopsychol.* (*Paris*), 1958, *1*(5), 815-822.

The schizophrenic patient is unable to give well-organized and kinesthetic responses in the Rorschach because the irradiation of the visual stimulus on the cortex is greatly limited by the pathologic process.

de ASSIS POCHECO, OLINDA. Osimbolo do movemento no crianca. (The symbolism of movement in children.) *Crianca Port.*, 1951, 1952, *11*, 129-139.

Compared Rorschach responses and free drawings in Terman-Merrill IQ's. The proportion of movement representation was found unfavorable as regards human movement, but favorable for animal movement. Only one element, the egotistical mental attitude of the child, is common to graphic representation and the interpretation of movement on the Rorschach.

DELAY, J., AND PICHOT, P. De la psychopathologie de la vision sur le test de Rorschach. (On the psychopathology of vision on the Rorschach.) *Encephale*, 1957, *46*, 547-563.

Found that K (i.e., M) is also a measure of perceptual acuity which is disrupted by organic epileptic pathology.

de RENZI, E., ISOTTI, M., AND SARAVAL, A. L'influenza del sesso e dell'eta sul test di Rorschach dell'italiano adulto normale. (The influence of sex and age on the Rorschach in the normal adult Italian.) *Arch. Psicol. Neurol.*, 1958, *19*, 497-507.

Ss between ages forty to sixty had a smaller number of rejections and m responses than those between twenty and forty.

DILLER, L., AND RIKLAN, M. Rorschach correlates in Parkinson's disease: M, motor inhibition, perceived cause of illness, and self-attitudes. *Psychosom. Med.*, 1957, *19*, 120-126.

Found that the person who sees M is the person who verbalizes a psychological cause for Parkinson's disease and negative self-statements.

DOUGLAS, ANNA G. A tachiscopic study of the order of emergence in the process of perception. *Psychol. Monogr.*, 1947, *61*(6), Whole No. 287, 133 pp.

Evidence indicates that M is of an interpretative order, self-stimulated in excess of the sensory facts.

DREGER, R. M. The relation between Rorschach M and TAT content categories as a measure of creative productivity in a representative high-level intelligence population. *J. Gen. Psychol.*, 1960, *63*, 29-33.

Main finding was that no significant correlations were obtained between Rorschach M or M% and TAT number of content categories.

EARL, C. J. A note on the validity of certain Rorschach symbols. *Rorschach Res. Exch.*, 1941, *5*, 51-61.

Tested hypothesis that responses to the Rorschach are capable of symbolic interpretation when the determinant is M, FM, m, K, KF or FK, but not when it is a pure F. Compared responses of five unstable, mentally defective boys made under hypnosis with their responses when not in this state. Results confirm hypothesis.

ECKHARDT, W. Stimulus determinants of "shading" responses. *J. Clin. Psychol.*, 1957, *13*, 172-173.

Used a regular set of Rorschach cards, a set with only two of gray and a set reproduced as a monotone. Only on the first set did texture, diffused movement and vista responses occur.

ENDECOTT, J. L. The Rorschach Test in postencephalitis. *Illinois Med. J.*, 1945, *88*, 256-258.

Fourteen postencephalitis cases were given the test. The pattern of responses of this group is distinguished primarily by poor interpretation of form and a predominance of color reponses over movement responses.

FABRIKANT, B. Rigidity and flexibility on the Rorschach. *J. Clin. Psychol.*, 1954, *10*, 255-258.

Studied six variables on a test-retest of the Rorschach, and found only one, M, to show a significant change where change was predicted. Concludes that the presence of four of the five signs does suggest rigidity, but the absence of the signs cannot be interpreted as a lack of rigidity.

FIELDING, B., AND BROWN, F. Prediction of intelligence from certain Rorschach factors. *J. Clin. Psychol.*, 1956, *12*, 196-197.

Abram's formula for obtaining an intelligence quotient from Rorschach determinants M, F+, W and R was tested on 107 male psychotic and psychoneurotic patients. The results were correlated with WB IQ's, and the formula was found satisfactory for the WB IQ range 90-110 and for the Rorschachs in which M is greater than three.

FISCHLE, W. H. Dis stirnhirnverletzte im Rorschachschen formdeutversuch. (Brain damage on the Rorschach Test.) *Beih. Schweiz. Psychol.*, 1954, No. 25, 48-80.

Found typical syndrome in brain-damaged patients: absence of movement responses, unstable experience type, perseveration and lowered intelligence.

FORD, M. The application of the Rorschach Test to young children. *Univ. Minn. Child Welf. Monogr.*, 1946, No. 33, xii and 114.

Test given to 123 children ages 3-0 to 7-11. Found that boys tended to give movement responses earlier than girls, with the reverse tendency for color responses.

FRIEDMANN, W. Die bewegungs und dynamik-deutungen in Rorschach test. (M responses and dynamic responses in the Rorschach Test.) *Rorschachiana*, 1952, *1*, 127-152.

Human content and restrained movement indicate introversion, stabilized affectivity and motility. The projection of movement responses results from instinctive urges.

GARRISON, M., JR. Relationships between Rorschach scores and clinical change in mental patients. *J. Personality*, 1948, *17*, 146-152.

Eight Rorschach scores (W, D, F, M, C, IRT, mean IRT/C and R) were intercorrelated with seventy-three scores from thirty-eight other tests for thirty-two topectomy patients. Results show validity for the method.

GEERTSMA, R. H. Factor analysis of Rorschach scoring categories for a population of normal subjects. *J. Consult. Psychol.*, 1962, *26*, 20-25.

Through a statistical analysis, it was found that the vista variable implies internal cognitive activity akin to that represented by the human movement variable.

GIBBY, R. G., STOTSKY, B. A., HARRINGTON, R. L., AND THOMAS, R. W. Rorschach determinant shift among hallucinatory and delusional patients. *J. Consult. Psychol.*, 1955, *19*, 44-46.

Found that patients who were hallucinating showed significantly more M and less FC and total C than delusional patients.

GOLDMAN, A. E., AND HERMAN, J. L. Studies in vicariousness: The effect of immobilization on Rorschach movement responses. *J. Project. Techn.*, 1961, *25*, 164-165.

Found a greater increase in FM% on achromatic cards for physically immobilized subjects.

GOLDSTONE, M. H. The relationship between certain Rorschach indicators and the magnitude of kinesthetic aftereffect. *Diss. Abstr.*, 1960, *21*, 1254.

KAE magnitude varies negatively with movement (M, FM, m). These factors were related to personality and stimulus ambiguity coping.

GRAHM, S. R. Histamine tolerance and perceived movement: A study of visually perceived movement as related to performance in the AK effect and Rorschach movement responses measured against histamine tolerance. *Diss. Abstr.*, 1955, *15*, 1202.

No relationship was found between Rorschach movement and histamine tolerance. No relationship was found between Rorschach movement and AK movement.

GUIRDHAM, A. The diagnosis of depression by the Rorschach Test. *Brit. J. Med. Psychol.*, 1936, *16*, 130-145.

In depression states there is a reduction in the appreciation of color and movement. Concludes that the test reflects a prevailing mood rather than an underlying fixed personality.

GUSTAN, A. Estimation of Rorschach scoring categories by means of an objective inventory. *J. Psychol.*, 1946, *22*, 253-260.

Administered an objective inventory and the Rorschach to 130 female college students. Found that the objective test significantly estimated W%, D%, Fc, M, FM, and ΣC.

HALPERN, F. Rorschach interpretation of the personality structure of schizophrenics who benefit from insulin therapy. *Psychiat. Quart.*, 1940, *14*, 826-833.

Compared schizophrenic patients who had had insulin therapy. Found a distinct difference between improved and unimproved patients' protocols which had been taken before therapy. Showed, among other things, more capacity for inner living, as shown by the movement responses.

HAMMER, E. F., AND JACHS, I. A study of Rorschach flexor and extensor human movement responses. *J. Clin. Psychol.*, 1955, *11*, 63-67.

Compared M responses to Card III made by assertively forceful rapists and passive pedophiles. Found the rapists emitted extensor M while the pedophiles emitted flexor M.

HAMMOND, K. R. A tabulation method for analyzing combinations of Rorschach scores. *J. Clin. Psychol.*, 1951, *7*, 276-279.

Gives a discussion of how to analyze Rorschach data — emphasis is given to movement.

HARRIMAN, P. L. The Rorschach Test applied to a group of college students. *Amer. J. Orthopsychiat.*, 1935, *5*, 116-120.

Test given to fifty college men and fifty college women. Perceptions of movement were slightly, but significantly, more numerous than color responses, indicating young adults have achieved a reasonable control of their affective and cognitive dispositions.

HARRIS, RILDA. A comparative study of two groups of boys, delinquent and non-delinquent, on the basis of their Wechsler and Rorschach Test performances. *Bull. Marit. Psychol. Ass.*, 1957, *6*, 21-28.

Found that the delinquent group of boys scored significantly higher in M responses (1 per cent level) than the nondelinquents.

HERMAN, J. L. Ideational and motor correlates of the Rorschach experience type. *Diss. Abstr.*, 1960, *20*, 3831.

Variables related to introversion and extroversion, and M:C were found in most cases to support the Rorschach experience type concept.

HERTZ, MARGUERITE R. The Rorschach Ink-blot Test: Historical summary. *Psychol. Bull.*, 1935, *32*, 33-66.

Includes a discussion of history and scoring of movement responses.

HERTZ, MARGUERITE R. Rorschach norms for an adolescent age group. *Child Develop.*, 1935, *6*, 69-76.

Gives norms for Rorschach based on three-hundred adolescent junior high school students. Found the average percentage of movement responses higher than those reported for adults and other groups of adolescents.

HERTZ, MARGUERITE R. Pubescence and personality. *Psychol. Bull.*, 1941, *38*, 598.

Relates periods of pubescence to five patterns of emotionality: M; Sum C; FC−; (C+CF); and M−.

HERTZ, MARGUERITE R. Personality patterns in adolescence as portrayed by the Rorschach ink-blot method: The movement factors. *J. Gen. Psychol.*, 1942, *27*, 119-188.

Relates M to intelligence and to personality in general.

HERTZMAN, M., ORLANSKY, D., AND SEITZ, C. P. Personality organization and anoxia tolerance. *Psychosom. Med.*, 1944, *6*, 317-331.

Tested forty male college students subjected to conditions simulating an altitude of 18,500 feet. The Rorschach signs characteristic of the poor tolerators of anoxia were shading shock, refusal to respond to slides (cards) and zero or one human movement response.

HERTZMAN, M., AND SEITZ, C. P. Rorschach reactions at high altitudes. *J. Psychol.*, 1942, *14*, 245-257.

Test given to thirteen males under oxygen conditions of sea level and of 16,000 feet. Without changing the basic Rorschach pattern, altitude brought decreases in movement and increases in color responses.

HURWITZ, I. A developmental study of the relationships between motor activity and perceptual processes as measured by the Rorschach Test. *Diss. Abstr.*, 1954, *14*, 1805.

The hypoactive group showed more measures of empathetic movement response (M) compared with the hyperactive group. This was related to development and pathology.

KALLSTEDT, FRANCES E. A Rorschach study of sixty-six adolescents. *J. Clin. Psychol.*, 1952, *8*, 129-132.

Compared sixty-six adolescents' scores with those obtained by Buhler and Lefever on adults. The adolescents showed less M, more FM>M, more m, more c, cF, Fc and more low W% than adults.

KAPLAN, B. Reflections of the acculturation process in the Rorschach Test. *J. Project. Techn.*, 1955, *19*, 30-35.

Found that veterans exceeded nonveterans on M and FC at the .05 level.

KELLEY, D. McG., AND BARRERA, S. E. Rorschach studies in acute experimental alcoholic intoxication. *Amer. J. Psychol.*, 1941, *97*, 1341-1363.

Gives discussion of meaning of movement responses and

relates this to alcoholic intoxication.

KIKUCHI, T., KITAMURA, S., AND OYAMA, M. Rorschach performance in alcoholic intoxication. *Tuhuku Psychol. Folia.*, 1961, *20*, 45-71.

Under mild intoxication, M is increased, FM is also increased.

KIKUCHI, T., KITAMURA, S., SATE, I., AND OYAMA, M. Rorschach performance in alcoholic intoxication. *Tuhuku Psychol. Folia.*, 1962-1963, *21*(1-2-3), 19-46.

Alcoholic intoxication increases M.

KIMBLE, G. A. Social influence on Rorschach records. *J. Abnorm. Soc. Psychol.*, 1945, *40*, 89-93.

Tests administered twice to fourteen students, once in a laboratory and again in a social atmosphere of a cafeteria. In this latter situation there was a striking increase of color responses and the color sum and a very slight tendency toward the production of more whole responses.

KING, G. F. A theoretical and experimental consideration of the Rorschach movement response: Its relation to the neuropsychiatric patient's orientation to his problem. *Diss. Abstr.*, 1954, *14*, 2127.

Interpretation of M as the ability in fantasy to project the self into time and space in the interpersonal sphere. M related to thinking and pathology.

KING, G. F. A theoretical and experimental consideration of the Rorschach human movement response. *Psychol. Monogr.*, 1958, *72*(5, Whole No. 458), 23 pp.

Found that high M producers showed greater tendency to recognize their problems as involving disturbances in interpersonal relations, project themselves backward in time accounting for their problem, utilize their interpersonal fantasy and project into the future.

KING, G. F. Rorschach human movement and delusional content. *J. Project. Techn.*, 1960, *24*, 161-163.

Found that paranoid schizophrenics with interpersonal delusions produced more M than did those with somatic delusions.

KLEBANOFF, S. G. The Rorschach Test in an analysis of personality in general paresis. *J. Personality*, 1949, *17*, 261-272.

Compared protocols of twenty-six paretics with twenty-six normals. Found significant differences at 10 per cent level: R, W%, Dd, F+%, P, M, FC, N, Z, (F+); at the 5 per cent level: S and Z.

KLINGENSMITH, S. W. Effects of different methods of structuring the Rorschach inquiry upon determinant scores. *J. Clin. Psychol.*, 1957, *13*, 279-282.

Found that an increased inclusiveness of the inquiry had most effect on C′ and V responses, least effect on M responses.

KLOPFER, B., AND MARGULIES, R. Rorschach reactions in early childhood. *Rorschach Res. Exch.*, 1941, *5*, 1-23.

Study based on 205 records of 155 children ages two to seven. Found the percentage of children using the major determinants increases consistently with age for M, FM and CF.

KOGAN, W. Shifts in Rorschach patterns during a critical period in the institutional experience of a group of delinquent boys. *Rorschach Res. Exch.*, 1940, *4*, 131-133.

Test given to six institutionalized delinquents twice over a month's span. An improvement in the balance between M and FM occurred.

KORNETSKY, C. Relationship between Rorschach determinants and psychosis in barbiturate withdrawal syndrome. *AMA Arch. Neurol. Psychiat.*, 1954, 72, 452-454.

Results indicated that those who became psychotic with barbiturate withdrawal had significantly less Sum C+M percepts than did those who did not develop a psychosis.

KORNETSKY, C., AND GERARD, D. L. Effect of increasing the number of Rorschach responses on *Sum C* and *M*: A note on Fishe and Baughman's study. *J. Abnorm. Soc. Psychol.*, 1954, 49, 592-593.

Results indicate that equating the number of responses will not equate the frequency of color or human movement responses.

KROPP, R. P. The Rorschach "Z" score. *J. Project. Techn.*, 1955, 19, 443-452.

Found that Z is highly related to W, M and R.

LAIR, C. V. Empathy and its relation to stimulus meaning. *J. Clin. Psychol.*, 1958, 14, 175-177.

Found a relationship between empathy (as measured by M and H) and the apprehension of meaning in external stimuli (as measured by seeing "mother" in VII and "father" in IV when forced to classify all responses into one of the two categories).

LANE, BARBARA M. A validation test of the Rorschach movement interpretations. *Amer. J. Orthopsychiat.*, 1948, 18, 292-296.

The author induced creativity and introversive mechanisms through hypnosis and found a significant rise in Sum M.

LEDWITH, NETTIE H. *Rorschach Responses of Elementary School Children.* Pittsburgh: Univ. Pittsburgh Press, 1959, ix, 185 pp.

A normative study of Rorschach protocols of 291 children, ages six to eleven. The following indices are given: R's; W; D; d; Dd; S; F; M; FM; m; CF; K; FK; c; C'; FC; A; H; and P.

LEIMAN, C. J. An investigation of the perception of movement on the Rorschach ink-blots. *Diss. Abstr.*, 1958, 18, 1107.

The intelligence of the individual and the individual's propensity to see human figures appear to be two important factors in the perception of movement on the Rorschach ink-blot.

LEVI, J., AND KRAEMER, DORIS. Significance of a preponderance of human movement responses on the Rorschach in children below age ten. *J. Project. Techn.*, 1952, 16, 361-365.

Findings indicate that, even with disturbed children, M responses are scarce, averaging less than one up to age ten.

LEVINE, M., GLASS, H., AND MELTZOFF, J., The inhibition process, Rorschach human movement responses, and intelligence. *J. Consult. Psychol.*, 1957, 21, 41-45.

Authors contend that the inhibition process, as measured by M and by specific tasks, can be identified in intelligence test performances.

LEVINE, M., AND SPIVACH, G. Human movement responses verbal expression in the Rorschach Test. *J. Project, Techn.*, 1962, 26(3), 299-304.

A positive relationship was found to exist between an index of repression score and movement responses.

LEVINE, M., SPIVACH, G., AND WIGHT, B. The inhibition process: Rorschach human movement responses, and intelligence: Some further data. *J. Consult. Psychol.*, 1959, 23, 306-312.

Found that M and IQ relationship seems consistant in almost any population: normals; schizophrenics; organics; etc.

LEVY, L. H. Movement as a "rhetorical embellishment" of human percepts. *J. Consult. Psychol.*, 1955, 19, 469-471.

Questions the justification for scoring both M and H in Rorschach Test analysis.

LINTON, HARRIET B. Rorschach correlates of response to suggestion. *J. Abnorm. Psychol.*, 1954, 49, 75-83.

Found eleven Rorschach measures associated with change of autokinetic judgments under the influence of judgments given by a plant.

LIUTKUS, S. Rorschach indicators of maturity: a statistical study of 200 males. *Diss. Abstr.*, Vol. 16, 1956, No. 10-12, 2525.

Changes in use of following variables with age was found: FM in the location area; M; FM; m; Fm and the determinants of EB.

LOTSOF, E. J., COMREY, A., BOGARTZ, W., AND ARNSFIELD, P. A factor analysis of WISC and Rorschach. *J. Project. Techn.*, 1958, 22, 297-301.

On a correlation matrix of twelve WISC scores and seventeen Rorschach scores, only five factors seemed to be interpretable: verbal intelligence; perceptual movement; performance speed.

MACHOVER, S. Rorschach study on the nature and origin of common factors in the personalities of Parkinsonians. *Psychosom. Med.*, 1957, 19, 332-338.

Found an inverse relationship between length of illness and Sum M responses.

MAJUMBER, A. K., AND ROY, A. B. Latent personality content of juvenile delinquents. *J. Psychol. Res. (Madras)*, 1962, (6)1, 4-8.

Fm predominates M in delinquent personalities.

MARGULIES, H. Rorschach responses of successful and unsuccessful students. *Arch. Psychol.*, 1942, 271, 61.

Test given to seventy-five girls and ninety-one boys who were differentiated by teacher ratings and grades. Among the results: The raw W/M did not differentiate between students at the success extremes, although certain patterns of W and M did distinguish between the two groups.

MEILI-DWORETZKI, G. Versuch einer Analyse der Bewegungsdeutungen im Rorschach-Test. (Attempt of an analysis of factor M in the Rorschach Test.) *Schweiz. Z. Psychol.*, 1952, 11, 265-382.

Theorizes that the M perception in adults may be regarded as part of an inner reality resulting from the same needs as the play activity in children.

MELTZER, H. Personality differences between stuttering and non-stuttering children as indicated by the Rorschach Test. *Psychol. Bull.*, 1933, *30*, 726-727.

As compared with problem children, stutterers are less repressive of movement responses.

MELTZOFF, J., SINGER, J. L., AND KORCHIN, S. J. Motor inhibition and Rorschach movement responses: A test of the sensory-tonic theory. *J. Personality*, 1953, *21*, 400-410.

Found a direct relationship between voluntary inhibition of motor activity and production of M responses.

MILLER, L., AND SALOMON, F. Test de Rorschach de medicins practiciens. *Bull. Soc. Franc. Rorschach meth. Project*, 1962, No. *13-14*, 20-27.

Physicians give few M.

MIRIN, B. The Rorschach movement response and role-taking behavior. *J. Nerv. Ment. Dis.*, 1955, *122*, 270-275. Studied thirty chronic male schizophrenics on relationship between human movement response and role-taking behavior. Results show that the nature of M is reflected directly in social behavior.

MOYA, G. Estudia de inteligencia, personalidad y comportaminento enun grupo de 165 soldados. (A study of intelligence, personality, and behavior in a group of 165 soldiers.) *Rev. Psicol. Gen. Appl. (Madrid)*, 1959, *14*, 321-389.

This group of soldiers showed R, W%, S%, M, FM, m and FC% greater than CF to be positively related to intelligence and cultural level.

McARTHUR, C. C., AND KING, S. Rorschach configurations associated with college achievement. *J. Educ. Psychol.*, 1954, *45*, 492-498.

Found that protocols dominated by inanimate movement and color responses were a significantly differentiating factor between successful and unsuccessful college students. Offered as evidence of validity of Vorhaus' types.

McCULLY, R. S. Human movement in the Rorschach materials of a group of preadolescent boys suffering from progressive muscular loss. *J. Project. Techn.*, 1961, *25*, 205-211.

Inconsistencies between behavior and Rorschach findings suggest greater complexity of the M response than encompassed by present meaning.

McFATE, MARGUERITE Q., AND ORR, FRANCES G. Through adolescence with the Rorschach. *Rorschach Res. Exch.*, 1949, *13*, 302-319.

Results indicate that the average use of R, K, M, F, P, H and A increases with age for both sexes. There is a decrease in FM and cF.

McNEELY, H. E. The influence of varied instructions on the response adequacy of certain Rorschach intelligence indicators. *Diss. Abstr.*, 1955, *15*, 628.

Human movement was correlated significantly with intelligence measures. No sex differences were found.

NEEL, ANN F. Inhibition and perception of movement on the Rorschach. *J. Consult. Psychol.*, 1960, *24*, 224-230. Studied ninety-three college students in five groups. Animal movement findings not significant. Results of inanimate movement were positive and indicative of tension and conflict due to inhibition of need and integration into behavior.

NORMAN, R. D., LIVERANT, S., AND REDLO, M. The influence of a superficial immediately preceding "set" upon responses to the Rorschach. *J. Consult. Psychol.*, 1952, *16*, 261-264.

Attempted to prove hypothesis that an immediately preceding set would not significantly influence the number and kind of responses. A food set and a movement set were evoked, using magazine ads as stimuli. Results confirm hypothesis.

OGDON, D. P., AND ALLEE, RUTH. Rorschach relationships with intelligence among familial mental defectives. *Amer. J. Ment. Defic.*, 1959, *63*, 889-896.

Found eight signs to relate significantly with intelligence: R; F; M; FM; W; etc.

OHKURO, K. Rorschach study with delinquents. *Jap. Fam. Court Mon.*, 1957, *9(5)*, 1-37.

Delinquents in comparison with normals showed no difference in W:D:Dd, W:M, FM:M and A%.

OKARSKI, J. F. Consisting of projective movement responses. *Psychol. Monogr.*, 1958, *72* (6, Whole No. 459), 26 pp. Concluded that the majority of Ss did not reveal M, FM and m responses related to deep-rooted, stable characteristics.

PAGE, H. A. Studies in fantasy-daydreaming frequency and Rorschach scoring categories. *J. Consult. Psychol.*, 1957, *21*, 111-114.

Found some evidence that the tendency to perceive movement in the Rorschach is associated with fantasy activity. Also that the frequent daydreamer tends to perceive movement in partial human figures, in unusual locations and with form of lower or minus quality.

PARKER, R. S. An investigation of the content of the Rorschach human movement response utilizing the subject's associations to their own M. *Diss. Abstr.*, 1959, *20*, 384.

The response pattern did not suggest that M is a derivative of unconscious fantasies. The subject tends to express the drives represented by M.

PAULSEN, A. Rorschach of school beginners. *Rorschach Res. Exch.*, 1941, 5, 24-29.

Studied eighty-two children, five years, seven months to seven years, 5 months. Found that the quality of whole, number of M, FM and FC, number of H responses, number of P responses and the F% and F+% were most closely associated with Binet scales of intelligence.

PEMBERTON, W. H. General semantics and the Rorschach Test. *Pop. Amer. Congr. Gen. Semant.*, 1943, 2, 251-260. "Since the ratio and nature of the form, movement and color responses change with age and maturity, deviation from the norm may be used as an index of the degree of regression or arrest of development." Gives a discussion of the significance of movement responses.

PESCOR, M. J. Marital status of delinquents in relationship to Rorschach Test scores. *Public Health Rep.*, 1939, Suppl. No. *153*, 6 pp.

Found an inclination for divorced, separated and widowed individuals to have a faster reaction time, and a higher total of general, motion, color, human anatomy and abstract responses than either married or single men.

PESCOR, M. J. A further study of the Rorschach Test applied to delinquents. *Public Health Rep.*, 1941, *56*, 381-395.

Applied test to 476 federal penitentiary inmates and found only six coefficients above 0.50: educational grade status *versus* total detail Rs; mental age *versus* total detail, color and motion Rs; and mental age *versus* analysis of cards by the general to detail and detail to general methods.

PHARES, E. J., STEWART, L. M., AND FOSTER, J. M. Instruction variation and Rorschach performances. *J. Project. Techn.*, 1960, *24*, 28-31.

Found that when subjects have to categorize their answers as either right or wrong, there were not significantly fewer total, movement or color responses.

PIOTROWSKI, Z. A. The M, FM, and m responses as indicators of change in personality. *Rorschach Res. Exch.*, 1936-37, *1*, 148-157.

Author believes that if the nature of the attitudes expressed in the categories, M, FM and m is the same, then the individual has not changed his essential attitude since childhood.

PIOTROWSKI, Z. A. Rorschach manifestations of improvement in insulin-treated schizophrenics. *Psychosom. Med.*, 1939, *1*, 508-524.

Improvement after successful insulin treatment was revealed in the Rorschach by, among other things, an increase in number and quality of movement responses.

PIOTROWSKI, Z. A. A simple experimental device for the prediction of outcome of insulin treatment in schizophrenics. *Psychiat. Quart.*, 1940, *14*, 267-273.

In the study of the pre-insulin treatment protocols of ninety-four schizophrenics, it was found that the presence of both meaningful color and good human movement responses in a record appreciably strengthens the possibility for improvement with this therapy.

PIOTROWSKI, Z. A. A comparative table of the main Rorschach symbols. *Psychiat. Quart.*, 1942, *16*, 30-37.

Author compares symbols used by Rorschach, Beck, Binder, Klopfer and himself. Except for the chiarosuro determinants and the FM, m and Cn used by Klopfer and himself, there is close agreement.

PIOTROWSKI, Z. A. *Perceptanalysis: A Fundamentally Reworked, Exampled, and Systematized Rorschach Method.* New York: Macmillan, 1957, xvii, 505.

Offers a discussion of scoring and meaning of movement responses.

PIOTROWSKI, Z. A., AND ABRAHAMSEN, D. Sexual crime, alcohol, and the Rorschach Test. *Psychiat. Quart.* [*Suppl.*], 1952, *26*, 248-260.

Found that individuals who produce more spontaneous animal movements than human movements are likely to be more aggressive and active when in a state of diminished consciousness. Also found converse to be true.

PIOTROWSKI, Z. A., *et al.* Rorschach signs in the selection of outstanding young male mechanics. *J. Psychol.*, 1944, *18*, 131-150.

The group Rorschach, as administered by Harrower-Erickson, differentiated between outstanding and mediocre workers. Of four signs, m (movement of neutral forces or inanimate objects) was the most important discriminator.

PRADOS, M. Rorschach studies on artists-painters. I. Quantitative analysis. *Rorschach Res. Exch.*, 1944, *8*, 178-183.

Tests were given to twenty professional creative artists. Found: overemphasis on W; underproduction of D; high F% with signs of refined control; large number M outnumbering FM; high CF:FC ratio; diluted Erlebnistype; W somewhat greater than M; and A% very low.

RATTLEF, A. Om teoridannelse om personlighedstests. (On the culture theory of personality tests.) *Nord. Psykol.*, 1959, *11*, 296-301.

Calls for further clarification and clinical evidence on M, FM and m.

RAUSCH DE TRAUBENBERG, NINA. La signification des kinesthesis: Rapport de travaux experimentaux recents. (The meaning of kinesthesis: Report of recent work.) *Psychol. Franc.*, 1960, *5*, 53-59.

Critical discussion of recent studies on Rorschach movement responses (18 ref.).

REISMAN, J. M. Types of movement in children's Rorschach. *J. Project. Techn.*, 1960, *24*, 46-48.

Found that with disturbed children, if a child's m is of an extreme (flexor, blocked) type, then it is highly probable that his record contains M and FM of this type. Suggests a positive correlation between the type of m, M and FM in children.

REISMAN, J. M. An interpretation of m. *J. Consult. Psychol.*, 1961, *25*(4), 367.

An analysis of adolescents' Rorschachs contradicts Piotrowski's hypothesis that types of movement in m responses are always different from M or FM.

REISS, AMMELIESE. A study of some genetic behavioral correlates of human movement responses in children's Rorschach protocols. *Diss. Abstr.*, 1958, *18*, 668.

M children displayed greater motor restraint than no M children. It was felt that planned behavior developed at the same time as the perception of M.

REITAN, R. M. The relation of Rorschach ratios to brain injury. *J. Gen. Psychol.*, 1955, *53*, 97-107.

Test given to brain-damaged and control patients. Mean values for a group of ratios reflecting relationships between traditional scoring categories were calculated for each group. Results indicate that, except for M, the formally scored variables do a much better job of differentiating the group than do the ratios.

RICHARDSON, L. H. A personality study of stutterers and non-stutterers. *J. Speech Hearing Dis.*, 1944, *9*, 152-160.

Found significant differences between stutterers and non-stutterers only in the M and C responses. No significant differences were noted with the TAT, which was also administered.

RICKERS-OVSIANKINA, MARIA. The Rorschach Test as applied to normal and schizophrenic subjects. *Brit. J. Med. Psychol.*, 1938, *17*, 227-257.

Schizophrenics show an excess of: more W, lacking normal details; prevalence of cover M; and more original responses.

ROBB, R. W., KOVITZ, B., AND RAPAPORT, D. Histamine in the treatment of psychosis: A psychiatric and objective study. *Amer. J. Psychiat.*, 1940, 97, 601-610.

Rorschachs were given before and after histamine treatment of catatonics. Found that there was an increased movement and color score after treatment, indicating a more free and responsive affectivity and psychomobility, as well as decreased blocking.

ROBIN, A. I., AND SANDERSON, M. H. An experimental inquiry into some Rorschach procedures. *J. Clin. Psychol.*, 1947, 3, 216-225.

Study presented cards in reversed order and found Card I to be the only one affected to any degree. In the reverse order, form quality is somewhat less good and S, M, Sum C and P are all used slightly less frequently.

ROE, ANNE. Analysis of group Rorschachs of biologists. *Rorschach Res. Exch.*, 1949, 13, 25-43.

Found that the biologists had a relatively high number of entries for above-average use of unused details, a very high incidence rate of shading and color shock and considerable restriction in the use of human movement.

ROGERS, L. S., AND HAMMOND, K. R. Prediction of the results of therapy by means of the Rorschach Test. *J. Consult. Psychol.*, 1953, 17, 8-15.

Found that extensor M's, when appearing alone in a Rorschach record, were associated with improvement therapy.

ROSENTHAL, M. Some behavior correlates of the Rorschach experience balance. *J. Project. Techn.*, 1962, 26(4), 442-446.

The M group showed more deliberateness and caution in its approach to matchstick test compared with the C group.

ROSENZWEIG, S. A note on Rorschach pre-history. *Rorschach Res. Exch.*, 1944, 8, 41-42.

Author reports discovery of early use of inkblots as a basis for inducing fantasy in a juvenile book, *Gobolinks*, 1896. The extremely high frequency of movement responses in the book tends to give a degree of general validation to the capacity for creative fantasy signified by the M type response.

RUST, R. M., AND RYAN, F. J. The relationship of some Rorschach variables to academic behavior. *J. Personality*, 1953, 21, 441-456.

Found that animal and animal movement responses indicate that superego status may be the factor responsible for persistance in making good grades.

SCHACHTEL, E. G. Projection and its relation to character attitude and creativity in the kinesthetic responses. *Psychiatry*, 1950, 13, 69-100.

Presents an exhaustive interpretation of M, FM and m responses to the Rorschach.

SCHENK, V. W. D., AND COLTOF, F. Changes in the Rorschach Test after insulin treatment. *Psychiat. Neurol. Bl. Amst.*, 1940, 44, 435-445.

Found that changes in the color and form-color answers and an increase in movement answers are favorable phenomena with insulin therapy.

SCHMIDT, H. O., AND FONDA, C. P. Rorschach scores in the manic state. *J. Psychol.*, 1954, 38, 427-437.

Compared scoring of forty-two manics and forty-two schizophrenics. Found manics' scores were higher from Sum C, Z, H and M. They were lower for lambda, TIR and TR.

SCHMIDT, H. O., FONDA, C. P., AND LESTER, J. R. Rorschach behavior as an index of color anaesthesia. *J. Psychol.*, 1955, 40, 95-102.

Found that reduction of the red areas on Card III facilitated perception of the black and white area as human figures engaged in passive, centripetal or flexor movement.

SCHULMAN, I. The relation between perception of movement on the Rorschach Test and levels of conceptualization: An experimental study and theoretical analysis of thought processes in the perception of movement on the Rorschach Test. *Diss. Abstr.*, 1954, 14, 303.

Movement responses, and particularly accurate movement responses, tend to be associated with abstract conceptual ability.

SCOTT, E. M., AND DOUGLAS, F. A comparison of Rorschach and Howard Tests on a schizophrenic population. *J. Clin. Psychol.*, 1957, 13, 79-81.

Found that the Howard produced very significantly more M, color and shading responses and pure C, but not significantly more F responses.

SEN, Z. A statistical study of the Rorschach Test. *Brit. J. Psychol. Statist. Sect.*, 1950, 3, 21-29.

Concludes that the inference commonly drawn from color and movement seems to rest more on preconceived hypothesis than on verifiable evidence.

SHATIN, L. The constriction-dilation dimension in Rorschach and TAT. *J. Clin. Psychol.*, 1958, 14, 150-154.

Found that M+ Sum C, number of O's and of rejects were more related to the TAT measures than were F%, R or A%.

SHEEHAN, J. G. Rorschach prognosis in psychotherapy and speech therapy. *J. Speech Hearing Dis.*, 1954, 19, 217-219.

Found that the movement variables and the prognostic score may be unsuccessful in sorting out those stutterers who are likely to drop out of therapy early and in predicting which will show the most progress psychotherapeutically.

SHERMAN, M. H. A psychoanalytic definition of Rorschach determinants. *Psychoanalysis*, 1955, 3(2), 68-76.

Movement responses correspond to superego functioning based on parental identification. Obsessives tend toward the M end of the CF/M continuum.

SIEGMAN, A. W. A culture and personality study based on a comparison of Rorschach performance. *J. Soc. Psychol.*, 1956, 44, 173-178.

Compared performance of American and Yeshiva students. Found that F%, sum M, Fc, C', M, FM, FM:M, color shock and W distinguished between the two groups.

SINGER, J. L., AND HERMAN, J. Motor and fantasy correlates

or Rorschach human movement responses. *J. Consult. Psychol.*, 1954, *18*, 325-331.

These two hypotheses were supported: (a) subjects differing in Rorschach M productivity will differ on tasks tapping motor control and fantasy; and (b) subjects will show "rough consistency" in their performance on motor and fantasy situations.

Singer, J. L., Meltzoff, J., and Goldman, G. D. Rorschach movement response following motor inhibition and hyperactivity. *J. Consult. Psychol.*, 1952, *16*, 359-364.

Found that after motor inhibition Ss showed an increase in M responses. Also found that Ss do not show a corresponding decrease of M after hyperactivity.

Sommer, R. Rorschach animal responses and intelligence. *J. Consult. Psychol.*, 1957, *21*, 358.

Found no overall relationship between the WB verbal IQ and sum of animal responses. Did find small, but significant, positive relationship between animal movement responses and IQ.

Sommer, R. Rorschach M responses and intelligence. *J. Clin. Psychol.*, 1958, *14*, 58-61

Found that for a psychiatric population, there is a definite relation between M and the Wechsler Verbal scale which exists.

Sommer, R., and Sommer, Dorothy T. Assultiveness and two types of Rorschach color responses. *J. Consult. Psychol.*, 1958, *22*, 57-62.

Found that Ss giving aggressive color responses showed more assultive behavior than the nonaggressive Ss. This trend was especially clear in cases where S gave both aggressive color and aggressive movement responses.

Sopchak, A. L. Prediction of college performance by commonly used tests. *J. Clin. Psychol.*, 1958, *14*, 194-197.

Compared with the usual single prediction measures of the GPA, only the M variable of the Rorschach had a very significant (.24) tetrachoric correlation.

Spivach, G., Levine, M., Fuschillo, J., and Travernier, Ann. Rorschach movement responses and inhibition processes in adolescents. *J. Project. Techn.*, 1959, *23*, 426-466.

Authors conclude that M differs in meaning in the protocol of adults and adolescents: General inhibition ability is usually found in adulthood but not in adolescence.

Spivach, G., Levine, M., and Sprigle, H. Barron M threshold values in emotionally disturbed adolescents. *J. Project. Techn.*, 1958, *22*, 446-449.

Found significant tetrachoric correlations between M threshold and IQ and M threshold and Rorschach M.

Stark, S. A note on time, intelligence, and Rorschach movement responses. *Percept. Motor Skills*, 1962, *15*(2), 267-272.

Movement may be regarded as an index of aptitude for creative foresight and planning.

Stein, H. A note on "A comparative analysis of Rorschach forms with altered stimulus characteristics" by E. E. Baughman. *J. Project. Tech.*, 1955, *19*, 465-467.

Author criticizes an inference made by Baughman concerning the independence of M% and FM% and the lack of identity in their underlying processes.

Stotsky, B. A. Factor analysis of Rorschach scores of schizophrenics. *J. Clin. Psychol.*, 1957. *13*, 275-285.

Found two factors as determinants of schizophrenic protocols — pure form and M responses clustered together and color and shading responses in a cluster.

Swift, J. W. Rorschach responses of eighty-two pre-school childen. *Rorschach Res. Exch.*, 1945, *7*, 74-84.

Average CA was 4-8 and average IQ, 124.6. Found categories P, A% and M+, FM+, m, to be related to CA; P, W% and F% were related to MA.

Tanaka, F. Rorschach no undo hanno to chino tono hankei. (Rorschach movement responses in relation to intelligence.) *Jap. J. Educ. Psychol.*, 1958, *6*, 85-91, 132-133. Results: (a) found a positive r between M and IQ: (b) no relation was found between FM and IQ.

Taulbee, E. S. The use of the Rorschach test in evaluating the intellectual levels of functioning in schizophrenics. *J. Project. Techn.*, 1955, *19*, 163-169.

Found that R, Z, M, W and F% individually and collectively failed to correlate significantly with WB IQ's of schizophrenics.

Thomas, H. F. The relationship of movement responses on the Rorschach Test to the defense mechanism of projection. *J. Abnorm. Soc. Psychol.*, 1955, *50*, 41-44. Results suggest a relationship between movement responses and projection; but quantity alone is not enough to differentiate between an extreme use of the mechanism and cases where it is not the primary mechanism.

Thompson, Grace M. MMPI correlates of certain movement responses in the group Rorschach of two college samples. *J. Consult. Psychol.*, 1948, *12*, 379-383.

Found two types of movement responses to correlate with maladjustment as measured by the MMPI. These were: human movement visualized in small detail blot areas; and animal movement responses in excess of three.

Thompson, Grace M. MMPI correlates of movement responses on the Rorschach. *Amer. Psychol.*, 1938, *3*, 348-349.

Using the M and FM response to the group Rorschach, certain correlates were drawn with the MMPI, such as degree of maladjustment.

Tucker, J. E. Rorschach human and other movement responses in relation to intelligence. *J. Consult. Psychol.*, 1950, *14*, 283-286.

Found that human movement (M) scores and summed animal and minor movement (FM + m) scores correlated at same level of significance with intelligence test scores (Wechsler-Bellevue Adult Intelligence Test).

Tumin, L. An experimental contribution to the study of psychic change in postencephalitic Parkinsonism. Dissertation, Bucharest, 1939, 48 pp.

Found patients' responses to the Rorschach pointed to a regression in the kinesthetic function, a weakening of the chromatic disposition and a lowered excitability of the subcortical centers.

Vianna, Guerra C. As respostas das criancas d 3-8 anos

ao psicodiagnostic de Rorschach. (The responses of children of 3-8 to the Rorschach.) *Bol. Inst. Psicol.,* 1958, *8,* 20-31.

Found that the M(FM,m)% increased 2.6 per cent (three years) to 14.5 per cent (eight years).

VIOLET-CONIL AND CONINET, N. Le test de Rorschach et le diagnostic de l'angoisse. (The Rorschach Test and the diagnosis of anxiety.) *Rorschachiana,* 1952, *1,* 78-127.

Anxiety may be disclosed by: Bohm's signs; few W, a special sort of Dd, Do and S; few M, often M-pure C; many shadings, shocks and special features in the contents.

WAGNER, E. E. The interaction of aggressive movement responses and anatomy responses on the Rorschach in producing anxiety. *J. Project. Techn.,* 1961, *25,* 212-215.

Found anxiety, as measured by the IPATA, to be positively correlated with aggressive movement and anatomy responses.

WARSHAW, L., LEISER, R., IZNER, S. M., AND STERNE, S. B. The clinical significance and theory of sodium amytal Rorschach testing. *J. Project. Techn.,* 1954, *18,* 248-251.

Found that the only essential change that sodium amytal seems to produce is the release of cortical inhibitory functions which will allow the individual a more marked responsiveness to inner stimuli (increase in M and FM).

WEBER, A. Der Rorschach'sche Formdeutversuch bei Kindern. (The Rorschach Test as applied to children.) *Schweiz. Arch. Neurol. Psychiat.,* 1944, *53,* 47-61.

The special childish characteristics are: a decrease in primary color responses, kinesthesia and total answers; increase in detail; perseveration; and inverse interpretations.

WERNER, H. Peceptual behavior of brain-injured, mentally defective children: An experimental study by means of the Rorschach techniques. *Genet. Psychol. Monogr.,* 1945, *31,* 51-110.

Compares two groups of mentally defective boys, one group having brain injury as the cause of deficiency. Found this group gave fewer responses, more whole responses, fewer movement responses, higher percentage of white space responses, etc.

WERTHEIMER, RITA R. Relationships between specific Rorschach variables and sociometric data. *J. Project. Techn.,* 1957, *21,* 94-97.

Compared socially accepted and socially rejected adolescents on H%, P%, FC greater than CF, Fc and Sum C greater than M and found no significant relationships.

WETHERHORN, M. Flexor-extensor movement on the Rorschach. *J. Consult. Psychol.,* 1956, *20,* 204.

Concludes that a flexor-extensor movement continuum does not measure the same dimensions of personality as the A-S Study or the Mf scale of the MMPI.

WOLF, ELIZABETH B. Investigation of the meaning and expression of the movement responses to the Rorschach Ink-blot Test in 216 juvenile delinquents. *Amer. Psychol.,* 1946, *1,* 461.

Studied M in relation to a number of characteristics of juvenile delinquents.

WYSOCKI, B. A. Assessment of intelligence level by the Rorschach Test as compared with objective tests. *J. Educ. Psychol.,* 1957, *48,* 113-117.

Per cent of human movement responses was found to correlate significantly with objective intelligence tests.

WYSOCKI, B. A. Differentiation between introvert-extrovert types by Rorschach methods as compared with other methods. *J. Psychol.,* 1957, *43,* 41-46.

Found that the ratio M to C fails to measure introversion-extroversion using a questionnaire and judge ratings as criteria. Also found that F to C is a better measure than M to C (used the group Rorschach).

WYSOCKI, B. A. A factorial study of Rorschach protocols. *Percept. Motor Skills,* 1960, *10,* 105-106.

Results indicate that the color to form, and not color to human movement, proportion is the primary index of experience balance.

ZEHRER, F. A. Investigation of Rorschach factors in children who have conclusive disorders and those who present problems in adjustment. *Amer. J. Psychiat.,* 1951, *21,* 292-302.

Found for children ages eight to fourteen with conclusive disorders a higher R, Dd%, CF, Sum C and lower FC, M and P.

COLOR

ADAMS, H. B., COOPER, G. D., AND CARRERA, R. N. The Rorschach and the MMPI: A concurrent validity study. *J. Clin. Psychol.,* 1963, *27,* 23-34.

Most of the correlations between color and the MMPI were in directions opposite to those originally expected, suggesting that color may not be directly related to ego functioning. Color correlated positively with the Hy scale. Subjects were from a veteran's hospital.

ALLEN, R. M. The influence of color in the Rorschach Test on reaction time in a normal population. *J. Project. Techn.,* 1951, *15,* 481-485.

There was no significant difference in the reaction times indices between those subjects who received the standard color plates and those who received the special achromatic Rorschach Plates II, III, VIII, IX and X.

There was no reliable delay in reaction between the five color and five noncolor standard Rorschach cards.

ALLEN, R. M. The M determinant and color in Rorschach's Test. *J. Clin. Psychol.,* 1953, *9,* 198-199.

M responses of twenty-five college students were compared on the usual and on an achromatic series of Rorschach cards; the tests were given individually by the same examiner using an ab-ba order. The production of M responses appeared independent of the presence or absence of color.

ALLEN, R. M., MANNE, S. H., AND STIFF, M. The influence of color on the consistency of responses in the Rorschach Test. *J. Clin. Psychol.,* 1952, *8,* 97-98.

No statistically significant difference in response consistency were found using either standard or achromatic

Rorschach cards with test-retest procedures.

ALLEN, R. M., MANNE, S. H., AND STIFF, M. Sobre el efecta del color del psicodiagnostico de Rorschach. (On the effect of color in the Rorschach Test.) *Rev. Neuro-Psiquiat.*, 1952, *15*, 228-238.

The normal population showed no rejection of either the standard chromatic or special achromatic Rorschach cards; the subjects who responded well on the colored cards also gave good responses on the achromatic cards. There was no significant difference in popular responses for Cards II, III, VIII, IX and X on both series; the localization factors W and D were not affected by the presence or absence of color.

ALLEN, R. M., STIFF, M. P., AND ROSENZWEIG, M. The role of color in Rorschach's Test: A preliminary survey of neurotic and psychotic groups. *J. Clin. Psychol.*, 1953, *9*, 81-83.

Ten hospitalized neurotics and nine hospitalized psychotics were tested on both a chromatic and an achromatic series of Rorschach cards, the order of presentation of the two forms being systematically varied. There was a six-week interval between testing. Color did not appear to have any effect on the records obtained.

BAER, A. Le test de Rorschach interprete du point de vue analytique. (The analytic interpretation of the Rorschach Test.) *Rev. Franc. Psychoanal.*, 1950, *14*, 455-503.

The aim of the investigation was the examination of repressed conceptual content. The deep dynamics of the test are guided by the opposition of movement to form and not by color to movement.

BAKER, C. M., AND HARRIS, J. S. The validation of Rorschach Test results against laboratory behavior. *J. Clin. Psychol.*, 1949, *5*, 161-164.

A positive correlation between variation in speech intensity under stress and the Rorschach form-color integration score fell just short of significance.

BASH, K. W. Ganzeigenschaften als Determinantentrager im Rorschach-Versuch mit besonderer Berucksichtigung der farbontworten. (Whole qualities as Rorschach determinants, with special consideration of color responses.) *Schweiz. Z. Psychol.*, 1957, *16*, 121-126.

The attempt was made to show that certain properties of wholes (above all, their essential physiognomy) are embodied in relatively pure forms in certain Rorschach determinants (above all in color), and that the psychological significance of the determinants is derived therefrom.

BAUGHMAN, E. E. A comparative analysis of Rorschach forms with altered stimulus characteristics. *J. Project. Techn.*, 1954, *18*, 151-164.

In addition to the standard Rorschach cards, four experimental forms of the Rorschach were devised having the same peripheral form as the originals but changes in color. Comparisons of the five forms administered to five groups of neurotic male veterans showed the following: (a) the effects of color and shading are less extensive than postulated by Rorschach theory; (b) the formation of certain percepts is dependent upon certain stimulus attributes, such as color.

BAUGHMAN, E. E. The role of the stimulus in Rorschach responses. *Psychol. Bull.*, 1958, *55*, 121-147.

Section on color as a stimulus.

BAUGHMAN, E. E. The effects of inquiry method on Rorschach color and shading scores. *J. Project. Techn.*, 1959, *23*, 3-7.

The Rorschach was administered to two groups of adult subjects equated for intelligence, education, age and sex. Shading and color scores were obtained for one group by the standard inquiry method, for the second group by the paired comparison technique. Color scores for the two groups were not significantly different.

BECK, S. J. Emotional experience as a necessary constituent in knowing. In Reymert, M. L. *Feelings and Emotions: The Mooseheart Symposium.* New York: McGraw-Hill, 1950, pp. 95-107.

"The C determined response on the Rorschach Test is definitely related to factors of emotional experience and to various degrees of maturation and of maladaptation. A certain amount of this response in any record is essen- the knowing of one's world so that one can adjust to it."

BELL, F. B. Some relationships between Rorschach responses and form or color choices. *Diss. Abstr.*, 1956, *16*, 2512.

This study revealed a significant relationship between color matching as measured by the Form-Color Matching Test and responsiveness to color on the Rorschach.

BENTON, A. L. The experimental validation of the Rorschach Test. *Brit. J. Med. Psychol.*, 1950, *23*, 45-58.

tial for normal functioning. There is a relation between the psychological components eliciting FC and CF and A selective critical review of the literature. One of the topics discussed is the color determined response.

BENTON, A. L. El test de Rorschach como prueba percep-tion. (The Rorschach Test as a perceptual test.) *Rev. Psicol. Gen. Appl.*, 1951, *6*, 443-457.

The theoretical basis of the Rorschach appears to be sound, but some of the important clinical interpretations have not survived rigorous experimental tests. The bulk of evidence on color indicates that color responses *per se* are not important.

BENTON, A. L. The experimental validation of the Rorschach Test. II. The significance of Rorschach color responses. *Amer. J. Orthopsychiat.*, 1952, *22*, 755-763.

The author examined the theoretical implications of the color responses. It seems that color *per se* is not important. The important factor may be the ability of the subject to utilize all elements in the visual stimulus situation.

BIERI, J., AND BLACKER, E. External and internal stimulus factors in Rorschach performance. *J. Consult. Psychol.*, 1956, *20*, 1-7.

In the present study, the Rorschach cards were modified, with one detail being selected from each blot. These were administered to the subjects in three consecutive series, yielding thirty responses from each of the forty subjects. Among the findings was the fact that the subjects in the M>Sum C group generally had significantly longer reaction times to the blots than did subjects in the Sum C>M group, a difference which was general to the performance of the subjects and was not specifically related to longer reaction times for movement responses or shorter reaction times to color responses.

BILLS, R. E. Rorschach characteristics of persons scoring high and low in acceptance of self. *J. Consult. Psychol.*, 1953, *17*, 36-38.

Low scorers on a measure of self-acceptance used fewer color responses but more "well-controlled" color represented by FC, whereas high scorers used a greater number of color responses and more "poorly-controlled" color represented by predominance of CF and C responses.

BLECHNER, J. E. Constancy of Rorschach color responses under educational conditioning. *J. Exp. Educ.*, 1954, *22*, 293-295.

The Rorschach was administered to two groups twice at an interval of about one month. Prior to the post-test, the experimental group was presented with lecture material, the Ishehara test of color-blindness and slides designed to increase the subjects' experience at formulation of color-dominated concepts. There was a significant increase in the number of color responses to both groups.

BOYNTON, P. L., AND WALSWORTH, B. M. Emotionality test scores of delinquent and non-delinquent girls. *J. Abnorm. Soc. Psychol.*, 1943, *38*, 87-92.

Results indicate that delinquent girls cannot be differentiated from nondelinquent girls on the basis of color responses on the Rorschach.

BRENNAN, M., AND REICHARD, S. Use of the Rorschach Test in the prediction of hypnotizability. *Bull. Menninger Clin.*, 1943, *7*, 183-187.

BRICKLIN, B. Clinical use of the n affiliation score. *J. Project. Techn.*, 1961, *25*, 277-281.

It was posited that the n affiliation score and positive color responses on the Rorschach would correlate, inasmuch as both represent, theoretically, a tendency to move toward others. A small and insignificant correlation was found between these two scores. Currently, the meaning of the n affiliation score appears more equivocal than that of the Rorschach positive color response.

BROCKWAY, A. L., GLESER, G. C., AND ULETT, G. A. Rorschach concepts of normality. *J. Consult. Psychol.*, 1954, *18*, 259-265.

There was a greater use of c, m, C', CF as determinants for maladjusted normal than for adjusted ones. Found CF greater than FC in the normal protocol.

BRODY, G. G. A study of the effects of color on Rorschach responses. *Genet. Psychol. Monogr.*, 1955, *48*, 261-311.

Standard and achromatic Rorschach cards were administered to fifty normal male college students and fifty neurotic male students. When the standard cards were responded to first, it was found that the neurotics were disturbed by color while the controls were not. When the achromatic cards were responded first, neither the neurotic nor controls were disturbed by the presence of color in the standard series to which they responded next.

BUHLER, C., AND LEFEVER, D. W. A Rorschach study on the psychological characteristics of alcoholics. *Quart. J. stud. Alcohol.*, 1947, *8*, 197-260.

Alcoholic subjects differed from psychopathic subjects in greater sensitivity (Fc), better emotional responsiveness (Sum C).

BUKER, S. L., AND WILLIAMS, M. Color as a determinant of responsiveness to Rorschach cards in schizophrenia. *J. Consult. Psychol.*, 1951, *15*, 196-202.

It was found that: (a) color as a discrete variable does not materially influence responsiveness to the Rorschach; (b) color increases initial reaction time to chromatic but not to achromatic cards; (c) color may have a depressant effect on the F+% for achromatic, but not affect F+% for chromatic cards.

CANTER, A. Rorschach response characteristics as a function of color and degree of emotional constriction. *J. Consult. Psychol.*, 1957, *21*, 46.

Found no significant relationship between emotional constriction scores and color scores.

CANTER, A. The effect of unshaded bright colors in the Rorschach upon form-color responses balance of psychotic patients. *J. Project. Techn.*, 1958, *22*, 390-393.

The results indicated that the color-dominated responses were significantly inhibited to the unshaded bright color series, while overall productivity remained the same from one type of cards to the other. Cards VIII, IX and X were used. It was concluded that there is an optimum combination of values in color saturation, shadedness and figure-ground which will produce a form-color balance of responses to differentiate the emotionally unstable subject.

CARLSON, V. R., AND LAZARUS, R. S. A repetition of Meyer Williams' study of intellectual control under stress and associated Rorschach factors. *J. Consult. Psychol.*, 1953, *17*, 247-253.

No relationship was found between Rorschach Sum C/ total C and decrement in performance under stress.

CARR, A. C. The relation of certain Rorschach variables to expression of affect in the TAT and SCT. *J. Project. Techn.*, 1956, *20*, 137-142.

The relationships between several Rorschach variables (Sum C) and the expression of affect inferred from the TAT and the Forer SCT were studied and found often to be in the opposite direction to that predicted in terms of Rorschach theory. The study demonstrated a relationship between Rorschach variable "Sum C>2" and variables on the other tests. This variable showed a consistent positive relationship with hostility variables on other tests and a negative relationship with those pertaining to positive feelings.

CAVALCANTI, B. J. G. Da psicologia de epilepticos genuinos. Respostas de cor primaria no psicodiagnostico de Rorschach. (The psychology of idiopathic epilepsy. Pure color responses in Rorschach records.) *Rev. Med. Pernambuco*, 1936, *6*, 185-187.

CERBUS, G., AND NICHOLS, R. C. Personality variables and

response to color. *Psychol. Bull.,* 1963, *60,* 566-575. Review of color research with the general conclusion that there is no relationship between responses to color on the Rorschach and personality variables.

CHRISTOFFEL. Affektivitat und Farben, speziell Angst und Halbdunkelerscheinungen. (Affectivity and color, specific anxiety and shading responses.) *Z. Neurol.,* 1923, *82.*

CLARK, J. H. Some MMPI correlates of color responses in the group Rorschach. *J. Consult. Psychol.,* 1948, *12,* 334-386.

The difference of the means on the MMPI subscales indicates that maladjustment tends to be correlated with higher Sum C scores.

CONSALVI, C., AND CANTER, A. Rorschach scores as a function of psychological factors. *J. Consult. Psychol.,* 1957, *21,* 47-51.

There is a factorial similarity among high form-dominant color and shading scores as well as a unique factor of low form-dominance which includes both color and shading. This suggests that the traditional method of separating determinants into the various color and shading categories may be unnecessary.

COSTELLO, C. G. The Rorschach records of suicidal patients. *J. Project. Techn.,* 1958, *22,* 272-275.

The mean number of m and C responses were significantly larger for the nonsuicide group than for the suicide group.

COX, F. M., AND SARASON, S. B. Test anxiety and Rorschach performance. *J. Abnorm. Soc. Psychol.,* 1954, *49,* 371-377.

Two groups of twenty high- and twenty low-anxious college students were given the Rorschach under standard or ego-involving conditions. The high-anxious group did not give fewer weighted color responses than the low-anxious group under standard conditions, as was predicted.

CRUMPTON, E. The influence of color on the Rorschach Test. *J. Project. Techn.,* 1956, *20,* 150-158.

The standard and an achromatic Rorschach test were administered to two comparable groups of psychotics, neurotics and organics. The color stimulus was shown to influence the subject's performance when protocols were evaluated in a global way, but not when consideration was limited to color shock signs. The influence of color was apparent in the conceptual content of responses. The presence of color resulted in a shift in emphasis among content categories was conventionally scored; and it increased ratings of aggression and affect (especially unpleasant affect), as reflected in content. These results imply that the method of evaluation determines whether color is shown to influence Rorschach performance.

DALLA VOLTA, A. "Risposte primarie di colore" e "modi di apparire dei colori" nella prova di Rorschach. ("Primary color answers" and "modes of color appearance" in the Rorschach Test.) *Arch. Psicol. Neurol.,* 1949, *10,* 181-185.

Author maintains that a better classification of color responses in the Rorschach Test would be obtained by considering these responses from a phenomenological point of view.

DAWO, A. Nachweis psychischer Veränderungen gesunder Frauen während der Menstruation mittels des Rorschachversuches. *Rorschachiana,* 1952, *1,* 238-249.

Dawo reported a shift from introversive to extratensive experience types in female medical students tested in intermenstrum and again at onset of menstruation.

DELAY, J., AND PICHAT, P. De la psychopathologie de la vision au test de Rorschach. *Encephale,* 1957, *46,* 547-563.

Evidence has been found in epileptic protocols for positive diagnostic signs. Seventy-five percent of epileptics with grave character difficulties have Sum C>2, indicating strong correlation of affectivity with character disorder. These disorders are encountered basically in traumatic epileptics.

DRECHSLER, R. J. Affect-simulating effects of colors. *J. Abnorm. Soc. Psychol.,* 1960, *61,* 323-328.

The assumption that a subject's response to color on the Rorschach is related to affect was tested by presenting subjects with screen projections of various colors (bright red, green and gray geometric designs) followed by a list of words (devoid of affect-laden items) to which associations were elicited. Analysis of reaction time showed the most clear-cut evidence supporting the hypothesis that color (particularly red and green) would intrude on the associative processes more than the neutral gray, and red more so than green.

DROHOCKI, Z. Die typologische Bedeutung der Orientierung mittels Farbenordergestalt. (Color and form perception and typology.) *Pol. Arch. Psychol.,* 1932, 5(a).

DROHOCKI, Z. Smaczenie typologiczne orjentacji przy pomosy barwy lub kaztalter. Studium nad znaczeniem diagnostycznem testow Rorschacho. (The typological significance of orientation with the use of color or form. A study of the diagnostic significance of the Rorschach Test.) *Pol. Arch. Psychol.,* 1932, *5,* 406-426. (b)

DUBITSCHER, F. Der Rorschachsche Formendeutversuch als diagnostisches Hilfsmittel. (Rorschach's form-interpretation experiment as an aid in diagnosis.) *Z. Ges. Neur. Psychiat.,* 1932, *138,* 515-535.

Normal asthenics showed a marked displeasure toward color. Pyknics showed pleasure toward color.

DUBROVNER, R. J., VON LACKERM, W. J., AND JOST, H. A study of the effect of color on productivity and reaction time in the Rorschach Test. *J. Clin. Psychol.,* 1950, *6,* 331-336.

Standard Rorschach cards and achromatic cards were administered to one group of subjects in ab order and to the other in ba order with two weeks between the two tests. None of the data offered support for the hypothesis that the presence of color on Rorschach figures influence either productivity of responses or speed of reaction time.

EICHLER, R. M. Experimental stress and alleged Rorschach indices of anxiety. *J. Abnorm. Soc. Psychol.,* 1951. *46,* 344-356.

The total number of weighed color responses was less

for the stress than the nonstress group, but it did not reach statistical significance.

EXNER, J. E., Jr. The influence of chromatic and achromatic color in the Rorschach. *J. Project. Techn.*, 1959, *23*, 418-425.

When Card I of the Rorschach was modified in color only, it was found that the change influences the subject's responses. The author suggests the development of better methods of inquiry to differentiate "perceptual" and "projective" responses and to weigh color responses.

EXNER, J. E., Jr. Achromatic color in Cards IV and VI of the Rorschach. *J. Project. Techn.*, 1961, *25*, 38-40.

Blue colored chromatic variations of Cards IV and VI were administered to a group of college students, and their responses were compared with those of a group administered standard cards. Average reaction times for first responses were significantly greater to the standard cards than to the chromatic variations. Shading and form seem to be major determinants of popular responses to these cards.

EXNER, J. E., JR. The effect of color on productivity in Cards VIII, IX, X of the Rorschach. *J. Project. Techn.*, 1962, *21*, 30-33.

Results with college students tend to indicate that color does affect Rorschach productivity on Cards VIII, IX, X. Achromatic cards do not appear to affect the development of popular responses "animal'" and "spider" or "crab" on VIII and X respectively.

FABRIKONT, B. Suggestibility and the Rorschach. *J. Clin. Psychol.*, 1955, *11*, 309-310.

The Rorschach was administered to two groups of veterans under normal instructions and under instructions with a set to change M, C and c responses. These instructions were given for the retest of the Rorschach after a two week interval from the first testing. The group with the "set" instructions gave more M, C and c responses during retest than the group with the normal instructions.

FELZER, S. B. A statistical study of sex differences on the Rorschach. *J. Project. Techn.*, 1955, *19*, 382-386.

Females gave significantly more FC responses, showing a more ready control over emotional situations without loss of responsiveness. The feminine and nonfeminine females as well as masculine males gave significantly more FC responses than nonmasculine males.

FINNEY, B. C. Rorschach Test correlates of assultive behavior. *J. Project. Techn.*, 1950, *14*, 15-30.

Comparing assultive psychiatric patients with others who had never been assultive during their hospitalization, Finney found significantly more CF and Sum C in the records of the former group but no differences emerged in M.

FINNEY, B. C. Rorschach Test correlates of assultive behavior. *J. Project. Techn.*, 1955, *19*, 6-16.

The assultive groups showed more C and CF responses than the nonassultive group. Hypothesized FC— and CF—, CF>FC and fewer FC responses for the assultive group was not borne out.

FISHER, S. Rorschach patterns in conversion hysteria. *J. Project. Techn.*, 1951, *15*, 98-108 (a).

Hysterics gave few responses indicating controlled sensitivity to color and few loose color (C or CF) responses. This latter finding stands in contradiction to the general belief that hysterics give considerable loose color.

FISHER, S. The value of the Rorschach for detecting suicidal trends. *J. Project. Techn.*, 1951, *15*, 250-254 (b).

Only the number of FC's and average initial reaction time significantly differentiated the suicides from the nonsuicides, with the nonsuicides giving more FC responses and having shorter reaction times. They were not different on C and CF responses.

FORD, M. The application of the Rorschach Test to young children. *Univ. Minn. Child Welf. Monogr.*, 1946, *23*.

The Rorschach Test was administered to 123 nursery and elementary school children ranging in age from 3-0 to 7-11 years. Girls tended to give more color responses than boys, while boys tended to give more movement responses.

FORSYTH, R. P. The influence of color, shading and Welsh anxiety level on Elizur Rorschach content analyses of anxiety and hostility. *J. Project Techn.*, 1959, *23*, 207-213.

Subjects were divided into high, low and middle anxiety groups on the basis of k scale of the MMPI and the Welsh Anxiety scale. The results suggest that color facilitates the production of Elizur Anxiety scores unless all ten cards are considered together, and that there is a difference between the Rorschach relative to Elizur anxiety and hostility. The anxiety scores used here should not be equated. K is related to Elizur anxiety and hostility negatively in the middle group and positively in the low anxiety group.

FORTIER, R. H. The response to color and ego functions. *Psychol. Bull.*, 1953, *50*, 41-63.

Author presents a theory of the nature of the relation of the response to color and personality dynamics. Includes a review on color in the Rorschach.

FORTIER, R. H. An appraisal of Keehn's critique of "The response to color and ego functioning." *Psychol. Bull.*, 1954, *51*, 67-69.

This reply is directed at the principal criticisms levied by Keehn.

FRIEDMAN, H. A comparison of a group of hebephrenic and catatonic schizophrenics with two groups of normal adults by means of certain variables of the Rorschach Test. *J. Project. Techn.*, 1952, *16*, 352-360.

No significant differences in responses to color between schizophrenics and normals.

GARDNER, R. W. Impulsivity as indicated by Rorschach Test factors. *J. Consult. Psychol.*, 1951, *15*, 464-468.

High positive correlations were obtained between impulsivity ratings based on long-term acquaintance, P-F responses and responses to color on the Rorschach.

GEORGE, C. E., AND BONNEY, W. C. Rorschach's affect-color hypothesis and adaptation-level theory. *Psychol. Rev.*, 1956, *63*, 294-298.

Authors contend that many findings concerning color responses can be explained by reference to adaptation-level theory.

GIBBY, R. G., STOTSKY, B. A., HARRINGTON, R. L., AND THOMAS, R. W. Rorschach determinant shift among hallucinatory and delusional patients. *J. Consult. Psychol.*, 1955, *19*, 44-46.

Patients who were hallucinating showed significantly more M and less FC and total C on the Rorschach than delusional patients. Delusional patients showed more determinant shift from free association to inquiry with significant differences for F, FY, FC, total Y and total C.

GILL, H. S. Delay of response in problem solving and color response to Rorschach stimuli. *Diss. Abstr.*, 1961, *22*, 1252.

It was found that people characterized by inability to delay responses in problem-solving were, on a perceptual task like the Rorschach, less capable of integrating color of a stimulus with its form properties as compared to those who are characterized by delay of response.

GILLENSON, G. A study of the effects of color on Rorschach responses. *Diss. Abstr.*, 1953, *12*, 103.

Control and neurotic subjects were presented with standard and achromatic Rorschach cards. Difference in the number of responses to each variable did not seem to depend on color in the series, but were associated with the structural elements in the blot material. Control subjects were not disturbed by color, but neurotic subjects were.

GOLDFARB, W. Rorschach Test differences between family-reared, institution-reared and schizophrenic children. *Amer. J. Orthopsychiat.*, 1949, *19*, 624-633.

Children raised from very early life under impersonal institutional conditions show primitive and markedly extratensive Rorschach characteristics in addition to difficulties in delaying capacity and conceptualization.

GOLDSTONE, M. H. The relationship between certain Rorschach indicators and the magnitude of kinesthetic after-effect. *Diss. Abstr.*, 1960, *21*, 1254.

KAE magnitude varied insignificantly with color. Subjects were sixty male adolescent heroin addicts.

GOODMAN, H. W. An experimental investigation of the affective value of color on the Rorschach Test. *Amer. Psychol.*, 1950, *5*, 321-322.

The purpose was to discover the relationship between response to color on the Rorschach and affect as determined by concomitant psychogalvanic activity. It was concluded that the assumption that color on the Rorschach is an emotional stimulus and is reacted to as such is not valid.

GOODSTEIN, L. D., AND GOLDBERGER, L. Manifest anxiety and Rorschach performance in a chronic patient population. *J. Consult. Psychol.*, 1955, *19*, 339-341.

Responses to color did not differentiate between high and low anxious patients as measured by the Taylor Anxiety Scale.

GRACIA, J. S, El Rorschach en los indios aguaranas. (The Rorschach among the Aguarana Indians.) *Rev. Psicol. Gen. Appl.*, 1959, *14*, 287-320.

Rorschach records of fifteen Aguarana Indians showed use of white space, elevated F%, constant use of texture, absence of achromatic color and a marked tendency to stereotopy. The response to bright color showed a marked pathological significance in terms of Occidental norms.

GRAYSON, H. M. Rorschach productivity and card preference as influenced by experimental variation of color and shading. *J. Project. Techn.*, 1956, *20*, 288-296.

The author devised ten different Rorschach sets in which are included: the original Rorschach; three achromatic sets, and six monochromatic sets running the rainbow gamut from blue through red. These were used on normal nurses. It was found that productivity was independent of color and shading and is influenced by design-color interaction.

GUTIERRIZ-NORIEGA, C., AND CRUZ SANCHEZ, G. Efecto de la intoxicacion producida por la Opuntia culindrica sobre los resultados del test de Rorschach. (Effect of intoxication produced by Opuntia cylindrica on the results of the Rorschach Test.) *Rev. Neuro. Psiquiat.*, 1948, *11*, 390-401.

Eleven persons were administered the Rorschach during a state of intoxication produced by the alkaloid of Opuntia cylindrica. They found an absolute and relative diminution in the number of chromatic responses produced in many cases.

HAFNER, A. J. Response time and Rorschach behavior. *J. Clin. Psychol.*, 1958, *14*, 154-155.

Two groups of college students were given the Rorschach. One group was given the test under standard conditions, the other with instructions to respond as quickly as possible and to give only two responses. The experimental group obtained significantly higher pure C, significantly lower D, P and F% scores.

HALPERN, F. Rorschach interpretation of the personality structure of schizophrenics who benefit from insulin therapy. *Psychiat. Quart.*, 1940, *14*, 826-833.

The improved group showed more active emotionality as shown by color responses and chiascuro responses.

HARRINGTON, R. W. Maladaptive responses to frustration predicted from Rorschach color responses. *J. Consult. Psychol.*, 1954, *18*, 455-458.

The group whose Rorschach color scores were predominantly of the C and/or CF type showed more impairment in performance on a code-subsituation test under frustration than did the group whose color responses were predominantly of the FC type. This did not hold for a mirror-tracing test.

HARRINGTON, R. W. Prediction of maladaptive response under conditions of habit-interference from Rorschach color responses. *Diss. Abstr.*, 1954, *14*, 555.

It was found that subjects who gave color responses in which the emphasis was predominantly on the color element C-CF showed a greater degree of impairment in performance under conditions of frustration than did subjects who gave primarily FC responses.

HERTZMAN, M., ORLANSKY, J., AND SEITZ, C. Personality organization and anoxia tolerance. *Psychosom. Med.*, 1944, *6*, 317-331.

These investigators found that the threshold for breakdown under anoxic conditions was lower for extratensives, suggesting greater response to environmental alterations by the high Sum C group.

HOLTZMAN, W. H. Validation studies of the Rorschach Test: Impulsiveness in the normal superior adult. *J. Clin. Psychol.*, 1950, 6, 348-351.

The most important single indicator of impulsiveness was the presence of one or more spontaneous immediate responses provoked by color. The use of single, isolated color ratios did not prove satisfactory for the prediction of impulsiveness as judged by the intimate associates of college men. Results were more promising when signs were considered together.

HOLTZMAN, W. H., ISCOE, I., AND CALVIN, A. D. Rorschach color responses and manifest anxiety in college women. *J. Consult. Psychol.*, 1954, 18, 317-324.

Colored versions of Cards II and III gave shorter reaction times and more responses than the achromatic versions of these cards. The colored-before-achromatic order of presenting cards resulted in shorter mean reaction time for Cards II and III than the reverse order of presentation.

HOLZBERG, J. D., AND SCHLEIFER, M. J. An experimental test of the Rorschach assumption of the impact of color on the perceptual and associative processes. *J. Project. Techn.*, 1955, 19, 130-137.

Thirty-nine mental hospital patients were given five tasks measuring a variety of perceptual and associative processes. These tasks were prepared in two forms — chromatic and achromatic. Their results offer evidence to support the assumption that color on the Rorschach has an impact on the perceptual and associative processes.

HUGHES, H., EPSTEIN, C. J., AND JOST, H. The relationship between certain measurable functions of autonomic nervous system activity and color responses on the Rorschach Test. *J. Clin. Psychol.*, 1951, 7, 244-249.

An attempt was made to analyze quantitatively affective tone to color responses on the Rorschach thru continuous measurements of respiration, relative blood pressure, heart rate and GSR as measured by the Keeler polygraph during the free association period of the Rorschach Test. Only one of the twenty t's computed between physiological reactions of thirty-two college women to noncolor and color responses on the colored cards was significant above the 5 per cent level. It was concluded that color and noncolor Rorschach responses were not associated with appreciably different physiological changes as measured in this study.

KEEHN, J. D. Rorschach validation. III: An examination of the role of color as a determinant in the Rorschach Test. *J. Ment. Sci.*, 1953, 99, 410-438.

Factor analysis of the results of administration of a battery of tests constructed to determine whether color-determined Rorschach responses depend upon color to two-hundred normals revealed two factors. A C-F factor, depending upon reaction or nonreaction to color was found, but Rorschach color score had no saturation upon this. The second was identified as reaction to the stimulus as a whole rather than to any part, and the Rorschach had a saturation of .6 upon this.

KEEHN, J. D. A re-evaluation of the role played by color in the Rorschach Test. *Brit. J. Med. Psychol.*, 1954, 27, 89-93.

This paper suggested that the general practice of weighing M against Sum C responses is insufficiently refined and that in all probability whole responses should also be taken into consideration. In addition, it is considered that C-determined responses occurring initially to the colored cards should be interpreted differently from those appearing later.

KEEHN, J. D. "The response to color and ego functions:" A critique in the light of recent experimental evidence. *Psychol. Bull.*, 1954, 51, 65-67.

"The use of the results of Rorschach studies either to support or to refute the color-emotionality hypothesis is invalid. Hence, the great majority of evidence put forward by Fortier in support of his hypothesis must be regarded as irrelevant."

KERNETSKY, C., AND GERARD, D. L. Effect of increasing the number of Rorschach responses on Sum C and M: A note on Fiske and Baughman's study. *J. Abnorm. Soc. Psychol.*, 1954, 49, 592-593.

The results indicated that equating the number of responses will not equate the frequency of color or human movement-determined responses. In terms of the problem raised by Fiske and Baughman, the results suggested that the frequency of C- and M-determined responses is probably not due to the influence of the number of responses as an independent variable.

KLATSKIN, E. H. An analysis of the effect of the test situation upon the Rorschach record: Forman scoring characteristics. *J. Project. Techn.*, 1952, 16, 193-199.

"From what little data is available, it would appear that when the subject is in a stress situation, the C and T determinants and contents are more susceptible than other aspects of his record to such influence."

KNOPF, I. J. The effects of recent perceptual training and experience on Rorschach performance. *J. Clin. Psychol.*, 1954, 10, 52-56.

Sixteen subjects were exposed to a nonpersonal film on color while another sixteen subjects learned a series of nonsense syllables. All subjects were given the Rorschach twice, spaced three weeks apart, with the experimental conditions immediately preceding the second Rorschach testing. The results indicate that the color experience had no appreciable effect on the Sum of C.

KOBLER, F. J., AND STIEL, A. The use of the Rorschach in involutional melancholia. *J. Consult. Psychol.*, 1953, 17, 365-370.

For this group of women, the sum of the chromatic responses was larger than the sum of the achromatic responses. The emotional responsiveness of the involutionals is indicated further in the predominance of the CF and C over the FC responses.

KRAL, V. A., AND DORKEN, H. The influence of subcortical brain lesions on emotionality as reflected in the Rorschach color responses. *Amer. J. Psychiat.*, 1951, 107, 839-843.

Found complete absence of color responses in nine people with diencephalic lesions.

KRAUSE, A. R. Shifts in the levels of operating defenses induced by blurring of inkblots slides. *J. Clin. Psychol.,* 1956, *12,* 337-341.

Zullinger inkblots were presented first maximally blurred and then clearly to thirty student nurses who had taken the Harrower-Ericksen previously and to fify-four others who had not had the Rorschach. For both groups, R and A were reduced, while vista, CF and C "blocked" M particularly, but also M, were greater under the blurred than under clear conditions.

LAX, R. F. An experimental investigation of the influence of color on the perception of movement in ink blots. *Psychol. Newsletter,* 1957, *8,* 61-75. N.Y.U.

Four inkblots in red, blue, green and black-gray, forming a series of sixteen, were presented to thirty college students matched in intelligence and ratio of men to women. The findings indicated tentatively that color influences movement responses in a unique fashion for each personality.

LAZARUS, R. S. An experimental analysis of the influence of color on the protocol of the Rorschach Test. *J. Personality,* 1948, *17,* 182-185.

The subjects were one-hundred high school seniors divided into two groups. The standard Rorschach and the noncolor version were presented to the two groups in ab-ba order. From the results it was concluded that the assumption that color widely influences performance in determinants other than color is not acceptable.

LAZARUS, R. S. The influence of color on the protocol of the Rorschach Test. *J. Abnorm. Soc. Psychol.,* 1949, *44,* 506-516.

High school students were administered the standard Rorschach and six weeks later an achromatic version. Few significant differences in scoring categories between color and noncolor series were found. It appeared that the presence or absence of color had little effect on the performance of the subjects with regard to the scoring categories.

LEVINE, K. N., GRASSI, J. R., AND GERSON, M. J. Hypnotically induced mood changes in the verbal and graphic Rorschach: A case study. *Rorschach Res. Exch.,* 1943, *7,* 130-144.

LEVY, L. H., AND KURZ, R. B. The connotative impact of color on the Rorschach and its relation to manifest anxiety. *J. Personality,* 1957, *25,* 617-625.

The study was designed to test the hypothesis that the connotative meaning of Rorschach cards will change with the presence or absence of color and that the amount of change will vary directly with the subject's anxiety level. The results were interpreted as supporting both the experimental hypotheses and providing the basis for an explanation of some of the discrepant findings with regard to the role of color in Rorschach performance.

LIGHT, B. H., AND AMICK, J. H. Rorschach responses of normal aged. *J. Project. Techn.,* 1956, *20,* 285-295.

The aged were characterized by low Sum C, infrequent use and underproduction of FC and CF.

LINTON, H. B. Rorschach correlates of response to suggestion. *J. Abnorm. Soc. Psychol.,* 1954, *49,* 75-83.

Purpose was to discover Rorschach measures associated with change of autokinetic judgments under the influence of planted judgments given by a confederate. Sum C was significantly and positively correlated with change of judgment, while C control and C trend had a low positive correlation with change of judgment.

LITTLE K. Connotations of the Rorschach inkblots. *J. Personality,* 1959, *27,* 397-406.

Nine semantic differential scales were completed by twenty male and twenty female college sophomores for the ten Rorschach inkblots and for six concepts. Achromatic cards on the average were considered less active, potent and "good" than the chromatic cards.

LOOSLI-USTERI, MARIA. Le test de Rorschach applique a differents groupes d'enfants de 10-13 ans. (Application of the Rorschach Test to different groups of children 10-13 years.) *Arch. Psychol.,* 1929, *22,* 51-106.

LOOSLI-USTERI, MARIA. Les interpretations dans le test de Rorschach. Interpretations-kinesthesique et interpretations-couleur. (Interpretations of the Rorschach Test. Kinesthetic and color interpretations.) *Arch. Psychol.,* 1932, *23,* 349-365.

The results from a study of the color interpretations agreed perfectly with those found for adults. The subjects were children.

LUCENA, J. Modifications des donnes du test de Rorschach pendant les phases du chod insulinique. (Modifications of Rorschach Test findings during phases of insulin shock.) *Rev. Psychol. Appl.,* 1958, *8,* 25-35.

The Rorschachs of those patients who improved were compared with those patients who did not. Rorschachs were given before the injection of insulin, during the phase of moderate hypoglycemia, again during the later phase of accentuated hypoglycemia, then immediately upon interruption of the coma and finally later in the day after the patient's first meal. Although comparisons of color responses were made, the results of these comparisons were not given in the abstract.

MANDEVILLE, P. F. A study of the relationship between responsiveness to color on the Rorschach Examination and impulsive behavior. *Diss. Abstr.,* 1954, *14,* 1251.

Average rating on impulsiveness was shown to be positively and significantly correlated with number of C + CF responses to chromatic cards, total number of responses given to all but the chromatic series of cards.

MANN, L. The relation of Rorschach indices of extratension and introversion to a measure of responsiveness to the immediate environment. *J. Consult. Psychol.,* 1956, *20,* 114-118.

Sum C was positively related to the criterion measure of responsiveness. C total was negatively related to the criterion measure of responsiveness. The criterion measure was defined in terms of words referring to the immediate environment written in the Binet association task.

MARADIE, L. S. The goal-spurt hypothesis and the Rorschach Test. *J. Consult. Psychol.,* 1956, *20,* 205-210.

The author believes that the goal-spurt hypothesis for the increment in productivity on the last three cards of the Rorschach "is more parsimonius, is objectively demonstratable, is based upon studies concerned with the laws of learning and mental work and, quite apart from the various qualities attributable to color, explains the increment in productivity in the later-appearing cards."

MATARAZZO, R. G., WATSON, R. I., AND ULETT, G. A. Relationship of Rorschach scoring categories to modes of perception induced by intermittent photic stimulation – a methodological study of perception. *J. Clin. Psychol.*, 1952, 8, 368-374.

The study was undertaken to discover whether or not the Rorschach categories were meaningful to perception in general. In the control population, the quantity of C and M as scored on Rorschach responses was related to the amount of color and movement produced in the subjective sensations resulting from intermittent photic stimulation. The above relationship was disturbed in patients with anxiety and in control subjects who were considered anxiety-prone.

MEYER, G. Some relationships between Rorschach scores in kindergarten and reading in the primary grades. *J. Project. Techn.*, 1953, 17, 414-425.

A larger proportion of achieving readers use a color determinant one or more times. A larger proportion of achieving readers use a FC+CF+C% of 14.0 or more. A larger proportion of achieving readers have a Sum C of three or more.

MILLER, C., AND SALOMON, F. Test de Rorschach de medecins praticiens. (Rorschach Test of practicing physicians.) *Bull. Soc. Franc. Rorschach Math. Project.*, 1962, 13-14, 20-27.

Protocols of twenty practicing physicians and ten physicians not in practice were used to indicate probable characteristics of responses of physicians for comparison with similar data from those in other professions. Tentative conclusions were that practicing physicians have greater W% and less D%, few M, relatively numerous CF and some S.

MULLENER, E. Rorschachbefunde bei Farbenblindheit. (Rorschach data in color blindness.) *Z. Diag. Psychol.*, 1956, 4, 3-23.

The Rorschach was administered to fifty-one red-green color blind men. In comparison to normal controls, their records yielded fewer C but more accurate F responses. Cards IX and X produced the most misjudgments.

NIIMI, Y., HASHIMOTO, H., MOCHIZUKI, K., AND OHNO, I. Galvanic skin response during Rorschach Test administration. *Jap. J. Psychol.*, 1956, 27, 175-184.

Psychotics, as compared with normals, showed marked increases in GSR to VI-X, differences that did not appear when non-Rorschach color stimuli were used.

NORMAN, R., AND SCOTT, W. Color and affect: A review and semantic evaluation. *J. Gen. Psychol.*, 1952, 46, 185-225.

Section on color in the Rorschach.

OESER, O. A. Some experiments on the abstraction of form and color: Part II. Rorschach Tests. *Brit. J. Psychol.*, 1932, 22, 287-323.

Found personality differences between form-dominated

peoples and color-dominated peoples. To the Rorschach blots, Cd people gave far more interpretation on the basis of color. Feeling plays a great part in their interpretations. The Fd's interpret on the basis of form, select small, clear details and are more introversive.

OHKURA, K. Rorschach study with delinquents. *Jap. Fam. Court. Monogr.*, 1957, 9, 1-37.

One hundred delinquents aged fourteen to nineteen were tested. On the whole, as compared to other studies on normals (a) relatively more color responses appear, especially C, (b) there is an extravert tendency as shown by 23 per cent M>C and 35 per cent C>M. In violent delinquents, C and K were frequently observed.

PASTO, T. A., AND KIVISTO, P. Group differences in color choice and rejection. *J. Clin. Psychol.*, 1956, 12, 279-281.

Two hundred-forty subjects were tested as to color preference on Rorschach Card X and a color chart. Normal females shifted their preference more than normal males. The psychotics were characterized by a greater range of color choice and rejection. The mental defectives rejected yellow more than the other groups. Blue and red were the popular choices among all the groups; gray and brown were the colors most rejected.

PATTIE, F. A. The effect of hypnotically induced hostility on Rorschach responses. *J. Clin. Psychol.*, 1954, 10, 161-164.

The Rorschach responses of fourteen subjects were studied when the test was given under normal conditions and with posthypnotically induced hostility toward the experimenter. The results offered no support whatever to the theory that color responses are indicators of outwardly directed hostility.

PERLMAN, J. A. Color and the validity of the Rorschach 8-9-10 per cent. *J. Consult. Psychol.*, 1951, 15, 122-126. The findings indicated that color did not bring variability in production over and above the potentialities of the achromatic blots. The author concludes that individual differences in the 8-9-10 per cent cannot be attributed to color.

PHARES, E. J., STEWART, L. M., AND FOSTER, J. M. Instruction variation and Rorschach performance. *J. Project. Techn.*, 1960, 24, 28-31.

It was predicted that when subjects categorize the Rorschach testing situation as one in which their responses are either right or wrong; the results would be fewer total, movement and color responses, more popular, animal and pure form responses, and a higher form-level. Results failed to confirm any of the hypotheses, although a significant difference was found between experimenters in total number of responses elicited.

PIOTROWSKI, Z. Tendonces actuelles du Rorschach. (The present trends of the Rorschach.) *Bull. Group. Franc. Rorschach*, 1953, 3, 2-4.

Short review of some recent interpretations of color.

PIOTROWSKI, Z. *Perceptanalysis: A Fundamentally Reworked, Expanded, and Systematized Rorschach Method.* New York: Macmillan, 1957.

Includes a discussion on color.

PIOTROWSKI, Z., AND SCHREIBER, M. Rorschach percept-analytic measurement of personality changes during and after intensive psychoanalytically oriented psychotherapy. In *Specialized Techniques in Psychotherapy.* New York: Basic Books, 1951.

Evidence for increases in dilation of the experience type in the course of psychoanalytic psychotherapy were found as contrasted with supportive therapy. Changes in both M and Sum C seemed to mirror changes in individual patients.

POPPLESTONE, J. A. Scoring color responses in paintings. *J. Clin. Psychol.,* 1955, *11,* 191-193.

Twenty hospital admissions were given the Rorschach and a painting task. Quantitative measures of ability to structure color and the responsiveness to it on the two tasks failed to reveal a relationship.

RABINOVITCH, M. S. Physiologic responses, perceptual threshold, and Rorschach Test anxiety indices. *J. Project. Techn.,* 1954, *18,* 379-386.

Rorschach Test responses determined by Rorschach signs of anxiety (strong use of color, shading or texture) were associated with greater GSR deflection and higher perceptual threshold than P or F+.

RABINOVITCH, M. S., KENNARD, MARGARET A., AND FISTER, W. P. Personality correlates of electroencephalographic findings. *Canad. J. Psychol.,* 1955, *9,* 29-41.

EEG distinctions were found between extremes in the experience types and evidence that high introversive subjects showed more "harmonizing activity" from various cortical areas.

RAPPAPORT, S. An experimental investigation of the effects and persistence of set directed toward increasing responses on the color variables in Rorschach. *Diss. Abstr.,* 1960, *21,* 369.

Found that under conditions of verbal-instruction set and task-induced set, there was a significant increase in color productivity as represented by variables of Sum C and FC. Increases in color score were largely FC. The effects of set on color was not maintained when subjects were retested four weeks later under standard procedures. Sum C was significantly negatively correlated with the Guilford-Zimmerman scale for emotional instability. It was not correlated with the other scales.

REECE, M. M. Color shock in the Rorschach: The effect of achromatic reproductions. In E. Baughman's The role of the stimulus in Rorschach responses. *Psychol. Bull.,* 1958, *55,* 121-147.

Standard and achromatic cards were administered to two groups of psychology students. Color did not affect liking of cards.

RICHARDS, T. W., AND MURRAY, D. C. Global evaluation of Rorschach performances *versus* scores: Sex differences in Rorschach performance. *J. Clin. Psychol.,* 1958, *14,* 61-64.

Color responses did not differentiate males and females.

RICKERS-OVSIANKINA, MARIA (ed.). *Rorschach Psychology.* New York: John Wiley & Sons, Inc., 1960.

Contains a chapter on color by David Shapiro.

RICKERS-OVSIANKINA, MARIA, KNAPP, R. H., AND McINTYRE, D. W. Factors affecting the psychodiagnostic significance of color perception. *J. Project. Techn.,* 1963, *27,* 461-466.

Subjects were adminstered the Rorschach and the Knapp Tartan Tests. The reactions of the subjects to the color on these tests were analyzed and discrepant results were found; i.e., subjects whose Rorschach reactions frequently fell into one of the warm color categories, clearly tended to avoid the choice of warm-colored tartans, and vice versa.

ROCKETT, F. C. Speed of form recognition as a function of stimulus factors and test anxiety. *J. Abnorm. Soc. Psychol.,* 1956, *53,* 197-202.

The influence of color, pattern of color, figure and anxiety on response time was investigated in 192 subjects. The hypothesis that highly anxious persons are greatly affected by colors was not concerned.

ROE, ANNE. Analysis of group Rorschachs of psychologists and anthropologists. *J. Project. Techn.,* 1952, *16,* 212-224.

Roe found that physicists show more M than the psychologists, who tended to be more productive of M and Sum C as compared with other scientists. It was suggested that a knowledge of ideal Rorschach patterns played some role in the reactions of the psychologists.

ROSEN, E. Connotative meanings of Rorschach inkblots, responses, and determinants. *J. Personality,* 1960, *28,* 413-426.

Connotations of chromatic blots were found to differ significantly from those of achromatic blots as measured by fifteen semantic-differential scales.

RUESCH, J., AND FINESINGER, J. E. The relation of the Rorschach color response to the use of color in drawing. *Psychosom. Med.,* 1941, *3,* 370-388.

High color scores in drawings correlated with high values for the number of Rorschach color responses.

SAPPENFIELD, B. R., AND BUKER, S. L. Validity of the Rorschach 8-9-10 per cent as an indicator of responsiveness to color. *J. Consult. Psychol.,* 1949, *13,* 268-271.

A group of college students was shown the Harrower-Erickson Rorschach series first and then an achromatic series; a second group received the cards in the reverse order. Productivity to the cards was the same in both series. The hypothesis that productivity to the test is a function of color was not supported.

SARASON, S. B., AND POTTER, E. H. Color in the Rorschach and Kohs block design. *J. Consult. Psychol.,* 1947, *11,* 202-206.

Poor performance on the colored Kohs block designs was associated with the inability to respond constructively to the colored Rorschach cards.

SCHACHTEL, E. G. On color and affect: Contributions to an understanding of Rorschach's Test. II. *Psychiatry,* 1943, *6,* 393-409.

Discussion is offered in terms of what constitutes the color experience, the affect experience, the relations between color- and affect-experience, the affective significance of single colors, negative reactions to color and color affect and extratensiveness.

SCHACHTEL, E. G. Notes on Rorschach Tests of 500 juvenile delinquents and a control group of 500 non-delinquent adolescents. *J. Project. Techn.*, 1951, *15*, 144-172.

None of the color responses that differentiated between the delinquents and nondelinquents seemed to be statistically significant. Nondelinquents gave more FC responses than delinquents, and delinquents gave more pure C responses than nondelinquents.

SCHMIDT, H. O., FONDA, C. P., AND LESTER, J. R. Rorschach behavior as an index of color anaesthesia. *J. Psychol.*, 1955, *40*, 95-102.

Red areas of Rorschach Card III were masked with opaque white ink, and special attention was paid to subjects who failed to give any color-determined responses in the Rorschach. In both instances, the functional relationship between the variables remained the same: Reduction in the salience of red areas facilitated perception of the black and white area as human figures engaged in passive, centripetal or flexor movement. This technique was advanced as an objective means for testing the hypothesis that color, for rigidly defensive personalities, is something disturbing and disorderly and hence to be avoided.

SCHOLL, R. Untersuchungen uber die terlinhaltliche beachtung von farbe und form bei erwachsinin und kindern. (Color and form in the perception of adults and children.) *Z. Psychol.*, 1926, 101.

SCHOLL, R. Zur theorie und typologie der teilinhaltlichen beachtung von form und fabre. (Theory and typology of the perception of color and form.) *Z. Psychol.*, 1928, 611.

SCHOLL, R. Die terlinhaltliche beachtung von form, farbe und grosse in vorschulpflichtigen kindersalter. (Form, color, and size in the perception of preschool children.) *Z. Psychol.*, 1930, *109*.

SCHWARTZ, F., AND KATES, S. L. Rorschach performance, anxiety level, and stress. *J. Project. Techn.*, 1957, *21*, 154-160.

The FC and CF variables were excluded from analysis because of low test-retest reliability.

SCHWARZ, W. Correlation between the Rorschach Test and the Lindberg Ring Test in demonstration personality psychograms. *Acta Psychiat.*, 1951, *26*, 199-212.

Children who give color on the Lindberg Ring test tended to have personality traits associated with emotional lability and spotaneity, give a greater color sum on the Rorschach, have the heaviest loading of factors for noncontrol or lability on the Rorschach. Children responding in noncolor or mixed fashion show Rorschach loading for nonlability or nonspontaneity.

SHAPIRO, D. Color-response and perceptual passivity. *J. Project. Techn.*, 1956, *20*, 52-69.

The author explores the meaning of color responses in the Rorschach.

SHATIN, L. Relationship between the Rorschach Test and the Thematic Apperception Test. *J. Project. Techn.*, 1955, *19*, 317-331.

Found a relationship of FC with portrayal of parental figures as benign and nurturant which suggested a desire for emotional rapport. Individuals with high Sum C were more prone to bring their personal problems into the TAT situation. A high uncontrolled color score was directly related to verbal and emotional aggression on the TAT. Subjects were drawn from a VA hospital.

SHERMAN, M. H. A psychoanalytic definition of Rorschach determinants. *Psychoanalysis*, 1955, *3*, 68-76.

Author maintains that color is related to indirect manifestations of the id. Hysterics tended to the C end of the CFM continuum.

SIIPOLA, ELSA M. The influence of color on reactions to ink blots. *J. Personality*, 1950, *18*, 358-382.

Two groups of subjects responded to either chromatic areas of the Rorschach or achromatic copies of the same areas. Color increased reaction time. Whether content of response was affected depended upon whether the color was appropriate to the content suggested by the form of the blot.

SIIPOLA, ELSA M., KUHNS, F., AND TAYLOR, V. Measurement of the individual's reaction to color in ink blots. *J. Personality*, 1950, *19*, 153-171.

Each experimental subject was presented with matched versions of chromatic and achromatic blots in succession with the effects of memory controlled. The results supported the theory that color in the Rorschach blots produces distinct effects on the character of the subject's conceptual processes.

SIIPOLA, ELSA M., AND TAYLOR, VIVIAN. Reactions to ink-blots under free and pressure conditions. *J. Personality*, 1952, *21*, 22-47.

Authors conclude that the M tendency, in contrast to the C tendency characterizes the person who excels in the "ability to delay."

SINGER, J. L., AND HERMAN, J. Motor and fantasy correlates of Rorschach human movement responses. *J. Consult. Psychol.*, 1954, *18*, 325-331.

This study provided evidence for the influence of experience type on the rated amount of activity in a waiting room. The amount of activity increased progressively through four subgroups of high M; low Sum C, high M: high Sum C, low M: low Sum C, low M: high Sum C, or, in other words, as the group ratios changed from marked introversion to marked extratension.

SOMMER, R., AND SOMMER, D. T. Assultiveness and two types of Rorschach color responses. *J. Consult. Psychol.*, 1958, *22*, 57-62.

Found that subjects who gave aggressive color responses showed more assultive behavior than the nonaggressive color subjects.

SPITAL, C. Prediction of emotional control in children with the Rorschach Test. *Diss. Abstr.*, 1956, *16*, 581.

Rorschach administered to forty-one emotionally disturbed children. Results indicated that the behavior of children who gave color responses on the Rorschach was predictable to a satisfying degree, while the behavior of others who did not show responses to color was difficult to predict with this group of children. Little besides the color factor contributed to the prediction of emotional control.

STANCAK, A., AND FRAENKEL, E. Faktorova analyza Rorschachovych nalezov u neuroz pred a po aplikacee etulalkoholu. (Factor analysis of Rorschach's findings regarding neurosis before and after the application of ethyl alcohol.) *Cesk. Psychol.*, 1961, 5, 363-372.

Factors C (color response) and F (form response) are stated after alcohol consumption. The analysis was done on the Rorschach protocols of forty-five neurotics.

STEISEL, I. M. The Rorschach Test and suggestibility. *J. Abnorm. Soc. Psychol.*, 1952, 47, 607-614.

Did not obtain the hypothesized positive relationship between the absolute number and/or percentage of responses scorable as CF and some measure of suggestibility.

STOPOL, M. S. Rorschach performance in relation to two types of stress. *J. Consult. Psychol.*, 1954, 18, 11-16.

No relationship was found for tolerance to either failure stress or task-induced stress and the hypothesized preponderance of FC over CF+ C.

STORA, RENEE. Le probleme des couleurs dans les Rorschach francais. (The problems of color in the Rorschach Tests of French subjects.) *Beih. Schweiz. Z. Psychol.*, 1950, 19, 797-887.

Some evidence was presented suggesting that C and CF responses do not necessarily indicate observable labile and impulsive behavioral characteristics.

STORMENT, C. T., AND FINNEY, B. C. Projection and behavior: A Rorschach study of assultive mental hospital patients. *J. Project. Techn.*, 1953, 17, 349-360.

Violent patients differed significantly from the nonviolent patients on the number and percentage of color-minus responses, with the former giving more. No other usage of color differentiated between them.

STOTSKY, B. A. A comparison of remitting and non-remitting schizophrenics on psychological tests. *J. Abnorm. Soc. Psychol.*, 1952, 47, 489-496.

The remitted group of schizophrenics gave more FC responses than the hospitalized group. The latter group gave more CF and C responses than the former group.

STOTSKY, B. A. Differential responses of normals, psychoneurotics, and psychotics on Rorschach determinant shift. *J. Consult. Psychol.*, 1955, 19, 335-338.

Normals, psychoneurotics and psychotics did not differ significantly on the total number of C responses.

TRANQUE, G. F. Color y charscuro en el "test" de Rorschach. (Color and black-white contrast in the Rorschach Test.) *Psicotecnia*, 1942, 3, 428-433.

Descriptive account of affective distinctions said by Rorschach students to correlate with differential responses to colored test figures.

VAN EECKHOUTTE, R. Contribution a l'etude affective de l'enfant au moyen des "responses-couleurs." (Contribution to the affective study of the child by means of color responses.) *Rev. Belg. Psychol. Pedag.*, 1950, 12, 105-126.

In an investigation of fifty-two children of both sexes from four to fourteen years old, it was found that there was always a dominance of preferred and of antagonistic color. These dominances correspond to types of affective reactions, as shown by the Rorschach Test.

VANEK, Z. The role of color in learning: An investigation of the role of color in learning and its relationship to the color rationale of the Rorschach Psychodiagnostic Test. *Diss. Abstr.*, 1954, 14, 2299.

The Sum C factor in the group Rorschach Test showed no statistically significant relationship to chromatic and achromatic nonsense syllable learning.

VAN METRE, D. An investigation of the relationship between inkblot color and personality traits. *Diss. Abstr.*, 1954, 14, 2406.

The purpose of the study was to investigate the relationship of color scores and the personality traits of social adaptability and emotional maturity as rated by teachers and other students. A low negative correlation was found between the form-color integration ratio and social adaptability ratings and between the form-color integration ratio and emotional maturity. A low positive correlation was found between FC responses and social adaptability ratings and between FC responses and emotional maturity ratings.

VIANNA GUERRA, C. As respostas das criancas de 3-8 anos ao psicodiagnostico de Rorschach. (The responses of children of 3 to 8 to the Rorschach.) *Bol. Inst. Psicol.*, 1958, 8, 20-31.

The F% was higher than the C (CF, FC)% for one hundred Brazilian children.

WALLEN, R. The nature of color shock. *J. Abnorm. Soc. Psychol.*, 1948, 43, 346-356.

Normals preferred colored versions of 8, 9, 10, achromatic versions for 3 and no difference for 2. Neurotics preferred 8 and 10 in color, tended to prefer 9 in color, no difference for 3 and tended to prefer achromatic 2.

WERTHEIMER, R. R. Relationship between specific Rorschach variables and sociometric data. *J. Project. Techn.*, 1957, 21, 94-97.

The Rorschachs of ninety-eight socially accepted and 102 socially rejected adolescents were compared on five Rorschach variables purported to be associated with social acceptance (H%, P%, FC>CF, Fc, Sum C>M). No significant relationships were found between these Rorschach variables and social acceptance by others.

WESTROPE, M. R. Relations among Rorschach indices, manifest anxiety, and performance under stress. *J. Abnorm. Soc. Psychol.*, 1953, 48, 515-525.

Form-color integration and modified form-color integration did not differentiate anxious from nonanxious subjects.

WILLIAMS, H. C., AND LAWRENCE, J. F. Comparison of the Rorschach and MMPI by means of factor analysis. *J. Consult. Psychol.*, 1954, 18, 193-198.

In factor I, many of the MMPI scales had high negative loadings, while the factor had positive loadings on Rorschach W, CF and the K variables, verbal IQ and MMPI Es and K. Factor III contained negative loadings on the movement variables, FC and the MMPI Ma scale.

WILLIAMS, M. An experimental study of intellectual control under stress and associated Rorschach measures. *J. Consult. Psychol.*, 1947, 11, 21-29.

Found a positive correlation (+ .354) between form-color integration and performance under stress.

WITTENBORN, J. R. Level of mental health as a factor in the implications of Rorschach scores. *J. Consult. Psychol.*, 1950, *14*, 469-472.

The whole responses, and the vista, texture and color response which are uncontrolled by form, cluster together to form a factor. The human and animal movement responses cluster together with the form-color and large detail response to form a separate factor.

WOLPIN, M., AND HAMLIN, R. M. Effect of form-color incongruity on responses to inkblots. *J. Clin. Psychol.*, 1959, *15*, 151-155.

Incongruity increased the use of color as a determinant. Subjects gave many more CF and C responses to incongruous stimuli than they did to congruous stimuli where the color seemed to go with the form.

WYSOCKI, B. A. Rorschach card preference as a diagnostic aid. *Psychol. Monogr.*, 1956, *70*, 413, 16.

Preference for cards appeared to be related to chromatic versus achromatic character of the card, while in other situations it was the color, form or content that appeared important.

YORK, R. H. The effect of color in the Rorschach Test and in selected intellectual tasks. In E. Baughman's The role of the stimulus in Rorschach responses. *Psychol. Bull.*, 1958, *55*, 121-147.

Chromatic and achromatic cards administered to neurotics. He found that color significantly impaired form perception. Variables other than color made the chromatic cards more difficult to interpret than the achromatic cards.

ZECCA, G. Alcuni aspetti delle risposte di colore nel Rorschach infantile. (Some aspects of color responses in the child's Rorschach.) *Arch. Psicol. Neurol.*, 1957, *18*, 401-418.

The child's color responses are discussed and illustrated, with emphasis on frequency of color responses, color naming, color shock, color response perseveration and color responses given to achromatic cards. Phenomenological aspects of the chromatic blots are emphasized.

ACHROMATIC COLOR

BALLOCH, J. C. The effect of degree of shading contrasts in inkblots on verbal responses. *J. Exp. Psychol.*, 1954, *48*, 113-118.

The author sought to determine the effect of degree of shading contrast on responses. C' was found to increase as contrast increased.

BARNETT, I. The influence of color and shading on the Rorschach Test. Ph.D. Dissertation, Univ. of Pittsburgh, 1950, unpublished.

BAUGHMAN, E. E. A comparative analysis of Rorschach forms with altered stimulus characteristics. *J. Project. Techn.*, 1954, *18*, 151-164.

The study investigated the effects of color, shading, figure-ground and form upon perceptual behavior. The basic form was found to be of overwhelming importance.

BAUGHMAN, E. E. The effects of inquiry method on Rorschach color and shading scores. *J. Project. Techn.*, 1959, *23*, 3-7.

The Rorschach Test was administered to two groups of adults matched for intelligence, education, age and sex. While color responses for both groups were not statistically different, shading scores were significantly more frequent.

BECK, S. J. Problems of further research in the Rorschach Test. *Amer. J. Orthopsychiat.*, 1935, *5*, 100-115.

The writer summarizes his reaction to the Rorschach as used in Zurich; he suggests some problems of further research including the establishment of frequency tables for the color responses and determination as to whether tables or the subject's report is the more dependable criterion for color responses.

BENTON, A. L. The experimental validation of the Rorschach Test. II. The significance of Rorschach color responses. *Amer. J. Orthopsychiat.*, 1952, *22*, 755-763.

schach color responses. He concludes that color is not important *per se;* rather, the S's ability to utilize all elements in the visual stimulus situation is deemed important.

BIERI, J., AND BLOCKER, E. External and internal stimulus factors in Rorschach performance. *J. Consult. Psychol.*, 1956, *20*, 1-7.

The authors divide responses into external and internal stimulus forms. An extrotensive-introtensive dicotomy is explored, using C' as one of the scoring characteristics.

BINDER, H. The "chiaroscuro" responses in the Rorschach Diagnostic Psychological Test (translation). *Sw. Fr. Zurich: Orell Fussle*, 1932, *6*, 123.

The author explored the diagnostic value of "chiaroscuro" and gray Rorschach responses in a psychopathic, neurotic and normal patient group. He concludes that central mood reactions are more important in psychopaths and in neurotics than in normals. Adaptivity to peripheral or environmental stimulus plays a lesser role in the psychopathic personality than in the neurotic and in the neurotic than the normal.

BINDER, H. The significance of light and dark in the psychodiagnostic experiment of Rorschach (translation). *Arch. Swiss Neurol.*, 1932, *30*, 1-67, 233-286.

The author directs his attention to the responses concerned with brightness and not color. These responses, strongly influenced by affective attitude and having a definite relation to responses of movement, appear in 1 per cent of the normals, 3.3 per cent in neurotics and 4.4 per cent in psychopaths. The author concludes a diagnostic value for these responses.

BRODY, G. G. A study of the effects of color on Rorschach responses. *Genet. Psychol. Monogr.*, 1953, *48*, 261-311.

Chromatic and achromatic cards were presented to fifty students and fifty neurotics. The neurotics were found to be more disturbed by color than the controls. Presentation of achromatic cards followed by chromatic cards showed no effect, while the opposite procedure resulted

in disorganization of the neurotics.

BROWN, F. An exploratory study of dynamic factors in the content of the Rorschach protocol. *J. Project. Techn.*, 1953, *17*, 251-279.

The author discusses C′ along with other scoring characteristics as they are usually elicited by various cards.

BUKER, S. L., AND WILLIAMS, M. Color as a determinant of responsiveness to Rorschach cards in schizophrenia. *J. Consult. Psychol.*, 1951, *15*, 196-202.

The authors using chromatic and achromatic cards found that color does not materially influence responsiveness.

DALLA VOLTA, A. "Primary color answers" and modes of color appearance in the Rorschach Test. *Arch. Psicol. Neurol.*, 1949, *10*, 181-185.

The author proposes a better classification of color responses by viewing these responses from the phenomenological point of view. The author includes in this primary color responses as well as the chiaroscuro responses.

DUBITSCHER, F. Rorschach's form-interpretation experiment as an aid in diagnosis (translation). *Z. Sch. Ges. Neurol. Psychiat.*, 1932, *138*, 515-535.

The 190 subjects were classified according to "disease-groups," Kretschmer type and affective temperament. Normal asthenics showed a marked displeasure toward color. Pyknics showed pleasure toward color.

EXNER, J. E., JR. The influence of chromatic and achromatic color in the Rorschach. *J. Project. Techn.*, 1959, *23*, 419-425.

The author concludes that achromatic and chromatic color stimuli have significant influences on the individual's response to a perception, regardless of his conscious awareness of the relation of this color to the response.

FORTIER, R. H. The response to color and ego function. *Psychol. Bull.*, 1953, *50*, 41-63.

Author presents a brief review of color responses and their relatedness to ego functions. C′ is discussed.

FOX, J. A note on Klopfer's hypotheses about shading responses. *J. Project. Techn.*, 1958, *22*, 398.

The writer offers responses of a normal 7½-year-old boy as evidence for Klopfer's view of shading as an affective need for physical content.

GRAYSON, H. M. Rorschach productivity and card preferences as influenced by experimental variation of color and shading. *J. Project. Techn.*, 1956, *20*, 288-296.

The author concludes that productivity is independent of color and shading, while card preference is significantly influenced by color and shading.

HALPERN, F. Rorschach interpretation of the personality structure of schizophrenics who benefit from insulin therapy. *Psychiat. Quart.*, 1940, *14*, 826-833.

Schizophrenics who improved under insulin therapy showed greater productivity of response, more active emotionality as shown by color responses and chiarascuro responses.

HERTZ, H. Binder's shading responses. *Rorschach Res. Exch.*, 1937-38, *2*, 79-89.

This article includes Binder's classifications and inter-pretation of Rorschach's shading responses.

HERTZ, M. R. The shading response in the Rorschach Ink-blot Test: A review of its scoring and interpretation. *J. Gen. Psychol.*, 1940, *23*, 123-167.

This represents a review of the chiaroscuro response to 1940.

HERTZ, M. R. Rorschach: Twenty years later. *Psychol. Bull.*, 1942, *39*, 529-572.

The author presents a review of work on the Rorschach and provides an extensive bibliography.

JACOBSEN, W. Characterological forms of interpreting light-dark pictures (translation). *Z. Psychol.*, 1937, *140*, 86-108.

The author presented twenty boys' (11½ to 12½ years old) modified Rorschach pictures; the pictures were without color and reproduction was made by drawings. It was concluded that extroversion and objectiveness of cyclothymes was due to their accessibility to fantasy while introverted, artistically inclined schizothymes have less accessibility to fantasy.

KELLEY, D. M., MARGUILES, H., AND BARRERA, S. E. The stability of the Rorschach method as demonstrated in electric convulsive therapy cases. *Rorschach Res. Exch.*, 1942, *5-6*, 35-43.

After ECT patients exhibited a decrease of small c and C′ factors in Rorschach protocols. This is taken as a result of the treatment after effects.

KLOPFER, B. The shading responses. *Rorschach Res. Exch.*, 1937-38, *2*, 76-79.

The author describes four types of shading responses and provides tentative interpretations.

KLOPFER, B., AND MAILE, F. R. An illustration of the Rorschach interpretation: The case of Anna T. *Rorschach Res. Exch.*, 1937-38, *2*, 126-153.

The authors provide a completed record and discuss some of the rational. C′ scoring is mentioned in relation to the entire record. C′ is taken as an indication of extratensiveness.

KLOPFER, B., AND SENDER, S. A system of refined scoring symbols. *Rorschach Res. Exch.*, 1936-37, *1*, 19-22.

A complete refined scoring system is presented for the Rorschach Test. A description and interpretative value of each characteristic is provided.

LAZARUS, R. S. An experimental analysis of the influence of color on the protocol of the Rorschach Test. *J. Personality*, 1948, *17*, 182-185.

One hundred high school seniors were divided into two groups, one group receiving the standard test and one a noncolor test. The authors rejected the idea that color influences performance in determinants other than color.

LEME, L. J. *Chiaroscuro Interpretations in Rorschach's Psychodiagnostics and States of Anxiety* (translation). Rio de Janeiro: Imprensa Nacional, 1943.

Interpretative differences between Klopfer's and Binder's investigations on the role of chiaroscuro responses are with the author's work. This response is related to anxiety, but not to psychotic melancholia.

LEVINE, M., SPIVACK, G., AND WRIGHT, B. The inhibition process, Rorschach human movement responses, and

intelligence. *J. Consult. Psychol.*, 1959, *4*, 23.

The author reviews studies deriving IQ from the Rorschach. He explores the derivation of an intellectual factor from R, M and C′ Rorschach variable.

LEVITT, E. E. Alleged Rorschach anxiety indices in children. *J. Project. Techn.*, 1957, *21*, 261.

This study found that frequency of shading responses can be considered to be an indication of anxiety in children.

LOOSLI-USTERI, M. Interpretations of the Rorschach Test (translation). *Arch. Psychol.*, 1932, *23*, 349-365.

The author hypothesized that kinesthetic interpretations represent introversion and color interpretations extroversion. The author concluded that the test was capable of analyzing the affective structure of the individual, but little relationship was found between introversion and extroversion.

MANN, L. The relation of Rorschach indices of extrotension and introversion to a measure of responsiveness to the immediate environment. *J. Consult. Psychol.*, 1956, *2*, 20.

The Rorschach indices M, C total, C Sum, M:C total, M:C Sum, Fc, c and C′ were found to be related to a criterion of introversion-extrotension at or below the .05 level.

MATTE, I., BORLONE, M., AND MARCONI, J. Investigations on the meaning of C′ and K in the Rorschach Test. *Rev. Psiquiat.*, 1951, *16*, 66-91.

A method is provided for classifying free associations of Rorschach responses. Correlation of .21 for C′ was found between the Rorschach method and the free association method.

MOHR, P. The black and very dark shading in the Rorschach pictures and their meaning for the test. *Schweiz. Arch. Neurol. Psychiat.*, 1944, *53*, 122-133.

An interpretation of form and color in relation to affectivity is provided. Mohr showed that Ss who had been in conflict with authority figures reacted to dark-colored Rorschach cards with anxiety, while those without such conflicts reacted with hominess and quietness.

MOHR, P. The black and dark color in the Rorschach places (translation). *Beih. Schweiz. Z Psychol.*, 1948, *13*, 24-36.

The author has executed a simple study using achromatic cards. Black is viewed as representing justice, guilt, rebellion, fear, avenging and pure evil.

NIIMI, Y., HASHIMOTO, H., MACHIZUKI, K., AND OHNO, I. Galvanic skin responses during Rorschach Test administration. *Jap. J. Psychol.*, 1956, *27*, 175-184.

The position of the Rorschach card in a series was found to be significant in eliciting GSR increases to Cards VI and X in psychotics in comparison to no difference to noncolor reproductions.

RICKERS-OVSIANKINA, MARIA. Some theoretical considerations regarding the Rorschach method. *Rorschach Res. Exch.*, 1943, *7*, 41-53.

The author argues for the development of theoretical principles which will tend to integrate it into the body of psychological research. She argues for fundamental research in the fields of chiarascuro, movement and other responses.

ROCKWELL, F. V., WELCH, L., KUBIS, J., AND FISICHELLI, V. Changes in Palmar skin resistance during the Rorschach Test. II. The affect of repetition with color removed. *Mschr. Psychiat. Neurol.*, 1956, *116*, 321-345.

Colored Rorschach cards were presented to twenty-three subjects. Their Palmar skin resistance and verbal responses were recorded. They were then presented achromatic cards. The authors observed color shock and concluded that these subjects were not as capable of effectively utilizing normal defensive maneuvers as the control group.

RUESCH, J., AND FINESINGER, J. E. The relation of the Rorschach color response to the use of color in drawing. *Psychosom. Med.*, 1941, *3*, 378-388.

The researchers tested a group of thirty-four psychoanalytic patients and twenty feebleminded to ascertain variations in color responses. The author observed a high preference for gray by the introversive type and by those who gave a low number of Rorschach color responses.

SHATIN, L. Relationships between the Rorschach Test and the Thematic Apperception Test. *J. Project. Techn.*, 1955, *19* (3), 317-331.

A statistical comparison of the Rorschach and the TAT found considerable interrelation between the tests. C′ was found to be associated with the quality of fantasy output, but not necessarily its richness. C′ represents a responsiveness to external stimuli but with a tendency to withdraw to the safer realm of less affective responses.

TRANGUE, G. F. Color and black-white contrast in the Rorschach Test (translation). *Psicotecnia*, 1942, *3*, 428-433.

The author presents a descriptive account of affective distinctions reputed to correlate with differential responses to colored test figures.

VERNON, P. E. Recent work on the Rorschach Test. *J. Ment. Sci.*, 1935, *81*, 894-920.

The author presents a literature review of Rorschach progress from 1933-1935. He discusses E, F, EB, chiarsocuro, originality and content.

WALLEN, R. The nature of color shock. *J. Abnorm. Soc. Psychol.*, 1948, *43*, 346-356.

Servicemen were asked to report whether they liked or disliked each of the Rorschach cards in various sequences and in achromatic or color reproduction. Multicolored cards were preferred to achromatic copies, but unstable persons preferred three of the achromatic cards.

WEINER, I. B. Three Rorschach scores indicative of schizophrenia. *J. Consult. Psychol.*, 1961, *25*, 436-439.

The likelihood of being diagnosed as schizophrenic is associated with the tendency to give one or two CF, a Sum C from 1.5 to 3.0 and a C or CF without C′ on the Rorschach.

WITTENBORN, J. R. A factor analysis of Rorschach scoring categories. *J. Consult. Psychol.*, 1950, *14* (4), 261-267.

In a factor analysis of twenty scoring categories, C was found to have its highest loading on factor one, which related to form-color response. The form-color responses were not easily differentiated from human movement variables.

WITTENBORN, J. R., AND HOLZBERG, J. D. The Rorschach and descriptive diagnosis. *J. Consult. Psychol.*, 1951, 15 (6), 460-463.

Using thirty-nine scoring categories including FC′, C′F and C′, only eight of the thirty-nine categories were statistically significant in distinguishing between diagnostic groups. CF was able to statistically distinguish between groups.

TEXTURE (T, c)

ABT, L. E. The efficiency of the Group Rorschach Test in the psychiatric screening of Marine Corps recruits. *J. Psychol.*, 1947, 23, 205-217.

A large percentage of Fc is an indication of poor combat ability.

AINSWORTH, MARY D., KUELHE, J. C. Texture responses in the Rorschach and in a sorting test. *J. Project. Techn.*, 1959, 23, 391-402.

"Sorting of rough, smooth and soft objects by university students and hospital patients was compared with their Rorschach responses. Texture sorting scores and Rorschach texture scores correlated positively only in the combined patient group and in the psychotic group, but not in the normal or non-psychotic group."

ALLERHAND, M. E. Chiaroscuro determinants of the Rorschach Test as an indicator of manifest anxiety. *J. Project. Tech.*, 1954, 18, 407-413.

"The texture determinant showed significant correlations (.40 to .60) with the subjects' (anxiety) responses to both the conflict and nonconflict situations as well as with the subjects' anxiety reactions during the rest period after the conflict situation."

BECK, S. J., BECK, ANNE G., LEVITT, E. E., AND MOLISH, H. B. *Rorschach's Test: I. Basic Process* (3rd ed.). New York: Grune & Stratton, 1961.

"This determinant (T) is a clue to affect hunger, at the core of which is erotic need, one persisting from the patient's earliest developmental years."

BINDER, H. Comments concerning the Beck-Klopfer discussion. *Rorschach Res. Exch.*, 1937, 2, 37-42.

Binder suggested the use of F (Fb) for shading responses involving fur or finely chiseled statues (Klopfer's c). He adds that this sort of response "betrays a gently accommodating and delicately submissive adaptation to the environment, accompanied by positively-toned emotions."

BORGATTA, E. F., AND ESCHENBACH, A. E. Factor analysis of Rorschach variables and behavioral observation. *Psychol. Rep.*, 1955, 1, 129-136.

Texture (T), among other determinants, is heavily loaded on Na content.

BRADWAY, K. P., LION, E. G., AND CORRIGAN, H. The use of the Rorschach in a psychiatric study of promiscuous girls. *Rorschach Res. Exch.*, 1946, 10, 105-110.

Forty-two per cent of the subjects gave Fc responses (between one and three). Fifty per cent gave c responses (between one and two). Fc is a favorable indication of successful treatment.

BREECHER, SYLVIA. The Rorschach reaction patterns of maternally overprotected and rejected schizophrenic patients. *J. Nerv. Ment. Dis.*, 1956, 123, 41-52.

The large number of texture responses in the overprotected patients suggested that they were submissive, highly anxious and needed a great deal of approval. The few texture responses in the rejected ones suggested a lack of repressive mechanisms, less anxiety and not as great a need to be liked.

BROCKWAY, ANN L. Rorschach concepts of normality. *J. Consult. Psychol.*, 1954, 18, 259-265.

Texture responses (c, cF) were used approximately twice as often in maladjusted individuals as in normal or psychotic subjects.

BROWN, M., BRESNOBAN, T. J., CHAKIE, F. R., PETERS, BARBARA, POSER, E. G., AND TOUGAS, R. V. Personality factors in duodenal ulcer: A Rorschach study. *Psychosom. Med.*, 1950, 12, 1-5.

The twenty-five veterans receiving treatment for duodenal ulcers had significantly fewer texture responses (Fc) than the twenty-five controls being treated for various other complaints.

BUHLER, C., BUHLER, K., AND LEFEVER, D. W. *Rorschach Standardization Studies. I: Development of the Basic Rorschach Score.* Los Angeles: mimeographed private printing, 1948.

Texture responses are a sign of social and sexual insecurity.

COAN, R. A factor analysis of Rorschach determinants. *J. Project. Techn.*, 1956, 20, 280-287.

High loadings of Fc and M suggest a responsiveness to inner stimuli that could be termed creativity or empathy.

COOK, P. H. The application of the Rorschach Test to a Samoan group. *Rorschach Res. Exch.*, 1942, 6, 51-60.

Texture responses (c or c combinations) were given infrequently in comparison to the other varieties of response.

DAVIDSON, HELEN H. A measure of adjustment obtained from the Rorschach protocol. *J. Project. Techn.*, 1950, 14, 3-38.

An individual adjusted to his environment will have more bright color responses than texture and achromatic color responses.

ECKHARDT, W. Stimulus determinants of "shading" responses. *J. Clin. Psychol.*, 1957, 13, 172-173.

Texture responses occurred only with the standard shading effect of ten Rorschach popular details. None were illicited on cards having only two tones of gray or with cards having only one shade of gray.

FOX, J. A note on Klopfer's hypothesis about shading responses. *J. Project. Techn.*, 1958, 22, 398.

"Visual perception of shading (c or c combinations) constitutes need for physical contact, and is suggestive of the subject's manner of relating to and handling of his affectional needs."

GARCIA, J. S. El Rorschach en los indios aguaranas. (The

Rorschach among the Aguarana Indians.) *Rev. Psicol. Gen. appl.* 1959, *14*, 287-320.

"Rorschach records of 15 Aguarana Indians showed . . . constant use of texture. . . ."

GUSTAV, A. An estimation of Rorschach scoring categories by means of an objective inventory. *J. Psychol.*, 1946, *22*, 253-260.

Gustav equates Fc with sensitivity.

HARUYP, H. A study of perceptual processes of Rorschach cards by tachistoscopic method on movement and shading responses. *J. Project. Techn.*, 1961, *25*, 44-53.

"Fc (cF) responses generally are more frequent under tachistoscopic presentation. With increased exposure time they begin to appear markedly."

HERTZ, MARGUERITE, R. The shading response in the Rorschach Inkblot Test: A review of its scoring and interpretation. *J. Gen. Psychol.*, 1940, *23*, 123-167.

Klopfer's Fc represents sensitivity to external stimuli. The crude c or cF is simply a desire for contact.

HERTZ, MARGUERITE R. Suicidal configurations in Rorschach records. *Rorschach Res. Exch.*, 1948, *12*, 3-58.

Texture responses, Fc and its variations, reflect "cautious behavior, sensitivity, and an attempt to come to grips with the otuside world."

KALLSTEDT, F. E. A Rorschach study of 66 adolescents. *J. Clin. Psychol.*, 1952, *8*, 129-132.

". . . . c and Fc are common determinants in adolescent profiles, but are more frequent in older girls approaching womanhood. They denote social and sexual insecurity."

KATES, S. L., AND SCHWARTZ, F. Stress, anxiety and response complexity on the Rorschach Test. *J. Project. Techn.*, 1958, *22*, 64-69.

A cF response requires little organization of different perceptual qualities.

KLEBANOFF, S. G. A Rorschach study of operational fatigue in Army Air Force's combat personnel. *Rorschach Res. Exch.*, 1946, *10*, 115-120.

Patients showed a definite tendency to retain the form factor in texture responses. Ninety-two per cent of them gave Fc responses, and 12 per cent gave c or cF responses.

KLOPFER, B. The shading responses. *Rorschach Res. Exch.*, 1937, *2*, 76-79.

Fc is equated with "a careful emotional approach to the environment." cF or c suggests "a simple desire for contact with the surroundings without consideration of finer nuances." Animal skin responses in the latter category are quite common.

KLOPFER, B. *Developments in the Rorschach Technique. Vol. II. Fields of Application.* New York: Harcourt, Brace & World, 1956.

"Shading insensitivity would indicate a complete crippling of the need for affection . . . Shading denial would indicate an extreme conscious effort to reject the need for affection . . . Shading evasion takes a middle position between these two extremes."

KLOPFER, B., AINSWORTH, MARY D., KLOPFER, W. G., AND HOLT, R. *Development in the Rorschach Technique*

(Vol. I). New York: Harcourt, Brace & World, 1954.

A large number of Fc responses and few cF responses indicates both " a strong awareness of affectional need . . . and an exaggerated need for affectionate responses from others."

KLOPFER, B., AND DAVIDSON, HELEN H. *The Rorschach Technique: An introductory manual.* New York: Harcourt, Brace & World, 1962.

"Precedence (the main determinant score) is given to Fc over every determinant except human movement and color."

KLOPFER, B., AND MIALE, F. R. An illustration of the technique of the Rorschach interpretation: The case of Anne T. *Rorschach Res. Exch.*, 1937-38, *2*, 126-153.

Fc can be interpreted as sensitivity about one's self and the effect that the action of others will have on one's self.

MARKS, P. Effect of texture and form on the popular response (top of card VI) on the Rorschach. *J. Clin. Psychol.*, 1961, *17*, 38-41.

Seventy-one Ss were given the standard and experimental cards. "A significant number of Ss responded to texture rather than form, but form was a sufficient stimulus for the popular response."

McFATE, MARGUERITE Q., AND ORR, F. G. Through adolescence with the Rorschach. *Rorschach Res. Exch.*, 1949, *13*, 302-319.

As adolescence progresses, there is a decrease in the frequency of cF.

MONTALTO, FANNIE D. Maternal behavior and child personality: A Rorschach study. *J. Project. Techn.*, 1952, *16*, 151-178.

Children between six and seven years old whose mothers were restrictive gave significantly more texture (Fc) responses than children whose mothers were democratic.

MOYA, G. Estudia de inteligencia, personalidad y comportamiento en un grupo de 165 soldados. Segunda parte. (A survey of intelligence, personality and behavior in a group of 165 soldiers. Part II.) *Rev. Psicol. Gen. Appl.*, 1959, *14*, 321-389.

"Texture responses, perspective, and records showing color shock or no shock at all seemed positively related."

MURSTEIN, B. I. Factor analysis of the Rorschach. *J. Consult. Psychol.*, 1960, *25*, 262-275.

The testee himself must communicate the idea of texture in a shading response. A limited vocabulary may hinder this.

PIOTROWSKI, Z. A. *Perceptanalysis.* New York: The Macmillan Co., 1957.

Zulliger underlined the favorable prognostic and educational value of the light-shading texture responses. Punishment means more and results in much greater improvement in behavior in juvenile thieves who have texture responses than those who do not.

RICHARDS, T. W. Personality of subjects who volunteer for research on a drug (mescaline). *J. Project. Techn.*, 1960, *24*, 424-428.

"No difference was found between the number of texture

responses (T) for "normal" volunteers and "normal" controls."

STEINER, MATILDA E. The use of the Rorschach method in industry. *Rorschach Res. Exch.*, 1947, *11*, 46-52.

A group of unsuccessful copy writers gave more texture (c or c combinations) responses than a successful group.

STERN, K., AND MALLAY, H. T. Rorschach studies on patients with paranoid features, with an analysis of 35 cases. *J. Clin. Psychol.*, 1945, *1*, 272-280.

One of the few consistent qualities is a low threshold for texture responses (c or c combinations).

SWIFT, J. W. Rorschach responses of eighty-two preschool children. *Rorschach Res. Exch.*, 1945, 9, 75-84.

Girls gave significantly (.02) more texture responses (c or c combinations) than boys.

VORHAUS, PAULINE G. The use of the Rorschach in preven-

tive mental hygiene. *J. Project. Techn.*, 1952, *16*, 179-192.

There is theoretical support for the idea that the response to shading in infancy would be c, indicating an "all embracing need for closeness."

WALTERS, R. H. A preliminary analysis of the Rorschach records of fifty inmates. *J. Project. Techn.*, 1953, *17*, 437-446.

Fc is closely connected with feelings of insecurity and anxiety. It is also associated with the acting out of impulses.

WITTENBORN, J. R. Level of mental health as a factor in the implications of Rorschach scores. *J. Consult. Psychol.*, 1950, *14*, 459-472.

The texture (T) responses, together with W, V and C, cluster together to form a perceptual control factor. The usual scoring and interpretative distinctions between texture and other determinants were not supported.

SHADING

ABT, L. E. The efficiency of the group Rorschach Test in the psychiatric screening of Marine Corps recruits. *J. Psychol.*, 1947, *23-24*, 205-217.

The study is designed to ascertain to what extent the group Rorschach Test can be used to predict success or failure of men in the recruit training program of U. S. Marine Corps. A large percentage of FK and FC were found to be an adverse sign for success.

ADLER, A. The problem of distance. In *The Practice and Theory of Individual Psychology.* New York: Harcourt, Brace & World, 1929, 100-108.

Adler clarifies the meaning of "V" in the Rorschach as the "feeling of inferiority."

ALLERHAND, M. E. Chiarascuro determinant of Rorschach Test as indicator of manifest anxiety. *J. Project. Techn.*, 1954, *18*, 407-417.

Correlations were determined between Rorschach chiarascuro responses and behavioral signs of anxiety in experimental nonconflict and conflict situations. None of the shading factors warranted prediction between behavioral reactions to the conflict and nonconflict situations.

BALLOCH, J. C. The effect of degree of shading contrast in inkblots on verbal response. *J. Exp. Psychol.*, 1952, *43*, 120-124.

An experiment was conducted to investigate the effects of several goal-setting techniques on the performance of a simple block-turning task. The obtained results indicated that none of the three goal-setting techniques used provided greater motivation than simple knowledge of results. Seventy-five Ss were shown inkblots reproduced under weak, medium and strong conditions of shading contrast. Responses utilizing the shading to give diffusion effects (K) did not vary with contrast, nor were there changes in the number of shading responses produced. When contrast on the cards were varied, differential vista responses resulted. The least-contrasted cards produced the least "V" while the medium-shaded cards produced the greatest number of "V."

BARNETT, I. The influence of color and shading on the Rorschach test. Ph.D. Thesis, Univ. of Pittsburgh, 1950,

Abstracts of Doctoral Dissertations, 1950-51, 251-255.

BAUGHMAN, E. E. A comparative analysis of Rorschach forms with altered stimulus characteristics. *J. Project. Techn.*, 1954, *18*, 151-164.

Vista responses occurred only on series A (achromatic) while no such trends were noticed for "Y." Data indicated that color impact suppresses or shifts manifestations of "V."

BAUGHMAN, E. E. The effect of inquiry method on Rorschach color and shading scores. *J. Project. Techn.*, 1959, *23*, 3-7.

The Rorschach was administered to two groups of adults. Ss were equated for intelligence, age, education and sex. Shading and color scores were determined for one group by the standard inquiry method, for the second group by the paired comparison technique. Shading scores were significantly more frequent with the paired comparison technique. A greater number of "V" responses were gathered by the paired comparison technique as compared to the standard inquiry method. This held true for Beck's other two shading categories, but not for color.

BECK, S. J. *Rorschach's Test. II. A Variety of Personality Pictures.* New York: Grune & Stratton, 1945, 33-35.

Beck discusses such psychological implications of "V" as self-appraisal, inferiority complex, and depression.

BECK, S. J., LEVITT, E. E., AND MOLISH, H. B. *Rorschach's Test. I. Basic Processes.* New York: Grune & Stratton, 1961, 109-116.

Beck outlines his concept of "V" in terms of representative responses.

BEIZMANN, G. La personalite epileptique et le Rorschach test. (The epileptic personality in the light of the Rorschach Test.) *Ann. Med. Psychol.*, 1954, *112*, 305-336.

BENVENISTE, S. J. A study of shading responses on the Rorschach Inkblot Test. *Diss. Abstr.*, 1956, *16*, 1171.

This study was undertaken to investigate some of the possible determinants of a group of responses on the Rorschach Inkblot Test: the shading responses. It was found that the frequency of shading responses was dependent, in part, upon the total number of responses furnished by the subject. While individual differences were a significant factor, the amount of experience with the reproductions did not seem to affect the number of shading responses.

BILLIG, O. The light-dark interpretations in the Rorschach experiment. *Rorschach Res. Exch.*, 1937, *2*, 37-42.

In the Rorschach investigation the author found a group of light-dark interpretations in which he could observe the same attitude toward the whole-impression of a black plate that is produced in everyday life by an intermingling of dark shadows. Some light-dark interpretations with their selection of relatively independent shadings interpreted as such, are the result of an approach which is usual to bright colors, but not to light-dark shadings.

BINDER, H. Die helldunkeldeutingen im psychodiagnos tischen experiment von Rorschach. (The significance of light and dark in the psychodiagnostic experiment of Rorschach. *Arch. Swiss. Neurol.*, 1932, *30*, 1-67.

Studies made with 271 Ss, 51 normals, 111 psychopaths, 58 neurotics, and 61 psychotics, with Rorschach Inkblot Test. In some responses, brightness is the center of interpretation. These responses, strongly influenced by the affective attitude and having a definite relation to responses of movement, appear in a small percentage of normals (1 per cent), but much more frequently in neurotics (3.3 per cent), and above all in psychopaths (4.4 per cent).

BINDER, H. *Shading Responses in Rorschach's Psychodiagnostic Experiment.* Bern, Switzerland: Hans Huber, 1959.

Included are Binder's early comments (1932) on the inkblots and his interpretation of shading responses in normal and psychiatric syndromes, illustrated with numerous case samples. Includes sixty-one references to pre-1932 literature.

BRADWAY, K., LION, E., AND CORRIGAN, H. The use of the Rorschach in a psychiatric study of promiscuous girls. *Rorschach Res. Exch.*, 1946, *9*, 105-110.

One of the objectives of the study of promiscuous girls was to determine the efficacy of psychiatric and case work treatment. It was found that the Rorschach factor FK was one of the factors related to treatability.

BUHLER, C. Rorschach studies on alcoholism. *Amer. Psychol.*, 1947, *2*, 405-406.

Abstract. Rorschachs were given to one hundred alcoholics. Two signs were found to be outstandingly significant on all alcoholic groups: low m and relatively high (k+K).

BUHLER, C., AND LEFEVER, D. A Rorschach study on the psychological characteristics of alcoholics. *Quart. J. Stud. Alcohol.*, 1947, *8*, 197-260.

Used in the study of one hundred chronic alcoholics is a diagnostic sign list of ninety-nine Rorschach signs for the discrimination of clinical groups. Presence of significantly high anxiety and apprehensions (k+K+FK) in conjunction with low tension tolerance (low m) distinguishes alcoholics from nonalcoholics. The alcoholics

differ from the psychopaths in greater self-criticism (FK).

CHRISTOFFEL, M. Affektivitat und farben speziell angst und halbdunkeler-scheinungen. (Affectivity and color: Specific anxiety and shading responses.) *Z. Neurol.*, 1923, *82*.

CONSALVI, C., AND CANTER, A. Rorschach scores as a function of four factors. *J. Consult. Psychol.*, 1958, *22*, 272-275.

The purpose of this study was to evaluate the factorial composition of the Rorschach Test in terms of intelligence and the formal processes involved in the scores. Fourteen scores were used for the factor analysis including FK+Fc+FK and K+c+K. The Rorschach variable having the highest loading on the intelligence factor was FK+Fc+Fk.

COX, F. N., AND SARASON, S. B. Test anxiety and Rorschach performance. *J. Abnorm. Soc. Psychol.*, 1954, *49*, 371-377.

This study was designed to test the validity of certain Rorschach anxiety indices which have been shown to reflect the effects of exposure to a stressful situation and to examine the generality of certain hypotheses derived from a theoretical framework. It was predicted that the high-anxiety group would yield more FK+K than low-anxiety groups, and this prediction was strongly supported and gave encouraging evidence as to the validity of these as anxiety indicators.

ECKHARDT, W. An experimental and theoretical analysis of movement and shading responses. *J. Project. Techn.*, 1955, *19*, 301-305.

An experimental demonstration determined that movement and "V" are determined by shape gradients. Angularity enhances "V" responses.

ECKHARDT, W. Stimulus determinants of "shading" responses. *J. Clin. Psychol.*, 1957, *13*, 172-173.

Ten Rorschach population details were reproduced to form three card sets. The first set reproduced the original; the second had only two tones of gray; ;the third set was reproduced as a monotone. Achromatic color and orthodox vista responses occurred equally frequently on all sets; it was inferred these responses were due to overall intensity, since only this variable was common to all cards. Transparency and toned-down depth responses occurred on the first two sets but not on the third set. It was inferred that these were due to brightness contrast.

EICHLER, R. M. Experimental stress and alleged Rorschach indices of anxiety. *J. Abnorm. Soc. Psychol.*, 1951, *46*, 344-345.

An investigation of the influence of a stress-produced anxiety on the occurrence of fifteen Rorschach factors alleged to be signs of anxiety reveals increased weighted shading determinants, decreased whole responses, decreased number of responses and increased number of oligophrenic details (Do) to reflect the differential conditions at a high or moderate level of statistical reliability.

FISKE, D. W., AND BAUGHMAN, E. E. Relationship between Rorschach scoring categories and the total number of responses. *J. Abnorm. Soc. Psychol.*, 1953, *48*, 25-30.

Outpatient group showed an increasing FV except for a

slight reversal as R = 30-35. The corresponding curve for normals was irregular.

FORSYTH, R. P. The influence of color, shading, and Welsh anxiety level on Elizur Rorschach content test analysis of anxiety and hostility. *J. Project. Techn.*, 1959, *23*, 207-213.

Subjects were divided into three groups (high, low and middle anxiety) on the basis of K and Welsh A scores. Modified Rorschach cards were used. K is related to Elizur A and H negatively in the middle group and positively in the low-anxiety group.

FOX, J. A note on Klopfer's hypothesis about shading responses. *J. Project. Techn.*, 1958, *22*, 398.

Three responses to Rorschach Cards IV and VII of a normal 7½-year-old boy are offered as evidence, presumably on the validity of Klopfer's interpretation of shading reactions, as being related to affective needs and needs for physical contact.

FRANKHAUSER, E. Uber wesen und bedeutung der affectivitat eine parallele zwischen affektivitat und licht — und farbenemp findung. (Nature and meaning of affectivity: A parallel betwen affectivity and light and color sensation.) *Monogr. Neurol. Psychiat. (Berlin)*, *19*, 1919.

GOODSTEIN, L., AND GOLDBERGER, L. Manifest anxiety and Rorschach performance in a chronic patient population. *J. Consult. Psychol.*, 1955, *19*, 339-343.

The Rorschach and the Taylor Manifest Anxiety Scale were used to test anxiety in a group of hospitalized psychiatric patients. It was found that the low A group gave a higher percentage of K responses than the high A groups. In light of this finding, one can scarcely argue that both K responses and high A scale scores indicate the presence of anxiety, at least not the same kind of anxiety.

HERTZ, H. Binder's shading responses. *Rorschach Res. Exch.*, 1937-38, *2*, 79-89.

It is Dr. Binder's postulation that most of the shading responses occur in D or Dd areas on the Rorschach plates. The paper discusses scoring difficulties and "the basic principles upon which Dr. Binder bases his assumptions for the distinction used in scoring shading responses."

HERTZ, MARGUERITE R. The shading response in the Rorschach Inkblot Test: A review of its scoring and interpretation. *J. Gen. Psychol.*, 1940, *23*, 123-167.

One of the many observations made of shading responses, Beck's "V" was found to evidence depression and fear. Also a general uneasiness is characteristic. The shading category is one of the important test factors in the Rorschach Test. Examiners applying it have felt the need for more finely differentiated categories. Klopfer distinguishes between the three-dimensional chiaroscuro responses (K, KF and FK). Klopfer's K-combinations are related to the central emotional life and express diffuse and deep emotions.

JACOBSON, W. Charaktertypische arten des deutens von hell-dunkelbildern. (Personality types in interpreting light-dark pictures.) *Z. Psychol.*, 1937, *140*, 86-108.

KLEBANOFF, S. A Rorschach study of operational fatigue in Army Air Force combat personnel. *Rorschach Res. Exch.*, 1946, *9*, 115-120.

The present study attempts an evaluation by a projective technique of the personality structure characterizing operational fatigue. Among the salient features of the Rorschach findings in the group of patients include a significant use of the shading determinants with particular emphasis upon Fc, K, FK and k responses.

KLOPFER, B. The shading responses. *Rorschach Res. Exch.*, 1937, *2*, 76-79.

Klopfer differentiates the different shading responses. The K response seems to be the expression of free floating anxiety, anxiety without the accompanying awareness which would make for self-consciousness.

KLOPFER, B., AINSWORTH, MARY D., KLOPFER, W. G., AND HOLT, R. *Developments in Rorschach Technique* (Vol. I & II). New York: Harcourt, Brace & World, 1959.

Comprehensive refinement of the 1942 work by Klopfer and Kelly. Includes sections on k and other anxiety indices as well as scoring and interpretation examples for all.

KLOPFER, B., AND KELLEY, D. M. *The Rorschach Technique.* New York: World Book Co., 1942.

Formal presentations of the Klopfer method in scoring, administering and interpretation of the Rorschach test. k, as well as other indices of anxiety, are discussed.

KLOPFER, B., AND SENDER, SADIE. A system of refined Rorschach scoring symbols. *Rorschach Res. Exch.*, 1936-37, *1*, 19-22.

Authors present a series of symbols to be employed in scoring, along with a description and explanation and an interpretative value for each. Among others, the chiaroscuro (k) is discussed.

KOBLER, F. The use of the Rorschach in involutional melancholia. *J. Consult. Psychol.*, 1953, *17*, 365-370.

The present investigation has for its purpose the analysis of the Rorschach records of forty-five cases of involutional melancholia. Despite readily observable intense clinical anxiety in the majority of these patients, the appearance of K, k and m responses was extremely rare.

LEBO, D., TOAL, R., AND BRICK, H. Rorschach performances in the amelioration and continuation of observable anxiety. *J. Gen. Psychol.*, 1960, *63*, 75-80.

Twenty-four matched prisoners were selected on basis of observable anxiety symptoms. Half of the subjects were given CO_2, and half received no amelioration for their anxiety. Pre- and post-therapy Rorschachs were given. The reduction in K responses after therapy was found to be significant.

LEME LOPES, J. *Das interpretacoes claroescuro no psicodiagnostico de Rorschach e os esta dos de ansiedade.* (Chiaroscuro interpretations in Rorschach psychodiagnostics and states of anxiety.) Rio de Janeiro: Imprensa National, 1943.

The chiaroscuro response is directly related to neuroticism (anxiety), but not to psychotic melancholia. A case is presented in which the Rorschach analysis determined the diagnostic decision.

LEVETT, E. E. Alleged Rorschach anxiety indices in children.

J. Project. Techn., 1957, *21*, 261-264.

A group of child clinic patients was compared with a group of normal children on a series of Rorschach variables commonly regarded as anxiety indices in adults. Of nine significant differences, only the frequency of shading responses was in the right direction. It was concluded that as far as present data go, only frequency of shading responses can be considered to be an anxiety indicator in children.

LIGHT, B. H., AND AMICK, J. Rorschach responses of normal aged. *J. Project. Techn.*, 1956, *20*, 185-195.

The purpose of this study was threefold: to present the Rorschach responses of a group of normal aged persons; to compare these responses with younger "normal" groups and other aged groups; and to evaluate the personality pattern of the aged. In all three of these cases, zero or very little K and FK were evoked from the subjects.

LUKE, B. The Rorschach method applied to delinquent and non-delinquent boys: Summary of research. *Bull. Canad. Psychol. Ass.*, 1943, *3*, 52-53.

The experimental delinquent group were less self-critical (V) than were the control group.

MATTE, I., BORLONE, M., AND MARCONI, J. Investigacion sobre el significado de C′ y K en el test de Rorschach. (Investigation on the meaning of C′ and K in the Rorschach Test.) *Rev. Psiquiat.*, 1951, *16*, 66-91.

A method is developed for classifying free associations provoked by certain responses, selected from the Rorschach test of a group of individuals. When a comparison is made between results of the Rorschach method and of the free association method, the following correlation coefficients were derived: F or C′, .21; for K, .21. None of these coefficients has any significance.

McFATE, M. Q., AND ORR, F. G. Through adolescence with the Rorschach. *Rorschach Res. Exch.*, 1949, *13*, 302-319.

This longitudinal study of a group of children analyzes their Rorschach protocols at four different age levels during the adolescent period. Results indicate that the average use of K along with other variables increases with age for both sexes.

MELTZER, H. Personality differences between stuttering and nonstuttering children as indicated by the Rorschach Test. *J. Psychol.*, 1944, *17*, 39-59.

Fifty stutterers showed significantly higher percentage of shading responses than did the control group. The "V" was prominent among the shading responses.

MOHR, P. Die schwarze und sehr dunkle tonung der Rorschachen tafeln und ihre dedeutung fur den versuch. (The black and very dark shading in the Rorschach pictures and their meaning for the test.) *Schweiz. Arch. Neurol. Psychiat.*, 1944, *53*, 122-133.

In a positive sense, black symbolizes unusualness, importance, unchangeableness, solemnity, the Deity and authority in general. Negatively, it symbolizes renunciation, guilt, rebellion, punishment and death. Mohr's protocols show that Ss who have been in conflict with authority react to dark-colored Rorschach pictures with distaste or anxiety, while those having no such conflicts react to the same pictures with answers denoting protection, hominess or quietness.

MOHR, P. Die schwarze und dunkle farbe der Rorschachtafeln. (The black and dark color in the Rorschach plates.) *Beih. Schweiz. Z. Psychol.*, 1948, *13*, 34-36.

A report is presented of responses determined by the dark and black plates of the Rorschach in four patients. Black symbolically represents guilt, rebellion, fear, avenging justice and pure evil. The case histories demonstrated how the symbolic value of the dark plates can change.

NEURINGER, C. Manifestations of anxiety on the Rorschach Test. *J. Project. Techn.*, 1962, *26*, 318-326.

Equivocal results reported in studies on Rorschach anxiety are discussed and reviewed. The value of the Rorschach Content Test in evaluating anxiety is upheld. Rorschach determinants (including shading) are found to differ in their relationship to lab-induced and real-life anxiety.

OHKURA, KAZUKO. Rorschach study with delinquents. *Jap. Fam. Court. Mon.*, 1957, *9*, 1-37.

One hundred delinquents aged fourteen to nineteen were tested. In the violent delinquents C and K were frequently observed.

PHILLIPS, L., AND SMITH, J. G. *Rorschach Interpretation: Advanced Technique.* New York: Grune & Stratton, 1953, 97-98.

Vista is associated with the tendency to stand aside and analyze one's activities in relation to others. "V" may also be a measure of maturation, for it is rare in children.

RABINOVITCH, S. Physiologic response, perceptual threshold and Rorschach Test anxiety indices. *J. Project. Techn.*, 1954, *18*, 379-386.

Three types of word stimuli were tachistoscopically presented to eleven patients of a psychiatric ward while they were connected to a GSR apparatus. Two of the stimulus types, anxiety and nonanxiety were determined by the subject's own Rorschach Test responses. The third type of word stimuli, nontest, were selected from lists of frequently seen words. The criteria for the anxiety stimuli are based on four categories of Rorschach test responses which are purported to reflect personal anxiety. One of these criteria is three-dimensionality (V or FK) and it was found to be associated with greater GSR deflections and perpetual thresholds than P or F+ responses.

REUSCH, J., AND FINESINGER, J. E. The relation of the Rorschach color response to the use of colors in drawings. *Psychosom. Med.*, 1941, *3*, 370-388.

In drawings, a high selectivity for gray was shown by subjects belonging to the introversive type as well as by those who gave a low number of Rorschach color responses.

ROMBOUTS, J. M. Untersuchungen mit undeutlichen (nebeligen) schattenbildern. (Investigations with unclear, hazy pictures.) *Psychiat. Neurol. Bl. Amst.*, 1939, *43*.

RORSCHACH, H., AND OBERHOLZER, E. Zur auswertung des formversuchs (translation). *J. Nerv. Ment. Dis.*, 1924, *60*, 225-248.

Rorschach acknowledges Vista associations and describes their "affective loading."

SARASON, S. B. Exageration, mythomanie et simulation a la lumiere du test psychodiagnostic de Rorschach. (Exaggeration, mythomania and simulation in the light of the Rorschach.) *Folia Psychiat. Neerl.,* 1951, *54,* 95-111.

SCHNEIDER, E. Eine diagnostiche untersuchung Rorschache auf grund der helldunkeldeutungen erganet. (A diagnostic investigation in the field of shading interpretations.) *Z. Ges. Neurol. Psychiat.,* 1937, *159,* 1-10.

SCHWARTZ, F., AND KATES, S. L. Behn Rorschach and Rorschach under standard and stress conditions. *J. Consult. Psychol.,* 1958, *22,* 335-338.

The present investigation is designed to evaluate the equivalence of Behn and Rorschach Tests under standard and stress conditions. It was hypothesized that they will be equal under standard conditions, and under stress situations the Rorschach will have more Fsh, FK, Fc and FC responses. It was concluded that any differences found between the two tests were due to differences in stimuli properties of the two tests.

SION, M., AKATLI, S., AND KEMALOF, SARA. De certaines responses d'anxiete dans les protocoles de Rorschach des medecins. (Anxiety responses in the Rorschach protocols of physicians.) *Beih. Schweiz. Z. Psychol.,* 1954, *25,* 155-173.

Analysis of the Rorschach protocols of one hundred physicians yielded a high proportion of anxiety responses, suggesting "a typology of anxiety signs in correlation with clinical symptoms." Discrepancies between test findings and manifest behavior are believed due to "a possible professional or ethnic influence," or "to either a normal adaptation to abnormal ways, or latent neurosis, or a neurosis integrated into adaptation."

SOBUL, I. Interpretations du "clairobscur" dans le test de Rorschach. (Interpretations of "shading responses" in the Rorschach Test.) *Bull. Group Franc. Rorschach,* 1954, *5-6.*

The significance of the shading responses in the Rorschach Test is discussed, with special reference to the formulation of Binder. These nosological groups are distinguished: normal; neurotic; and "constitutional psychopathologic." In this research, the frequency of K is also discussed.

SWIFT, J. W. Relation of behavioral and Rorschach measures of insecurity in preschool children. *J. Clin. Psychol.,* 1945, *1,* 196-205.

The present study was designed to investigate the relationship between insecurity as measured by the Rorschach method and behavior considered clinically to be symptomatic of it. One of the Rorschach categories used was presence of K responses in persons not insecure. The results indicate there is no direct relationship as measured by the Rorschach method.

TRANGUE, G. F. Color y daroscuro en el "test" de Rorschach. (Color and black-white contrast in the Rorschach Test.) *Psicotecnia,* 1942, *3,* 428-433.

Descriptive account of affective distinctions said by Rorschach students to correlate with differential responses to colored test figures.

VERNON, P. E. Recent work on the Rorschach Test. *J. Ment.* *Sci.,* 1935, *81,* 894-920.

The author collates the literature since his similar article in 1933. Among the headings discussed is the chiaroscuro response and its interpretation. The general tenet upheld is that the orientation of the test is clinical rather than psychometric and its main value is for making fine differential diagnoses.

VIOLET-CONIL, AND CANIVET, N. Le test de Rorschach et le diagnostic de l'angoisse. (The Rorschach Test and the diagnosis of anxiety.) *Bull. Group. Franc. Rorschach,* 1949, *3.*

Anxiety may be disclosed in Rorschach terms: Bohm's signs; few W; a special sort of Dd, Do and S; few M'; often M $-$; pure C; many shadings; and special features in content. Anxiety seems to be the cause of adult regressions.

WALLER, PATRICIA F. Correlates of Rorschach shading scores obtained with two methods of inquiry. *Diss. Abstr.,* 1960, *20,* 2912.

This study was designed to investigate the relationship between the shading response on the Rorschach and other indices of anxiety that are used in the clinic and how these relationships may be affected by the use of a paired comparison inquiry procedure. On index of change based on the relationship of shading scores on the regular inquiry to shading scores on the paired comparison showed no significant relationships to personality variables such as intelligence, word fluency and defensiveness. Shading scores on the regular inquiry are more closely related to intelligence than are shading scores on the paired comparison inquiry.

WALLER, PATRICIA F. The relationship between the Rorschach shading response and other indices of anxiety. *J. Project. Techn.,* 1960, *24,* 211-217.

Validity of the interpretation of anxiety from the Rorschach shading response was investigated. The author concluded: "It may be more accurate to refer to different kinds of anxiety or to use different terms for various types of behavior observed."

WIRT, R. D. Pattern analysis of the Rorschach. *J. Clin. Psychol.,* 1956, *12,* 382-384.

This is a report of an investigation of differences in patterning of response tendency for Rorschach cards and for Rorschach determinants among groups of normal and abnormal people. The relative patterns are not wholly those which might be expected. For example, the normal group, rather than the neurotic group, scored highest on K+K+FK, although it would be reasonable to predict that these indicators of anxiety would show up most clearly in a neurotic population.

WOLFENSBERGER, W. P., MILLER, M. B., FOSHEE, J. G., AND CROMWELL, R. L. Rorschach correlates of activity level in high school children. *J. Consult. Psychol.,* 1962, *26,* 269-272.

A sample of hypokinetic subjects revealed a greater variety of determinants which tended to be less form controlled. Among the determinants discussed, the k was also included.

YOUNG, R. A., AND HIGGINBOTHAM, S. A. Behavior checks on

the Rorschach method. *Amer. J. Orthopsychiat.*, 1942, 12, 87-94.

The Rorschachs of twenty-one boys are examined. It was concluded that successful evaluation of behavior tendencies could only be arrived at through careful analyisis of the total configuration; single determinants and simple relations were of little prognostic value. The determinants are discussed singly and included are k and K, as anxiety-related.

Zullinger, H. Die Angst im Formdeutversuch nach Dr. Rorschach. (Anxiety in the form interpretation test of Dr. Rorschach.) *Z. Psychoanal. Padag.*, 1933, 7, 418-420.

The value of the Rorschach Test for revealing the presense of fear or anxiety is indicated. A careful evaluation of the responses may show the nature of the fear. A more general use of this test is recommended.

REACTION TIME AND CARD PREFERENCE

Allen, R. M. The influence of color in the Rorschach Test on reaction time in a normal population. *J. Project. Techn.*, 1951, 15, 481-485.

A report of a study "to ascertain the effect on the reaction time of a normal college student population of the presence and absence of color in the Rorschach Cards II, III, VIII, IX, X."

Barison, F. Il fattore tempo nel reattivo di Rorschach. (The time factor in the Rorschach Test.) *Riv. Psicol. Norm. Pat.*, 1940, Jan.-June.

Reaction times on the Rorschach Test were compared with characterological teacher-ratings of seventy-four normal children.

Basaglia, F., and Della Barba, G. Il rifiuto alla V tavola di Rorschach. (Rejection of Card V of the Rorschach.) *Arch. Psicol. Neurol.*, 1957, 18, 17-24.

On theoretical and statistical grounds, the belief that rejection of card V can be considered pathognomic of schizophrenia is challenged.

Borelli, G. L. A study of the meanings of Rorschach cards through use of the Semantic Differential technique. *Diss. Abstr.*, 1961, 21(10), 3161-3162.

The study investigated the relationship between meanings a subject ascribes to Rorschach cards and meanings he ascribes to his verbal responses. A second purpose was to compare the meanings of Rorschach cards for males and females.

Burstein, A. G. A note on time of first responses in Rorschach protocols. *J. Consult. Psychol.*, 1961, 25(6), 549-550.

A recommendation is made for the use of the median, rather than the mean, as the measure of central tendency for time of first response.

Carvalhal Ribas, J. Psico-diagnostico de Rorschach. (The Rorschach Test.) *Rev. Clin. S. Paulo*, 1942, 11, 31-34.

An explanation is furnished of the manner in which the Rorschach investigator interprets number of responses, reaction time, individuality of responses and content.

Crokes, T. G., and Keller, Anna. Rorschach card rejection and I. Q. *J. Clin. Psychol.*, 1960, 16(4), 424-426.

A replication of Tamkin's report of negative correlation between IQ and number of Rorschach cards rejected by male patients was conducted.

Dublineau, J., and Soboul, I. L'intervention du facteur "temps" dans l'interpretation du test de Rorschach. (The influence of response time in the interpretation of the Rorschach.) *Bull. Group. Franc. Rorschach*, 1955, 7, 27-34.

Data are presented from a group of two hundred patients with respect to total time per card and total time taken over the test as a whole.

Fosberg, I. A. Rorschach reactions under varied instructions. *Rorschach Res. Exch.*, 1938, 3, 12-31.

The author gave the Rorschach to a group of individuals under four different instruction sets. The results showed no significant difference between the four different variations of instructions.

Geourge, C. E. Stimulus value of the Rorschach cards: A composite study. *J. Project. Techn.*, 1955, 19, 17-20.

The rank order of preference for the Rorschach cards by various groups are compared and correlated with each other, with the rank order for frequency of sex responses, with Beck's Z and with order of presentation.

Grayson, H. M. Rorschach productivity and card preferences as influenced by experimental variation of color and shading. *J. Project. Techn.*, 1956, 20, 288-296.

The author has divided ten different Rorschach sets (one hundred cards in all). There is no relationship between card preference and productivity.

Hafner, A. J. Response time and Rorschach behavior. *J. Clin. Psychol.*, 1958, 14, 154-155.

Two groups of thirty college students were given the Rorschach. One group was administered under regular instructions. The other group was told to respond "as quickly as possible." A significant difference was found with the faster time factor.

Hafner, J. E. Rorschach card stimulus values for children. *J. Project. Techn.*, 1961, 25, 166-169.

A group of eighty children were individually asked to select the Rorschach card that reminded them of their mother, their father, the cards they liked best and least and the card that was most frightening.

Hiltman, Hildegard. Das Versagen im Rorschachtest. (Rejections in Rorschach testing.) *Beih. Schweiz. Z. Psychol.*, 1948, 13, 123-130.

A review of Rorschach literature reveals that rejections of cards are rather frequent.

Hirschstein, R., and Rabin, I. Reactions to Rorschach Cards IV and VII as a function of parental availability in childhood. *J. Consult. Psychol.*, 1955, 19, 473-474.

Two groups of male delinquent subjects, matched for age and intelligence, but differing with respect to parental availability in early childhood, were compared on the basis of their reactions to Rorschach Cards IV and VII.

Horiuchi, H. A study of perceptual process of Rorschach

cards by tachistoscopic method on movement and shading responses. *J. Project. Techn.*, 1961, 25, 44-53.

The experiment was aimed at the analysis of the temporal development process of movement and shading.

HUSHENSON, HEANNE R. Preference of adolescents for Rorschach figures. *Child Develop.*, 1949, 20, 101-118.

Thirty high school juniors were given the complete Rorschach Test and then asked to rank the cards in order of preference.

KATAGUCHI, Y. An experimental analysis of Rorschach cards, attributes by means of four modified series. *Rorschachiana Japonica*, 1960, 3, 23-28.

LEVY, E. Stimulus-values of Rorschach cards for children. *J. Project. Techn.*, 1958, 22, 293-296.

The study was undertaken to determine whether support could be found for Halpern's hypothesis that young children respond to Card IV as a "father" card and Card VII as the "mother" card. Significance was inconclusive.

LUCENA, J. Modifications des donnees du Test de Rorschach pendant les phases du choc insulinique. (Modifications of Rorschach Test findings during the phases of insulin shock.) *Rev. Psychol. Appl.*, 1958, 8, 25-35.

It was found that changes in Rorschach indices of personality organization changed significantly more often from preinjection test to either the test during or after hyperglycemia.

MARADIE, L. J. Productivity on the Rorschach as a function of order of presentation. *J. Consult. Psychol.*, 1953, 17, 32-35.

MATARAZZO, J. D., AND MENSH, I. N. Reaction time characteristics of the Rorschach Test. *J. Consult. Psychol.*, 1952, 16, 132-139.

Reaction variables of the Rorschach were studied, emphasis being on "card by card comparisons within and between diagnostic groups."

MEER, B. The relative difficulty of the Rorschach cards. *J Project. Techn.*, 1955, 19, 43-53.

It was hypothesized that the Rorschach cards are not of equal difficulty. High rank order correlations between reaction time, form level of the first response and subjective judgments of ease of difficulty support the hypothesis.

MEER, B., AND SINGER, J. L. A note on the "father" and "mother" cards in the Rorschach inkblots. *J. Consult. Psychol.*, 1950, 14, 482-484.

Fifty college fraternity men were given individual Rorschachs. At the end of test each was asked to select two cards, one which would represent a "mother" card and one which would represent a "father" card.

MENSH, I. N., AND MATARAZZO, J. D. Rorschach card rejection in psychodiagnosis. *J. Consult. Psychol.*, 1954, 18, 271-275.

MITCHELL, MILDRED B. Preferences for Rorschach cards *J. Project. Techn.*, 1952, 16, 203-211.

Two hundred mental hygiene clinic patients, twenty-seven hospitalized mental patients, and forty-two non-patients selected the Rorschach cards they liked best and least and gave their reasons.

NELSON, M. O., WOLFSON, W., AND LoCASCIO, R. Sexual identification in responses to Rorschach Card III. *J. Project. Techn.*, 1959, 23, 354-358.

The Rorschach Card III blot is found to be seen more often as a "male" or "neutral" than as "female" by both males and females, patients or nonpatients in a psychiatric hospital.

RABIN, A. I., AND SANDERSON, M. H. An experimental inquiry into some Rorschach procedures. *J. Clin. Psychol.*, 1947, 3, 216-225.

Presented the Rorschach cards to two groups of nurses in the usual order and in reverse order.

ROCKETT, F. C. Speed of form recognition as a function of stimulus factors and text anxiety. *J. Abnorm. Soc. Psychol.*, 1956, 53, 197-202.

Found drive level and figure difficulty were related to response time in that highly anxious persons became slower with increasing difficulty of figure during warm-up trials. During test series the predicted relationship was not found.

SCHACHTEL, E., AND HARTOCH, A. The curve of the reactions in the Rorschach Test: A contribution to the theory and practice of Rorschach's Psychodiagnostic Inkblot Test. *Amer. J. Orthopsychiat.*, 1937, 7, 320-348.

The authors stress the necessity for psychologist not only to give an inventory of modes of reaction, but also to describe and to explain the typical sequences in which the ingredients of this inventory become effective.

SCHNEIDER, B. H. The effect of varying time intervals on the reproduction and recall of Rorschach responses on retest. *Diss. Abstr.*, 1955, 15, 1653-1654.

The study investigated the differential effects of the passage of time on the persistence, change and recall of Rorschach responses on retest.

SIPOLA, E., AND TAYLOR, U. Reactions to inkblots under free and pressure conditions. *J. Personality*, 1952, 21, 22-47.

The study investigated responses given under free conditions and highly structured conditions.

SISSON, B. D., TAULBEE, E. S., AND GASTON, C. O. Rorschach card rejection in normal and psychiatric groups. *J. Clin. Psychol.*, 1956, 12, 85-88.

Two groups, one normal and the other a psychiatric group, were studied on card rejection.

STEIN, M. I. Personality factors in Rorschach responses. *Rorschach Res. Exch.*, 1949, 13, 355-413.

Tachistoscopic presentation of Rorschach cards at varying exposure times was used.

STEIN, M. I. Personality factors in the temporal development of Rorschach responses. Unpublished Ph.D. Thesis, 1949, Harvard U.

STONE, H. T. An experimental investigation of the effect of mode of color stimulation on inkblot response times. *Diss. Abstr.*, 1959, 20, 2391-2392.

An attempt was made to determine whether color shock could be "built in" to a set of inkblots by manipulation of the color aspects of such blots. A further variable studied was reaction time and time per response.

TAMKIN, A. S. Rorschach card rejection by psychiatric

patients. *J. Consult Psychol.*, 1958, 22, 441-444.

A chi square test failed to reach significance for the relationship between Rorschach card rejection and various personality traits.

TAMKIN, A. S. Intelligence as a determinant of Rorschach card rejection. *J. Clin. Psychol.*, 1959, 15, 63-64.

Card rejection was tested by comparing the Wechsler-Bellevue IQ's of 37 Ss who had no rejections with twenty-nine Ss who had one or more rejections. It was concluded that intellectual functioning was a factor in rejection.

TOLOR, A., GLASS, H. L., AND MERMELSTEIN, M. D. Rorschach card rejection as a correlate of intelligence in children. *J. Project. Techn.*, 1960, 24, 71-73.

Rorschach records and intellectual evaluations of 268 emotionally disturbed children aged four to eighteen years were studied. Results failed to confirm the hypothesis that Rorschach card rejection is a correlate of intelligence in emotionally disturbed children.

TYCKO, MILICENT. Rorschach response as a function of exposure time. *Diss. Abstr.*, 1957, 17, 899.

The study attempted to differentiate between projective reactions elicited under four conditions to temporal exposure.

UHELING, H. F. Rorschach "shock" for two special populations. *J. Consult. Psychol.*, 1952, 16, 224-225.

Reaction times to the ten Rorschach cards were obtained from two kinds of prison populations: guards and inmates.

VLES, S. J. De Behn-Rorschach-keuze-test. (The Behn-Ror-schach-Choice Test.) *Nederl. T. Psychol.*, 1950, 5, 343-356.

The Behn-Rorschach-Choice Test is described.

VLES, S. J. Enkele beschouwingen over de Bero-keuze test. (Reflections on the Behn-Rorschach-choice test.) *Psychol. Achtergr.*, 1953, 5, 124-127.

An introduction to the author's own technique with the Behn-Rorschach cards. Subjects are asked to choose cards they like most and cards they like least.

WEINER, I. B. Rorschach tempo as a schizophrenic indicator. *Percept. Motor Skills*, 1962, 15(1), 139-141.

Four indices of deviant Rorschach tempo were derived from normal expected response rates. In two samples of eighty-two and eighty-three patients, the presence of any one of these indices was significantly associated with a diagnosis of schizophrenia.

WILLIAMS, M. H., JR. The influence of variations in instructions on Rorschach reaction time. *Diss. Abstr.*, 1954, 14, 2131.

Investigated some problems involved in the use of reaction time to the cards of the Rorschach Psychodiagnostic.

ZAMPARO, D. Dati statistici e significati psicologici del tempo nel Rorschach. (Statistical and psychological significance of the time in the Rorschach.) *Rass. Neuropsichiat.*, 1954, 8, 2.

ZAX, M., AND LOISELLE, R. H. The influence of card order on the stimulus value of the Rorschach inkblots. *J. Project. Techn.*, 1960, 24, 218-221.

Applied the Semantic Differential in an investigation of the influence of the order of presentation on the stimulus value of the Rorscach inkblots.

SEQUENCE AND APPROACH

AMES, LOUISE B., LEARNED, JANET, METRAUX, RUTH W., AND WALKER, R. N. Rorschach Responses in Old Age. New York: Harper, 1954.

One chapter is devoted to location and the percentage of W, D and Dd responses with respect to age, socioeconomic status, institutionalization and sex differences. The differences between normals, preseniles and seniles are also presented with respect to approach.

AMES, LOUISE B., LEARNED, JANET, METRAUX, RUTH W., AND WALKER, R. N. Child Rorschach Responses. New York: Harper, 1956.

Mean values (percentages) for W, D and Dd are given for the ages two through ten, with a discussion of sex differences, also.

AMES, LOUISE B., METRAUX, RUTH W., AND WALKER, R. N. Adolescent Rorschach Responses. New York: Harper, 1959.

Approach is discussed for ages ten through sixteen, male and female, with the percentages.

BECK, S. J. Rorschach's Test I: Basic Processes. New York: Grune & Stratton, 1944.

The author devotes one chapter to approach and sequence.

BECK, S. J. Rorschach's Test II: A Variety of Personality Pictures. New York: Grune & Stratton, 1945.

The author discusses the concepts of approach and sequence in relation to personality structures.

BECK, S. J. Rorschach's Test III: Advances in Interpretation. New York: Grune & Stratton, 1952.

Approach and sequence are discussed in relation to their interpretative significance.

HALPERN, FLORENCE. A Clinical Approach to Children's Rorschachs. New York: Grune & Stratton, 1953.

Three paragraphs are devoted to a discussion of approach and sequence, after a discussion of location scoring. The significance of these concepts is discussed.

HARROWER, M. R., AND STEINER, M. E. Large Scale Rorschach Techniques (2nd ed.). Illinois, 1951.

Percentages of location responses are given for four main groups (college age, adult, prisoners and psychotics and psychopathic offenders) and for a breakdown of college age group into various professions. A discusion follows.

KLOPFER, B., AINSWORTH, MARY D., KLOPFER, W. G., AND HOLT, R. R. Developments in the Rorschach Technique (Vol. I). New York: World Book, 1954.

The authors thoroughly discuss sequence and approach from both scoring and interpretive standpoints.

KLOPFER, B., AINSWORTH, MARY D., KLOPFER, W. G., AND HOLT, R. R. Developments in the Rorschach Technique (Vol. II). New York: World Book, 1956.

In this second volume, sequence and approach are studied in relation to children's records and case studies.

LINN, L. A note on "manner of approach" in the Rorschach

Test as a measure of psychic energy. *Psychiat. Quart.,* 1948, 22, 634-537.

The manner of approach is herein considered an index to the quantity of psychic energy an individual has available for useful and effective contact with his environment, W being a measure of energy which is effectively controlled and directed by the individual.

MARINESCO, G., KREINDLER, A., AND COPELMANN, L. Le test de Rorschach et la dynamique de l'ecorle cerebrale d' apres les lois des reflexes conditionnels de Pavlov. *Ann. Medicopsychol. (Paris)*, 1935, 93(1), 614-623.

The proportion of W and D responses is cited as being dependent upon the balance of excitation and concentration in the cerebral cortex. Different diagnostic categories and their predisposition to different responses are cited.

RABIN, A. I., AND SANDERSON, M. H. An experimental inquiry into some Rorschach procedures. *J. Clin. Psychol.,* 1947, 3, 216-225.

Reversal on card order and the resulting effect upon various scorings, including approach, is discussed.

SCALES, MARGARET B. A study of intellectual functioning in terms of Rorschach location scores and free verbal expression. *Diss. Abstr.,* 1955, 15, 879-880.

This study was concerned with relationships between two sets of operations defining five traits of intellectual functioning, one set being the traditional manner of Rorschach approach scores, the other, verbalizations during a group therapy session. Some correlations for certain traits were found, whereas with some there was no correlation.

SCHACHTEL, E., AND HARTOCH, A. The curve of reactions in the Rorschach Test: A contribution to the theory and practice of Rorschach's Psychodiagnostic Inkblot Test. *Amer. J. Orthopsychiat.,* 1937, 7, 320-348.

The author cites Rorschach's ratios of modes of reaction and stresses importance of sequence or reactions. He includes a "curve of reactions" and explains and interprets same.

VERNON, P. E. Recent work on the Rorschach technique. *J. Ment. Sci.,* 1935, 81, 894-920.

Technique, subject's manner and attitude, and several scoring concepts including "erfassungstypus" (approach) are discussed in relation to diagnosis.

ZUBIN, J. A quantitative approach to measuring regularity of succession in the Rorschach experiment. *Character and Personality,* 1941, 10, 67-78.

The author gives a quantitative index for determining a preference for either progressive or regressive shifts (D to W, W to D, etc.) in Rorschach responses.

EXAMINER INTERACTION

ALDEN, PRISCILLA, AND BENTON, A. L, Relationship of sex of examiner to incidence of Rorschach responses with sexual content. *J. Project., Techn.,* 1951, 15, 231-234.

Fifty records secured by male and fifty by female examiners showed no significant difference in incidence of hidden and/or frank sexual responses. The implications of this are then discussed in relation to the testee-tester relationship.

ALLEN, R. M. *Introduction to the Rorschach Technique.* New York: International Universities Press, Inc., 1953.

Administration, including directions and rapport is discussed in the course of the book, briefly.

BAUGHMAN, E. E. Rorschach scores as a function of examiner difference. *J. Project. Techn.,* 1951, 15, 243-249.

A statistical analysis of 633 Rorschach protocols by fifteen examiners showed a significant difference in sixteen of twenty-two scoring categories. These differences were attributed by the author to differences in the relationships effected by the examiners and to differences in scoring.

BECK, S. J. Autism in Rorschach scoring: A feeling comment. *Character and Personality,* 1936, 5, 83-85.

Two other authors are criticized for suggesting that one "feel himself into" every response, as there are needs for more objectivity and less subjectivity in scoring the Rorschach. It is the feeling of the client and not the examiner which is to be tested, the author states.

BERGER, D. Examiner influence on the Rorschach. *J. Clin. Psychol.,* 1954, 10, 245-249.

Influences of eight examiners on patients in a VA hospital as to their Rorschach scores are discussed. The authority value of the examiner is cited as a factor influencing the Rorschach protocols.

CAMPBELL, FRANCES A., AND FIDDLEMAN, P. B. The effect of examiner status upon Rorschach performance. *J. Project. Techn.,* 1959, 23, 303-306.

The status of the examiner was shown to influence the number of responses but not the number of content categories nor the number of W responses.

CLEVELAND, S. E. The relationship between examiner anxiety and subject's Rorschach scores. *Microfilm Abstr.,* 1951, 11(2), 415-416. Abstract of Ph.D. thesis, 1951, University of Michigan. Microfilm of complete manuscript, 127 pp., $1.59, University Microfilms, Ann Arbor, Michigan, Publ. No. 2388.

DINOFF, M. Subject awareness of examiner influence in a testing situation. *J. Consult. Psychol.,* 1960, 24, 465.

With twenty-eight subjects, the author showed that it is possible for the examiner to influence Rorschach protocols.

FOSBERG, I. A. Rorschach reactions under varied instructions. *Rorschach Res. Exch.,* 1938, 3, 12-31.

With the Rorschach administered four times to the same individuals with different instructions each time ("standard," "make best impression," "make worse impression," and to check for various things, one at a time), no significant difference in the interpreted results was found between the different groups.

GIBBY, R. G. Examiner influence on Rorschach inquiry. *J. Consult. Psychol.,* 1952, 16, 449-455.

The study used twelve experimenters administering Rorschachs to 240 subjects with nonstandarized inquiry techniques, and nine experimenters administering to 135 subjects with standardized inquiry techniques. Although the former differed among themselves as to the changes that occurred between the free association and the final response of the inquiry, the latter also differed. The study, according to the author, points up the importance of considering the stimulus value of the experimenter in the production of Rorschach responses.

HAASE, W. Rorschach diagnosis, socio-economic class, and examiner bias. *Diss. Abstr.*, 1956, *16*, 1283.

HALPERN, FLORENCE. *A Clinical Approach to Children's Rorschachs.* New York: Grune & Stratton, 1953.
Administration to children is discussed, with the special problems encountered considered.

KRAMER, G. H., JR. The influence of training and personality characteristics of the examiner on Rorschach scores. *Diss. Abstr.*, 1956, *16*, 572.

LORD, EDITH. Experimentally induced variations in Rorschach performance. *Psychol. Monogr.*, 1950, *64*(10), 34.
Neutral, negative and positive attitude states were introduced by instructing the administrators to follow prescribed behavior patterns. The largest and most frequent variations in Rorschach performance were associated with examiner difference, however.

MARSH, J. T. An investigation of some examiner influences on productivity in the Rorschach Test. Unpublished Ph. D. thesis, 1952, Univ. of California, Los Angeles.

McNEELY, H. E. The influence of varied instructions on the response adequacy of certain Rorschach intelligence indicators. *Diss. Abstr.*, 1955, *15*, 628-629.
Experimental instructions varied Human M and W responses in predicted directions as to quality of the responses, but not as to quantity.

MILLER, D. R., SANDERS, RICHARD, AND CLEVELAND, S. E. The relationship between examiner personality and obtained Rorschach protocols: An application of interpersonal relations theory. *Amer. Psychol.*, 1950, *5*, 322-323.
Nine examiners gave thirty Rorschachs apiece which were scored randomly by the authors. The examiner's rankings for anxiety and hostility on the Rorschach, TAT and MMPI were then correlated with their corresponding Rorschach protocols. The results were discussed.

PHARES, E. J., STEWART, L. M., AND FOSTER, J. M. Instruction variation and Rorschach performance. *J. Project. Techn.*, 1960, *24*, 28-31.
The study failed to support the hypothesis that when subjects categorized the Rorschach testing situation as one in which responses are right or wrong, the result would be fewer total, movement and color responses, and more P, Z and F responses, with a higher form

level; but it did show a significant difference between examiners in the total number of responses elicited.

RABIN, A., NELSON, W., AND CLARK, MARGARET. Rorschach content as a function of perceptual experience and sex of examiner. *J. Clin. Psychol.*, 1954, *10*, 188-190.
The authors found that the sex of the examiner altered the production of sex responses but not anatomy responses, the former being more frequent with the male examiner. Other, situational, variables also are discussed.

SANDERS, R. The relationship between examiner hostility and subject's Rorschach scores. *Microfilm Abstr.*, 1951, 11(2), 433-34. Abstract of Ph.D. thesis, 1951, University of Michigan. Microfilm of complete manuscript, 122 pp. $1.53. University Microfilms, Ann Arbor, Mich., Publ. No. 2443.

SANDERS, R., AND CLEVELAND, S. E. The relationship between certain examiner personality variables and subject's Rorschach scores. *J. Project. Techn.*, 1953, *17*, 34-50.
The findings of this study, derived from thirty tests given by each of nine trained graduate assistants and scored by two expert clinical psychologists, show that the personality of the examiner is signicantly related to the type of Rorschach protocol which he obtains from a subject.

SARASON, S. B. *The Clinical Interaction: With Special Reference to the Rorschach.* New York: Harper, 1954.
This work is concerned with the belief that all clinical problems are concerned with data obtained from an interpersonal interaction and the subsequent variables, with particular emphasis on the Rorschach Test.

SCHAFER, R. *Psychoanalytic Interpretation in Rorschach Testing.* New York: Grune & Stratton, 1954, Chap. 2.
Offers an excellent discussion of the dynamics of the testing situation in terms of the examiner-subject relation, the impact of the examiner as a stimulus variable and the implication of the relationship for interpretation.

THOMAS, R. R. Instructional effects on Rorschach variables in relation to subject characteristics. *Diss. Abstr.*, 1954, 1816-1817.
Differences in instructions produced differences in responses equally among normals and psychiatric patients.

WILLIAMS, M. H., JR. The influence of variations in instructions on Rorschach reaction time. *Diss. Abstr.*, 1954, *14*, 2131.
With thirty male and thirty female subjects split fifty-fifty into control and experimental groups, the experimental group getting instructions to respond as quickly as possible, no differences were found as to the response time. Only F + % was found to differ in one group, and that was opposite to the expected direction and was considered a chance deviation. The author goes on to explain his results.

THE ANXIETY RESPONSE

ALLERHAND, M. E. Chiaroscuro determinant of Rorschach Test as an indicator of manifest anxiety. *J. Project. Techn.*, 1954, *18*, 407-413.
Correlations were determined between Rorschach chiaroscuro responses and behavioral signs of anxiety in

experimental nonconflict and conflict situations. None of the shading factors warranted prediction of the differences between behavioral reactions to the conflict and nonconflict situations.

BENA, E. Anxiety and emotional impoverishment in men

under stress. *Brit. J. Med. Psychol.*, 1961, *34*, 281-289.

Hungarian refugees were studied with the Rorschach, a sentence completion test and a questionnaire. The results are interpreted as showing that anxiety, guilt, depression and reduced emotion occurred frequently in these subjects. Emphasis is placed on effects of stress which did not occur early in life.

BINDER, H. The "light-dark" interpretation in Rorschach's experiment. *Rorschach Res. Exch.*, 1937, *2*, 37-42.

Discussion of sample chiaroscuro responses and their interpretations in relation to "anxiety mood." Also presented are Binder's unique scoring symbols and evaluative criteria.

BINDER, H. Die Helldunkeldeutungen im psychodiagnostischen Experiment von Rorschach. (The significance of light and dark in the psychodiagnostic experiment of Rorschach) *Arch. Suiss. Neurol.*, 1932, *3*, 1-67, 233-286.

Study made with normals, neurotics, psychotics and psychopaths indicates that responses of brightness — strongly influenced by affection attitude and having a definite relation to responses of movement — appear in a small percentage in normals (1 per cent), but much more frequently in neurotics (3.3 per cent) and above all in psychopaths (4.4 per cent).

BINDER, H. Die Helldunkeldeutungen im psychodiagnostischen Experiment von Rorschach. Zugleich ein Beitrag zur theoretischen Begründung des Experimentes. (The "chiaroscuro" responses in the Rorschach Diagnostic Psychological Test. A contribution to the theoretical basis of the test.) In, Bohm, E. Lehrbuch der Rorschach Psychodiagnostik (1st ed.). Berne, Hans Huber, 1951.

The author discusses the diagnostic value of the chiaroscuro and gray responses from a clinical study. On the basis of the results, author concludes that relatively more importance must be attached to the central mood reactions in psychopathic personalities than in neurotic, and in neurotic than in normal; conversely, adaptivity to the peripheral an environmental stimulus plays a lesser role in the psychopathic personality than in the neurotic, and in neurotic less than in normal.

BINSWANGER, W. Uber den Rorschach'schen Formdeutversuch bei akuten Schizophrenia. (The Rorschach Test in acute schizophrenics.) *Schweiz. Arch. Neurol. Psychiat.*, 1944, *53*, 101-121.

Those schizophrenics diagnosed as rationalizing their problems as an indefinite internal or external threat showed anxiety. The second group who "experienced a storm from without" did not demonstrate this characteristic.

BOLIN, B. J. An investigation of relationship between birth duration and childhood anxieties. *J. Ment. Sci.*, 1959, *105*, 1045-1052

Difference in Rorschach scores between two groups of twenty-three children, one group with average birth time 17.5 hours and one with average birth time 3.08 hours suggested that higher anxiety is related to prolonged birth time.

BUHLER, C., AND LEFEUER, D. A Rorschach study on the psychological characteristics of alcoholics. *Quart. J. Stud. Alcohol.*, 1947, *8*, 197-260.

Alcoholics distinguished from nonalcoholics by high anxiety and low tolerance to tension. Psychoneurotics showed greater anxiety, and psychopaths have little anxiety.

COX, F. N. AND SARASON, S. B. Test anxiety and Rorschach performance. *J. Abnorm. Soc. Psychol.*, 1954, *49*, 371-377.

This study was designed to test the validity of certain Rorschach anxiety indices. The results provide encouraging evidence as to the validity of certain anxiety indicators and support the theoretical assumptions from which most of them were derived.

DA CUNHA ARLINDO J. ADEOCLATO. O psicodiagnostico de Rorschach no estudo das maes soteras. (A Rorschach study of the unmarried mother.) *Rev. Psicol. Norm. Patol.*, 1960, *6*, 141-181.

Two groups of unmarried mothers were studied, one with a steady companion or protector in home and the other without. The test protocol did not distinguish between the two groups, but both were found to be anxious, insecure and depressed.

EICHLER, R. M. Experimental stress and alleged Rorschach indices of anxiety. *J. Abnorm. Soc. Psychol.*, 1951, *46*, 344-355.

Study of the influence of stress provoked anxiety on assumed indices of anxiety on the Rorschach. Results were increased shading and decreased W and R.

ELIZER, A. Content analysis of the Rorschach with regard to anxiety and hostility. *Rorschach Res. Exch.*, 1949, *13*, 247-284.

Responses which showed anxiety were assigned an "A." Subjects producing many "A" responses were found to suffer from phobias. Also, they lacked self-confidence.

FISHER, R. The effect of a disturbing situation upon the stability of various projective tests. *Psychol. Monogr.*, 1958, *72*(14, Whole No. 467).

A study concerned with determining whether responses to a series of projective tests would be significantly influenced by the stress growing out of temporary situational embarrassment or anxiety. The tests studied were TAT, Rorschach, Figure Drawing and Word Association. The projective tests studied were not significantly sensitive to the effects of embarrassment and anxiety in the experimental Ss.

FORSYTH, R. P. The influence of color, shading and Welsh anxiety level on Elizur Rorschach Content Test Analysis of Anxiety and Hostility. *J. Project. Techn.*, 1959, *23*, 207-213.

Ss were divided into three groups (high, low and middle anxiety) on the basis of K and Welsh A scores. Modified Rorschach cards were used. K is related to Elizur A and H, negatively in the middle group and positively in the low anxiety group.

GOLDSTEIN, K., AND ROTHMAN, E. Physiognomic phenomena in Rorschach responses. *Rorschach Res. Exch.*, 1945, *9*, 1-7.

A Rorschach was administered to a twenty-year-old college girl suffering from anxiety and compulsion. A marked predominance of physiognomic responses were obtained on the protocol.

GOODSTEIN, L. Interrelationships among several measures of anxiety and hostility. *J. Consult. Psychol.*, 1954, *18*, 35-39.

Selected tests were compared with respect to their ability to measure anxiety. Tests employed were MAS, Elizur Rorschach Content Test of Anxiety and Iowa Multiple-Choice Picture Interpretation.

GOODSTEIN, L., AND GOLDBERGER, L. Manifest anxiety and Rorschach performance in a chronic patient population. *J. Consult. Psychol.*, 1955, *19*, 339-343.

The Rorschach and the Taylor Manifest Anxiety Scale were used to test anxiety in a group of psychiatric patients. The results indicated that anxiety indices on the Rorschach and the MAS do not correlate.

GORLOW, L., ZIMET, G. N., AND FINE, H. J. The validity of anxiety and hostility Rorschach content scores among adolescents. *J. Consult. Psychol.*, 1952, *16*, 73-75.

Elizur's method of content analysis of anxiety and hostility were tested to discriminate delinquent from non-delinquent.

GUIRDHAM, A. The diagnosis of depression by the Rorschach Test. *Brit. J. Med. Psychol.*, 1936, *16*, 130-145.

In depression there is reduction in the appreciation of color and movement. It is possible to diagnose depression occurring in various states with both an EB score and the degree of stereotypy. The Rorschach seems to reflect a prevailing mood rather than an underlying fixed personality. During depression there appears an accentuation of the whole and small detail responses as opposed to the ordinary detail response.

GUIRDHAM, A. Simple psychological data in melancholia. *J. Ment. Sci.*, 1936, *82*, 649-653.

The findings in general illustrate certain traits of melancholia. Author goes on to differentiate these responses from those obtained from normals, depressive states of dementia praecox or delusional insanity and psychoneurotic anxiety. It is pointed out that no differentiation can be made between the clinical varieties of melancholia on only Rorschach responses.

HAMMUS, J. A., AND OSBORNE, R. T. Discrimination of manifest anxiety by the structured-objective Rorschach Test. *Percept. Motor Skills*, 1962, *15*, 59-62.

Thirty-eight low-anxious and thirty-one high-anxious Ss selected on the basis of a manifest anxiety scale were given the Structured-Objective Rorschach Test. Of twenty-six Rorschach factors, only Dd and S were found to be discriminative.

HARROWER-ERICKSON, M. R. The value and limitations of the so called "neurotic signs." *Rorschach Res. Exch.*, 1942, *6*, 109-114.

The author points out that no single "sign" proved to be unequivocally characteristic of a particular psychoneurosis. However, among the important indices of psychoneuroses is included shading shock — an anxiety indicator.

HERTZ, H. Binder's shading responses. *Rorschach Res. Exch.*, 1937-38, *2*, 79-89.

This includes Binder's classifications and interpretations of Rorschach "shading responses." Scoring difficulties which may be enumerated are illustrated.

HERTZ, MARGUERITE R. The "popular" response factor in the Rorschach scoring. *J. Psychol.*, 1938, *6*, 3-31.

Norms, scoring criteria, reliability and validity are all topics under discussion concerning the "popular" response. Apart from the point that, in combination with certain other factors, the P reflects upon the intelligence of the individual, it was brought out that cases of maladjustment, antisocial behavior and groups possessing neurotic tendencies all exhibit a marked low P%.

HERTZ, MARGUERITE R. Suicidal configurations in Rorschach records. *Rorschach Res. Exch.*, 1948, *12*, 3-58.

Ten configurations were found to be prevalent in the records of patients with suicidal tendencies. Among these is deep anxiety.

HERTAMAN, M., SMITH, G. M., AND CLARK, K. B. The relationship between changes in the angioscotoma and certain Rorschach signs under prolonged mild anoxia. *J. Gen. Psychol.*, 1949, *41*, 263-271.

Anoxia tolerance was measured by angioscotoma changes in twenty male college students. Rorschach results indicated that those who could not well tolerate anoxia were characterized by deep-seated anxiety.

HOLTZMAN, W. H., ISCOE, I., AND CALVIN, A. D. Rorschach color responses and manifest anxiety in college women. *J. Consult. Psychol.*, 1954, *18*, 317-324.

This experiment was designed to investigate the relationships of anxiety color, stimulus configuration, order of presentation and examiner with a number of different Rorschach variables. The Ss were high- and low-anxiety groups of college women. Color revisions of Cards II and III gave shorter reaction times and more responses than the achromatic versions of these cards.

KALDEGG, A., AND O'NEILL, D. Rorschach pattern in duodenal ulcer. *J. Ment. Sci.*, 1950, *96*, 190-198.

Twenty chronic cases of ulcers were given Rorschach Tests. They demonstrated anxiety and immaturity. No specific responses nor definite personality types were found.

KATES, S. L. Objective Rorschach response patterns differentiates anxiety reactions from obsessive-compulsive reactions. *J. Consult. Psychol.*, 1950, *14*, 226-229.

Inspection by Munroe Technique revealed more maladjustment and fewer responses among anxiety patients.

KATES, S. L., AND SCHWARTZ, F. Stress, anxiety and response complexity on the Rorschach Test. *J. Project. Techn.*, 1958, *22*, 64-69.

The present study investigated the effects of psychological stress and manifest anxiety level on the complexity of response organization in the Rorschach Test. It was noted that high manifest anxiety subjects tend to exhibit less complexity stress and control conditions.

KAUFMAN, L. Rorschach responses associated with experimentally induced anxiety. *Diss. Abstr.*, 1954, *14*, 187-188.

The influence of stress was determined by comparing the Rorschach performance of two subjects, one given after a stress experience and one given under standard conditions. Of the fifteen alleged indices of anxiety investigated, seven reflected the differential conditions in the manner hypothesized at an acceptable level of statistical reliability.

KLEBANOFF, S. G. A Rorschach study of operational fatigue in Army Air Forces combat personnel. *Rorschach Res. Exch.*, 1946, *10*, 115-120.

Sixty enlisted men diagnosed as having operational fatigue were given Rorschachs. Analysis showed the most frequent pattern was anxiety hysteria.

KRUGMAN, M. Psychosomatic study of 15 stuttering children. Roundtable. IV. Rorschach study. *Amer. J. Orthopsychiat.*, 1946, *16*, 127-133.

Great anxiety is a characteristic trend in a large proportion of stutterers.

LEBO, D., TOAL, R., AND ERICH, H. Rorschach performance in the amelioration and continuation of observable anxiety. *J. Gen. Psychol.*, 1960, *63*, 75-80.

Twenty-four matched prisoners, living under conditions of environmental stress, emphasizing anxiety symptoms were studied. 50 per cent were given CO_2 and 50 per cent nothing. Fourteen Rorschach signs of anxiety were selected for intergroup comparison. Three of the indices were significantly reduced in the experimental group; two in the control group.

LEME, LOPES J. *Das Interpretagoes Chiaroscuro no Psico-diagnostice de Rorschach e os Estados de Ansiedade (Chiaroscuro Interpretations in Rorschach's Psychodiagnostics, and States of Anxiety)* Rio de Janeiro: Imprensa Nacional, 1943.

Interpretative differences between Klopfer's and Binder's investigations are related to author's formulation of role of chiaroscuro response. This response is directly related to neuroticism (anxiety) but not psychotic melancholia. Case presented.

LEVITT, E. E. Alleged Rorschach anxiety indices in children. *J. Project. Techn.*, 1957, *21*, 261-264.

A group of child clinic patients were compared with a group of normal children on a series of Rorschach variables commonly indicated as anxiety indices in adults. Of nonsignificant differences, only the frequency of shading regions was in the predicted direction. It therefore was concluded that only frequency of shading responses can be considered to be an anxiety indicator in children.

LEVITT, E. E., AND GROSZ, H. H. A comparison of quanitifiable Rorschach anxiety indicators in hypnotically induced anxiety and normal states. *J. Consult. Psychol.*, 1960, *24*, 31-34.

Rorschach records were obtained from normal Ss in hypnosis and in induced anxiety. Anxiety state is reflected statistically.

LUKE, B. La methode de Rorschach appliquee a un groupe controle. (The Rorschach method applied to delinquent and control groups.) *Bull. Inst. Pedag. Saint-Georges.* 1942, *5*, 58.

Delinquent boys showed a stronger tendency towards anxiety and normal states. *J. Consult. Psychol.*, 1960, quents.

LUKE, B. The Rorschach method applied to delinquent and non-delinquent boys; summary of research. *Bull. Canad. Psychol. Ass.*, 1943, *3*, 52-53.

A group of eighty unselected delinquents were found to be "more afflicted by anxiety" than the equivalent control group.

McFATE, M. AND ORR, F. Through adolescence with the Rorschach. *Rorschach Res. Exch.*, 1949, *13*, 302-319.

Longitudinal study of a group of children at four age levels. While the girls consistently produced more color responses, the boys evidenced a greater number of anxiety indicators.

MIALE, F. R., AND HARROWER-ERICKSON, M. R. Personality structure in the psychoneuroses. *Rorschach Res. Exch.*, 1940, *4*, 71-74.

Nine "signs" appear to differentiate the protocols of psychoneurotics from those of normals. Among those suggested is shading shock.

MOGAR, R. E. Anxiety indices in human figure drawings: A replication and extension. *J. Consult. Psychol.*, 1962, *26*, 108 (See 36, 5622).

Draw-A-Person anxiety indicators are significantly related to Rorschach content scores. Neither is related to manifest anxiety.

MOHR, P. Die schwarze and sehr dunkle Tönung der Rorschach'schen Tafeln und ihre Bedeutung für den Versuch. (The black and the very dark shading in the Rorschach pictures and their meaning for the test.) *Schweiz. Arch. Neurol. Psychiat.*, 1944, *53*, 122-133.

Interpretations of form and color are closely related to affectivity. If it is pleasant, interpretation not inhibited; if not, then interpretation is inhibited, and picture is poorly perceived and answer is symbolic or complex. Protocols also show that subjects in conflict with authority react to dark-colored pictures with anxiety; those without such conflict answer with answers denoting protection or quietness.

NEURINGER, C. Manifestations of anxiety on the Rorschach Test. *J. Project. Techn.*, 1962, *26*, 318-326.

The value of the Rorschach Content Test in assessing anxiety is upheld. Rorschach determinants are found to differ in their relationship to lab-induced and real-life anxiety.

PIOTROWSKI, Z. A. Rorschach records of children with a tic syndrome. *Nerve Child.*, 1945, *4*, 342-352.

Rorschach responses of twelve children with tics indicated "marked neurotic anxiety."

RABIN, A. I. Homicide and attempted suicide: A Rorschach study. *Amer. J. Orthopsychiat.*, 1946, *16*, 516-524.

Longitudinal study of one person. The Rorschach administered before the homicide showed extreme anxiety and shading shock. This was not prevalent in the test given after the homicide.

RABINOVITCH, S. M. Physiologic response, perceptual threshold and Rorschach Test anxiety indices. *J. Project. Techn.*, 1954, *18*, 379-386.

Rorschach Test responses determined by Rorschach signs of anxiety are associated with greater GSR deflections and higher perceptual threshold than popular or good form responses.

Ross, W. D. The "anxiety neurosis" Rorschach record compared with the typical basically neurotic record. *Rorschach Res. Exch.*, 1940, *4*, 134-137.
An intracranial operation victim's protocols are examined. The protocol of "just after the operation" is compared with the protocol of five months later. The first showed two of nine neurotic signs; the second, five of nine. It was suggested that the first "showed the mode of comprehension suggestive of an anxiety state," while the second did not.

Sanches, L. J. Aplicacion del psicodiagnostico de Rorschach en psiquitria clinica y forense. (Application of the Rorschach psychodiagnosis in clinical and forensic psychiatry.) *Rev. Med. Legal., Colombia*, 1946, *8*, 86-110.
Case of a youth of twenty-three who indulged in homosexuality and masturbation. The Rorschach revealed a predisposition toward anxiety.

Sarason, S. B., Davidson, K., Lightfall, F., and Waite, R. Rorschach behavior and performance of high and low anxious children. *Child Develop.*, 1958, *29*, 277-285.
Rorschach protocols were obtained from thirty-two matched pairs of grade school children who differed in scores on the Test Anxiety and General Anxiety Scales. Results indicate differences between high- and low-anxious Ss and between boys and girls.

Schachtel, E. G. Subjective definitions of the Rorschach Test situation and their effects on test performance. *Psychiatry*, 1945, *8*, 419-448.
Increased self-control as demonstrated by a high A% is a function of anxiety. It is an attempt to prevent the conscious expression of thoughts.

Schwartz, F., and Kates, S. L. Rorschach performance, anxiety level and stress. *J. Project. Techn.*, 1957, *21*, 154-160.
The Rorschachs of college sophomores scoring in the upper and lower 20 per cent of the distribution of scores on the Taylor Manifest Anxiety Scale were compared under stress and nonstress conditions. The Rorschach is sensitive to differences between high and low anxious Ss as defined by the MAS. The responses elicited in the high anxious group imply a degree of personality impoverishment.

Singer, M. The validity of a multiple choice projective test in psychopathological screening. *Psychol. Monogr.*, 1950, *64*, No. 314.
"Fair" validity was obtained on a multiple choice Rorschach with anxiety reactions and schizoprenics.

Sion, M., Akatli, S., and Kemalof, S. De certaines responses d'anxiete dans les protocols de Rorschach des medecins. (Anxiety responses in the Rorschach protocols of physicians.) *Z. Psychol.*, 1954, *25*, 155-173.
Analysis of the Rorschach protocols of one hundred physicians yielded a high proportion of anxiety responses suggesting a "typology" of anxiety signs in correlation with clinical symptoms. English and German summaries.

Tuompo, A. Erfahrungen mit dem Rorschachversuch an der finnishen Front. (Experiences with the Rorschach Test on the Finnish Front.) *Beih. Schweiz. Z. Psychol.*, 1948, *13*, 114-122.
Rorschachs were administered to 110 soldiers and the same number of high school students. The soldiers demonstrated more anxiety on their records.

Violet-Conil and Canivet, V. Le test de Rorschach et le diagnostic de l'angoisse. (The Rorschach and the diagnosis of anxiety.) *Rorschachiana*, 1952, *1*, 78-127.
Anxiety disclosed in few W, Do and S, few M, pure C and many shading and shock responses. Anxiety seen as a cause of psychological regression.

Waller, P. F. Correlates of Rorschach shading scores obtained with two methods of inquiry. *Diss. Abstr.*, 1960, *20*, 2912.
The study was designed to investigate the relationship between the shading response on the Rorschach and other indices of anxiety that are used in the clinic.

Waller, P. F. The relationship between the Rorschach shading response and other indices of anxiety. *J. Project. Techn.*, 1960, *24*, 211-217.
Validity of the interpretations of anxiety from the Rorschach shading response was investigated. Rorschach inquiry was compared with Baughman's paired comparison inquiry, using sixty psychiatric patients as Ss. It appears that anxiety, as the term is used clinically, is closely related to the method of measurement. It may be more accurate to refer to different types of anxiety.

Westrope, M. R. Relations among Rorschach indices, manifest anxiety, and performance under stress. *J. Abnorm. Soc. Psychol.*, 1953, *48*, 515-524.
The relationships between Rorschach measures of anxiety and of intellectual control and manifest anxiety and the relationship between Rorschach measures of intellectual control and of anxiety and changes in Digit symbol performance under stress conditions were studied.

Wharton, L. H. Effect to stress-produced anxiety on Rorschach, draw-a-person and visual performance. *Diss. Abstr.*, 1953, *13*, 1268-1269.
Two groups of forty college students were administered these three tests, one a stress group and one a control group. Fifteen indices of anxiety on the Rorschach were investigated. Only one (number of responses) of the fifteen anxiety signs tended to differentiate the two groups.

Wise, F. Effect of chronic and stress induced anxiety on Rorschach determinants. *Diss. Abstr.*, 1957, *17*, 1603.
Of the fifteen alleged indices of anxiety on the Rorschach, four (number of responses, number of rejected plates, oligophrenic details and shading shock signs) differentiated among groups in the manner hypothesized and at an acceptable level of significance.

Zulliger, H. Die Angst im Formdeutversuch nach Dr. Rorschach. (Anxiety in the form interpretation test of Dr. Rorschach.) *Z. Psychoanal. Padag.*, 1933, *7*, 418-420.
The value of the test for revealing presence of fear or anxiety indicated. Careful evaluation of responses may show nature of fear.

THE RORSCHACH AND INTELLIGENCE

ABITMAN, H. D. Rorschach determinants in mentally defective and normal subjects. *Train Sch. Bull.*, 1953, *50*, 143-151.

The Rorschach was administered to fifty subjects with a mean MA of 7-4. Lower R, D, M and higher FM were typical of the records. With mentally deficient subjects, the Do response is so infrequent that it is suggested that it be abandoned as an oligophrenic response.

ABRAMS, E. N. Prediction of intelligence from certain Rorschach factors. *J. Clin. Psychol.*, 1955, *11*, 81-83.

A multiple correlation of .53 between F+%, M, W, R and the Wechsler-Bellevue full scale IQ was obtained from the protocols of four hundred VA mental hygiene clinic patients. The author presents a formula for estimating IQ from the Rorschach.

ADCOCK, C. V. A factorial approach to Rorschach interpretation. *J. Gen. Psychol.*, 1951, *44*, 261-272.

Intelligence was shown to be a factor in the analysis of Rorschach protocols of both native children of Cook Island and of New Zealand children.

ALLEN, R. M. The Rorschach records of a superior child. *J. Genet. Psychol.*, 1957, *91*, 115-118.

The Stanford-Binet, Leitter International Performance Scale, the WISC and the Rorschach were administered to one child at regular intervals. One Rorschach protocol disclosed a wide discrepancy with the IQ test data. The author states that this discrepancy may be attributable to situational variables.

ALLEN, R. M., AND LUCHTENSTEIN, D. The Rorschach and intelligence: A note of caution. *J. Genet. Psychol.*, 1960, *97*, 169-171.

It is suggested that tests other than the Rorschach should be used to ascertain intellectual ability. The author bases this on a subject's retest after six months on which the Rorschach elements which are usually considered to be significant for inferring IQ differed sufficiently to yield varying IQ levels.

ALTUS, W. D., AND ALTUS, GRACE T. Rorschach movement variables and verbal intelligence. *J. Abnorm. Soc. Psychol.* 1952, *47*, 531-533.

Popular M, FM and m correlate with intelligence at a relatively low level, the unstereotyped, fairly original M appears to be the Rorschach movement response which is saturated with the intelligence factor. The curvilinear regression of M on intelligence appears to be a function of the unstereotyped M.

ALTUS, W. D., AND THOMPSON, GRACE M. The Rorschach as a measure of intelligence. *J. Consult. Psychol.*, 1949, *13*, 341-347.

The group Rorschach and group IQ tests were administered to 228 college students. The results indicate that the most reliable and valid indicator of IQ on the Rorschach is the absolute number of M's, a large number of M's appearing to be evidence of relatively superior IQ. However, the relationship of M to IQ appears to depart significantly from linearity. The absolute number of W's is also a valid and reliable indicator of IQ, although less so than M.

ARMITAGE, S. G., GREENBERG, P. D., PEARL, D., BERGER, G., AND DASTON, P. G. Predicting intelligence from the Rorschach. *J. Consult. Psychol.*, 1955, *19*, 321-329.

A useful estimate of IQ was not obtained by statistically relating Wechsler-Bellevue IQ's and single or composite Rorschach scoring variables. When clinicians judged the psychograms of these protocols, a somewhat greater accuracy of prediction resulted. Use of the protocol itself enabled the clinicians to yield fairly accurate estimates of intellectual functioning.

BARRELL, R. P. Subcategories of Rorschach human movement responses: A classification system and some experimental results. *J. Consult. Psychol.*, 1953, *17*, 254-260.

On the basis of a new system of classification of M responses, the analysis of Rorschach protocols of 121 graduate students in psychology indicated that the various subcategories of M are differentially related to various categories of intellectual functioning.

BARRON, F. Threshold for the perception of human movement in inkblots. *J. Consult. Psychol.*, 1955, *19*, 33-38.

Although it was found that the threshold for human movement perceptions was unrelated to measures of intelligence, staff psychologists judged to be more intelligent those subjects with higher M responses.

BASH, K. W., AND LAMPL, E. Intelligenz- und Ausdrucksmerkmale in Rorschach-Test und in Kinderzeichnungen. (Characteristics of intelligence and expression in the Rorschach Test and in children's drawings.) *Z. Kinderpsychiat.*

IQ's derived from the Rorschach protocols of seventy children ages eleven and twelve were compared with Goodenough Draw-A-Man IQ's and experience type and Hd responses were compared with the children's free drawing.

BECK, S. J. Personality diagnosis by means of the Rorschach Test. *Amer. J.. Orthopsychiat.*, 1930, *1*, 81-88.

An explanation is given of the Rorschach Test in relation to its function as an IQ estimator.

BECK,, S. J. The Rorschach Test and personality diagnosis: The feebleminded. *Amer. J. Psychiat.*, 1930, *10*, 19-52.

Rorschach's principal concepts were substantiated and one of his findings unsubstantiated in an analysis of the Rorschach protocols of sixty-seven institutionalized feebleminded children.

BECK, S. J. The Rorschach Test as applied to a feebleminded group. *Arch. Psychol.*, 1932, *136*, 84.

An analysis of Rorschach records of eighty-seven children whose Stanford-Binet IQ's ranged from 21-77, with a mean of 55.10 yielded the following results: a correlation of .474 between W and MA, of .64 between F+% and M.A. and no linear relationship between A% and M.A.

BETT, H. V. An investigation of the significance of the Rorschach Z score. Unpublished Ph.D. Dissertation, U. of Nebraska, 1953.

Statistically significant correlations of .49 and .46 were found between the verbal and reasoning subtests of the

Primary Mental Abilities Test and weighted Z scores from the Rorschach protocols of thirty-two high school students.

BIALICK, I., AND HAMLIN, ROY M. The clinician as judge: Details of procedure in judging projective material. *J. Consult. Psychol.*, 1954, *18*, 239-242.

Valid and reliable judgments of subject's IQ's were made on the basis of the subject's Rorschach W responses. A procedure for judging instructed test material is also presented.

BINDER, H. Die klinische Bedeutung des Rorschach'schen Versuches. (Clinical meaning of the Rorschach Test.) *Schweiz. Arch. Neurol. Psychiat.*, 1944, *53*, 12-99.

The author discusses the Rorschach and states that being free from educational and linguistic elements, it is the best intelligence test.

BLECHKNER, JANET E. The responses of average and gifted students on the group Rorschach Test. *Calif. J. Educ. Res.*, 1959, *10*, 200-206.

One hundred children of 120 or above IQ's and eighty-seven children having IQ's of 90-110 were tested on the group Rorschach and the California Test of Mental Maturity. For the categories employed, no statistically significant differences were found between the responses given by the two groups.

BOISSON, G. La elaboracion perceptiva en los no intelligentes. (Perceptual elaboration in the unintelligent.) *Rev. Psicol. Gen. appl.*, 1952, *7*, 217-236.

The author states that for the diagnosis of low intelligence, the Rorschach seems to be the most promising test. His sample consisted of one hundred males who, although not feebleminded or abnormal, fell in the lowest IQ bracket. The results are in contradiction to those of some previous investigators in that there was not an extreme paucity of W, and that there was frequent A, perseveration, PA and card rejection.

BURNHAM, CATHARINE A. A study of the degree of relationship between Rorschach H% and Wechsler-Bellevue picture arrangement scores. *Rorschach Res. Exch.*, 1949, *13*, 206-209.

Subjects were ninety male World War II veterans, patients in a mental hygiene clinic. IQ's on the Wechsler-Bellevue ranged from 56 to 137. A correlation of .09 was obtained between Rorschach H% and the Wechsler picture arrangement subtest.

CALTONARO, E. Le interpeetasioni kinestet uche snel Rorschach di fanciulli deboli mentali. (Kinesthetic interpretations in the Rorschach of mentally defective children.) *Arch. Psicol. Neurol.*, 1959, *20*, 309-323.

A lack of Rorschach movement responses was found in the protocols of fifty-three feebleminded children, ages seven to thirteen. The Author attributes this to a failure in development of body image and a lack of kinesthetic sensation.

CARLSON, V. R., AND LAZARUS, R. S. A repetition of Meyer Williams' study of intellectual control under stress and associated Rorschach factors. *J. Consult. Psychol.*, 1953, *17*, 247-253.

This replication of Meyer Williams' study failed to sub-stantiate his conclusion that there is a relationship between intellectual control as measured by the Rorschach and actual intellectual performance under stress.

CARUSO, I. A. Intelligenz- und affektivgefarbte Do-Deutung im Rorschach'schen Formdeutversuch. (Intelligence and affective colored Do interpretation in Rorschach form interpretation experiment.) *Schweiz. Z. Psychol.*, 1948, *7*, 309.

CARUSO, I. A. Intelligenz- und affektivgefarbte Do-Deutung im Rorschach'schen Formdeutversuch. (Intelligence and affectively-toned Do-responses in the Rorschach Test.) *Wien. Z. Prakt. Psychol.*, 1949, *1*, 17-20.

The author discusses the Do (oligophrenic) response and states that the appearance of such a response in a Rorschach record is a result of emotionality, not intellectual deficiency.

CABAGNA, C. Il reattivo di Rorschach nei fanciulli anormali dell'intelligenza. *Note Psichiat., Pesaro*, 1948, *74*, 93-108.

In comparison with normal children, the Rorschach psychograms of ninety oligophrenic children, ages nine to fourteen were characterized by serious stereotype, poverty of interpretation, low number of G, very low F+%, very frequent Po and very high 0%.

CONSALVI, C., AND CANTER, A. Rorschach scores as a function of four factors. *J. Consult. Psychol.*, 1957, *21*, 48-51.

There is a single general intelligence factor in the Rorschach. M was found to be loaded on intelligence, productivity minimally related and Fm not related.

COX, S. M. A factorial study of the Rorschach responses of normal and maladjusted boys. *J. Genet. Psychol.*, 1951, *79*, 95-115.

One of the factors extracted from a factor analysis of the Rorschach protocols of 120 boys was intelligence *versus* lack of intelligence.

CROKES, T. G., AND KELLER, ANNA. Rorschach card rejection and IQ. *J. Clin. Psychol.*, 1960, *16*(4), 424-426.

In a replication of Tamkin's study in which a correlation was found between IQ and the number of Rorschach cards rejected, 293 female adult psychotic patients and 217 children were tested on the Rorschach, Wechsler-Bellevue, WISC and Stanford-Binet. Tomkin's results were confirmed.

DAVIDSON, H. H., AND KLOPFER, B. Rorschach statistics: Part I. Mentally retarded, normal, and superior adults. *Rorschach Res. Exch.*, 1937, 1938, *2*, 164-169.

A tabulation of findings appearing in the literature related to the various types of responses obtained from adults classified as mentally retarded, normal or superior.

DAVIS, HANNAH SUSAN. Judgments of intellectual level from various features of the Rorschach including vocabulary. *J. Project. Techn.*, 1961, *25*, 155-157.

The author found significantly high correlations between various Rorschach determinants and appraisal of Rorschach vocabulary and IQ scores of the subjects tested.

DREGER, R. M. The relation between Rorschach M and TAT content categories as measures of creative productivity in a representative high-level intelligence population. *J. Gen. Psychol.*, 1960, *63*, 29-33.

The relationship between R, M or M% and the Wonderlic Personnel Test were found to be low or absent in a population of sixty subjects of a high level of intelligence.

EGAS, E. D. Components of the intelligence and erlebnistype in the Rorschach method. Unpublished M.A. Thesis, Ohio State U., 1945, 146 pps.

FIELDING, B., AND BROWN, F. Prediction of intelligence from certain Rorschach responses. *J. Clin. Psychol.*, 1956. *12*, 196-197.

The formula advocated by Abrams for estimating an IQ from M, F+, W and R was tested, using Rorschach protocols of 107 male psychotics and psychoneurotics. For those subjects whose Wechsler-Bellevue IQ scores were above 110, the correlation between the WB IQ's and the formula IQ's was not significantly above 0. However, it was indicated that the formula is satisfactory for IQ's ranging from 90 to 110 and for those protocols in which there were more than three M responses.

FORD, M. The application of the Rorschach Test to young children. *Univ. Minn. Child Welf. Monogr.*, 1946, No. *23*, 114.

The validity of several Rorschach response categories as a measure of intelligence was substantiated by the comparison of the responses obtained from 123 children ages 3 to 7-11 with teacher's ratings and standardized test results.

FUCHS, C. Hohe Intelligenz: Versuch zur experimentellen Erfassung mit dem Rorschachtest. (Superior intelligence: An attempt at an experimental determination by means of the Rorschach Test.) *Z. Psychol.*, 1942, *142*, 30.

The author states that individuals of superior IQ yield Rorschach records which resemble those elicited from abnormal subjects.

GAIR, M. Rorschach characteristics of a group of very superior seven-year-old children. *Rorschach Res. Exch.*, 1944, *8*, 31-37.

Analysis of the Rorschach records of twenty-nine children of a mean Stanford-Binet IQ of 146 yielded the following trends in comparison with the average child: increased R and W, fewer D, wider range of content, greater maturity in the use of F%, m and FC combinations and an increase in CF.

GANZ, E., AND LOOSLI-USTERI, M. Le test de Rorschach applique a 43 garcons abnormaux. (The Rorschach Test applied to 43 abnormal boys.) *Arch. Psychol. Geneve.*, 1934, *24*, 245-255.

The Rorschach was administered to forty-three feebleminded and imbecilic boys ages ten to fourteen. In comparison to normals, these subjects projected themselves more easily, gave more interpretations and gave more small detail responses. Rorschach's oligophrenic details were found to appear more often in normals.

GARDNER, C. E. Rorschach Test replies and results in 100 normal adults of average IQ. *Amer. J. Orthopsychiat.*, 1936, *6*, 32-60.

A tabulation is presented of Rorschach responses of one-hundred normal adults of average intelligence.

GARMENDIA DE OTAOLA, A. El Test de Rorschach y el examen de los talentos. (The Rorschach Test and the examination of talents.) *Rev. Priscol. Pedag. apl.*, 1952, *3*, 237-250.

The author states that the Rorschach, rather than being useful in the derivation of IQ, instead is useful in the examination of the formal aspects of intelligence.

GIBBY, R. G. The stability of certain Rorschach variables under conditions of experimentally induced sets: 1. The intellectual variables. *J. Project. Techn.*, 1951, *15*, 3, 25.

Various experimental sets affected Rorschach intelligence variables. All intelligence variables were not found to be equally stable, F+%, A%, content and R being the most stable. The author cautions against estimating IQ from the Rorschach unless there is precise knowledge of the external conditions of administration and of the particular population to which the subject belongs.

GOLDFARB, W. Organization activity in the Rorschach examination. *Amer. J. Orthopsychiat.*, 1945, *15*, 525-528.

Thirty normal adolescents of a mean age of 12-3 administered the block design and similarities test of the Wechsler-Bellevue, the Weigl color Form Test, the Vigotsky Test of Abstraction. The Klopfer and Davidson Rorschach form-level rating scale was reliably related to the tests while Beck's Sum Z plus score was not.

GOLDFRIED, M. R. Some normative data on Rorschach developmental level "card pull" in a psychiatric population. *J. Project. Techn.*, 1962, *26*(3), 283-287.

A correlation was demonstrated between the level of perceptual organization in Rorschach responses and IQ level of 110 male psychiatric patients.

GREBSTEIN, L. C. Relative accuracy of actuarial prediction, experienced clinicians and graduate students in a clinical judgment task. *J. Consult. Psychol.*, 1963, *27*(2), 127-132.

A multiple regression equation and clinical judgments of Rorschach psychograms were used to predict Wechsler-Bellevue IQ scores. Both methods resulted in significantly better-than-chance prediction, with no significant difference in accuracy between the equation and the judges. Accuracy of prediction did not increase significantly with amount of clinical experience.

GREPPI-SADINO, A. Investigacion sobre los determinantes indicativos de inteligencia en el test de Rorschach. (Investigation on the determinants indicative of intelligence in the Rorschach Test.) *Rev. Psiquiat.*, 1951, *16*, 108-128.

The Wechsler and the Rorschach were administered to seventeen subjects, ages sixteen to twenty. A statistically significant correlation was obtained between full scale IQ scores and diverse factors of the Rorschach which have been related to IQ in previous investigations.

HERTZ, MARGUERITE R. The Rorschach Ink-Blot Test: Historical summary. *Psych. Bull.*, 1935, *32*, 33-36.

A correlation of .25 between the number of Rorschach M responses and Wechsler-Bellevue IQ scores is reported.

HERTZ, MARGUERITE R. The "popular" response factor in the Rorschach scoring. *J. Psychol.*, 1938, *6*, 3-31.

The author presents a summary of the norms for the Rorschach P% in relation to groups of varying intelligence and personality categories. It is concluded that the P% is higher for the intelligent than for the less intelligent subject.

HERTZ, MARGUERITE R. The organization activity. *Rorschach Psychology* (Rickers-Ovsiankina, M. A., ed.). New York: Wiley and Sons, 1961, 25-55.

The author discusses the organization activity in the Rorschach and reviews the literature concerning the relationship between various organization scores and intelligence.

HERTZ, MARGUERITE R., AND KENNEDY, S. The M factor in estimating intelligence. *Rorschach Res. Exch.* (abstract), 1940, *4*, 105-106. (Found in Rickers-Ovsiankina, Maria A., ed. *Rorschach Psychology.* New York: John Wiley and Sons, 1961, 49-50.)

The Rorschach was administered to 137 children, ages fourteen and fifteen, having a Stanford-Binet IQ range of 96 to 159. M's which were Mg and DMg and DMO plus g were given reliably more often by the group rated as having superior intelligence.

HOLZBERG, J. D., AND BELMONT, LILLIAN. The relationship between factors on the Wechsler-Bellevue and Rorschach having common psychological rationale. *J. Consult. Psychol.*, 1952, *16*, 23-29.

A correlation of Rorschach determinants and Wechsler-Bellevue subtests led to the following statistically significant relationships: a positive correlation between F+% and block design, F+% and FC with similarities, and M with information and a negative correlation between F% and similarities. Subjects for this research were fifty mental health patients.

INTI LUNA, R. Ensayo de la prusba de Rorschach en 104 ninos (Study of the Rorschach Test with 104 children.) *Rev. Neuropsiquiat.*, 1941, *4*, 249-262.

As a result of testing 104 subjects whose ages ranged from nine to sixteen years of age, the author concludes that the value of the Rorschach for yielding evidence of IQ level is comparatively small.

JOLLES, I. The diagnostic implications of Rorschach's Test in case studies of mental defectives. *Genet. Psychol. Monogr.*, 1947, *36*, 89-198.

On the basis of research with sixty-six children of ten to fifteen years of age and IQ's of 65 to 79, Jolles concluded that adequate F+, adequate range of content and high Z in conjunction with qualitatively good W and M contraindicate mental deficiency. In addition, it is reported that correlations between total Z scores and Binet and Wechsler-Bellevue IQ scores were insignificant.

KAY, L. W., AND VORHAUS, P. G. Rorschach reactions in early childhood. Part II. Intellectual aspects of personality development. *Rorschach Res. Exch.*, 1943, *7*, 71-77.

Research in the development of cognitive factors in personality of 138 children ages 2 to 6-11 by means of the Rorschach result in the following conclusions — number of R, W, D+d, W+, pseudopsychotic Ws and percentage of subjects using P, percentage of rejection and percentage of arbitrary and perseverated Ws increased with age.

KELLER, A. Normals und unternormale Intelligenz im Rorschachtest. (Normal and below normal intelligence in the Rorschach Test.) Cologne: Orthen., 1939, 54.

KELLEY, D. M., AND BARRERA, S. E. The Rorschach method in the study of mental deficiency: A resume. *Amer. J. Ment. Defic.*, 1941, *45*, 401-407.

The primary use of the Rorschach with mental defectives is stated to be the determination of the influence of the emotional life on intellectual functioning. Factors used in estimating IQ and response patterns of mental defectives are presented.

KERR, M. The Rorschach Test applied to children. *Brit. J. Psychol.*, 1934, *25*, 170-185.

A relationship between certain Rorschach criteria and IQ was demonstrated using a sample consisting of normal children ages seven to twelve, mentally defective children ages eleven to fourteen and children who were child guidance clinic patients.

KLOPFER, B. The interplay between intellectual and emotional factors in personality diagnosis. *Proc. 6th Inst. Except. Child, Child Res. Clin.*, 1939, 41-47.

It is stated that it is possible to differentiate capacity and efficiency levels by means of the Rorschach.

KLOPFER, B., AND DAVIDSON, H. H. Form-level rating: A preliminary proposal for appraising mode and level of thinking as expressed in Rorschach records. *Rorschach Res. Exch.*, 1944, *8*, 164-177.

A discussion of form level ratings and their suggested uses in relation to estimating intelligence.

KLOPFER, W. G., ALLEN, B. V., AND ETHER, D. Content diversity on the Rorschach and "range of interests." *J. Project. Techn.*, 1960, *24*, 290-291.

An insignificant correlation was found between the WAIS full scale IQ and the total number of Rorschach responses.

KROPP, R. P. The Rorschach "Z" score. *J. Project. Techn.*, 1955, *19*, 443-452.

Beck's rationale for Z scores is criticized, and evidence is presented to show that: Z is highly related to W, M and R; that it doesn't relate to the operationally defined IQ of current tests; and that it does relate moderately to IQ test raw scores.

LAL, RAM SURAT. Rorschach Test and assessment of intelligence under Indian conditions. *Brit. J. Educ. Psychol.*, 1956, *26*, 112-116.

Estimates of IQ derived from the Rorschach resources of thirty-nine normal subjects, ages nine to twenty-three, correlated .51 with the subjects Stanford-Binet IQ scores. There was also a positive, although somewhat smaller correlation with a group test and a battery of performance tests.

LEVINE, M., SPIVACK, G., AND WRIGHT, B. The inhibition process, Rorschach human movement responses, and intelligence: some further data. *J. Consult. Psychol.*, 1959, *23*, 306-312.

There was no significant difference found in the number of Rorschach M responses between organics and other diagnostic categories in an adult population. In an adolescent population diagnosed as chronic brain syndrome, schizophrenic, personality disorders, and emotional disorders, it was found that those subjects with higher IQs produced more movement responses.

LIEFMANN, E. Zur Frage des Rorschach-Versuches als Intelligenztest. (Concerning the question of the Rorschach as an intelligence test.) *Beih. Schweiz. Z. Psychol.*, 1950, *19*, 102-109.

An attempt is made to show that inaccurate indices of intelligence are obtained by the use of quantitative formula derived from the Rorschach test. It is concluded that the overall quality of an individual's protocol provides a more adequate estimate of his intellectual level.

LODERER, C. Die intellektuelle Entwicklung im Spiegel des Rorschachschen Formdeutversuches. (Intellectual development as seen in Rorschach records.) *Nervenartz*, 1942, *15*, 512.

LOTSOFF, E. V., COMREY, V., BOGARTZ, W., AND ARNSFIELD, P. A factor analysis of the WISC and Rorschach. *J. Project. Techn.*, 1958, *22*, 297-301.

It was found that Rorschach determinants were not loaded on the verbal intelligence factor. The authors, therefore, question the use of the Rorschach in estimating IQ.

LOOSLI-USTERI, M. Les interpretations dans le test de Rorschach. Interpretations Kinesthesiques et interpretations-couteur. (Interpretations of the use of the Rorschach Test. Kinesthetic and color interpretations.) *Arch. Psychol.*, 1932, *23*, 349-365.

The author tested boys, ages nine to fourteen, sixty-three of whom were clinic patients and sixty-three normals. It was found that kinesthetic interpretations were not normal for this age range and that they have nothing to do with intelligence. It is concluded that from the age of nine, the Rorschach permits an analysis of the child's IQ.

LOTSOF, E. J. Intelligence, verbal fluency, and the Rorschach Test. *J. Consult. Psychol.*, 1953, *17*, 21-24.

The results of an intercorrelation and factor analysis of Rorschach determinants and three verbal description scores of thirty college students had the author to state that it appears that Rorschach scoring categories are related to language measures.

McGOVERN, J. D. Validity of Rorschach components as measures of intellectual efficiency in the psychoneuroses. Unpublished M.A. thesis, Catholic U., 1949.

McNEELY, H. The influence of varied instructions on the response adequacy of certain Rorschach intelligence indicators. *Diss. Abstr.*, 1955, *15*(4), 628-629.

MOYA, G. Estudio de inteligencia, personalidad y comportamiento en un grupo de 165 soldados (A study of intelligence, personality and behavior in a group of 165 soldiers.) *Rev. Psicol. Gen. Appl.*, 1959, *14*, 615-705.

An analysis of Rorschach protocols yielded the following results: (a) ambi-equality, extrodensiveness, 0%, and 0+ covary with intelligence; (b) coarctation, extratensiveness, A%, Sex% and 0− vary inversely with IQ; (c) P% is highest with average intelligence; (d) H% and At% show no relation to IQ; (e) above the mental deficiency level response times lengthen as IQ decreases.

MURSTEIN, B. I. Factor analysis of the Rorschach. *J. Consult. Psychol.*, 1960, *24*, 262-275.

The article is a review and critique of factor analytic studies which have been done on the Rorschach, including those in which intelligence has been one of the factors extracted.

NEFF, W. S., AND LIDZ, T. Rorschach pattern of normal subjects of graded intelligence. *J. Project. Techn.*, 1951, *15*, 45-57.

The evaluation of Rorschach protocols of one hundred soldiers resulted in the conclusion that a somewhat above-average IQ is necessary to produce a record adequate to be considered normal. According to the Harrower-Erickson and the Ross and Ross systems of diagnostic signs, both the average and inferior IQ groups produced patterns which would be considered neurotic.

OGDON, D. P., AND ALLEE, RUTH. Rorschach relationships with intelligence among familial mental defectives. *Amer. J. Ment. Defic.*, 1959, *63*, 889-986.

Analysis of the Rorschach records of sixty familial mental defectives yielded the following correlations with the subjects' Wechsler-Bellevue IQ scores: (a) levels of R, F, M, FM, W, number of P, number of content categories and number of pure C correlated significantly, pure C tending to increase as IQ decreased, the other correlating positively; (b) number of M, FC and CF did not correlate significantly, number of M being severely depressed and Fc appearing rarely; (c) Fc+cF and the form level of FC correlated at the .01 level; (d) CF form level correlated at the .05 level.

PALMER, V. O. Rorschach's Experience Balance: The concept, general popular characteristics, and intellectual correlates. *J. Project. Techn.*, 1955.

On the basis of Rorschach protocols of psychiatric patients, normal adolescents and adults, the author concludes that an ambi-equal E.B. appears to be positively related to Wechsler-Bellevue IQ scores.

PAULSEN, A. Rorschachs of school beginners. *Rorschach Res. Exch.*, 1941, *5*, 24-29.

The Rorschach factors most closely associated with the Stanford-Binet scores of eighty-two children, ages 5-11 to 7-5 were: the equality of W; number of M; FM; and FC; number of H; number of P; F%; and F+ %.

PECHOUS, R., AND MERY, A. Test de Rorschach et intelligence (The Rorschach Test and intelligence.) *Rev. Psychol. Appl.*, 1960, *10*, 151-164.

The author describes an existential parameter derived from the Rorschach and reports that a statistically significant correlation of .28 was found between various tests of aptitude or intelligence and this measure.

PFIOTER, O. Ergebnisse des Rorschachschen Versuches bei Oligophrenen. (Results of the Rorschach Test with oligophrenics.) *Allg. Z. Psychiat.*, 1925, *82*, 198-223.

PIOTROWSKI, Z. A. A comparison of congenitally defective children with schizophrenic children in regard to personality structure and intelligence type. *Proc. Amer. Ass. Ment. Defic.*, 1937, *42*, 78-90.

A comparison of Rorschach protocols of ten schizophrenic and sixteen high grade unstable mentally defective children led the author to conclude that the main differences lie in the approach to the task and the qualitative aspects of their thinking.

PORTA, V. La valutazione dell' intelligenza col test di Rorschach (The measure of intelligence with the Rorschach Test.) *Arch. Psicol. Neurol.*, 1951, *12*, 337-349.

Seventeen factors are included in a quantitative method for determining IQ from the Rorschach. Using this method a correlation of .68 was found between the Kerman and the Rorschach.

RICCI, A. Studi di diangosi differenziale col reattivo del Rorschach (Studies on the differential diagnosis attained with the Rorschach Test.) *Cervello*, 1939, No. *1*, 11-20.

The Rorschach responses of one hundred normal and thirty feebleminded boys are compared.

RORSCHACH, H. *Psychodiagnostics*. Bern, Hans Huber., 1942, 56-66.

Based on a study of 120 individuals of superior intelligence, Rorschach postulated the following would characterize Rorschach protocols of high IQ subjects: optimum F+%, many M, high W%, orderly sequence within each card and throughout the test, low A% and optimum original responses.

ROSS, W. D., AND ROSS, S. Some Rorschach ratings of clinical value. *Rorschach Res. Exch.*, 1944, *8*, 1-9.

The research revealed that imbeciles yield Rorschach M and related introversive responses. There was some evidence that familial imbeciles produce fewer M responses than do imbeciles of injury or developmental origin.

SARASON, ESTHER K. The discriminatory value of the Rorschach test between two etiologically different mentally defective groups. Clark U., *Abstracts of Dissertations*, 1950, *22*, 44-48.

Correlations of −.55 and −.63 were found between Z−% and the MA's for the two mentally defective groups tested. However, no relationship existed between the Z scores and MA's.

SCALES, MARGARET B. A study of intellectual functioning in terms of Rorschach location scores free verbal association. *Diss. Abstr.*, 1955, *15*(5), 879-880.

SCHARMANN, T. Die Zwischenraumdeutungen im Rorschachtest. Versuch einer gestaltpsychologischen Erkläung. (White space responses on the Rorschach Test. An attempted gestalt psychological explanation.) *Beih. Schweiz. Z. Psychol.*, 1950, No. *19*, 64-72.

According to a gestalt interpretation, Rorschach S responses are a phenomena of perception and intelligence. The subjects tested had brain injuries and lesions. The twenty-four protocols with S response (one to five) gave evidence of greater flexibility of intellectual and apperceptive processes than did the thirty-one records containing no S responses.

SCHNEIDER, E. Intelligences noteiksana ar Rorsachu experimentu (Intelligence testing with the Rorschach Test.) *Musunakot, Riga.*, 1925, 11-14.

SCHNEIDER, E. Die Bedeutung des Rorschachschen Formdeutversuches zur Ermittlung Intellektuell Gehemmter. (The significance of the Rorschach Test for diagnosis of intellectual retardation.) *Z. Angew. Psychol.*, 1929, *32*, 102-163.

SEN, A. A study of the Rorschach Test. *Brit. J. Psychol. Statist. Sect.*, 1950, *3*, 21-39.

M was found to be highly loaded on the intelligence factor in a factor analysis of Rorschach protocols and IQ test scores of one hundred Indian college students.

SISSON, B. D., AND TAULBEE, E. S. Organizational activity on the Rorschach Test. *J. Consult. Psychol.*, 1955, *19*, 29-31.

The authors state that the Rorschach organization factor, Z, shows a direct relationship with intelligence. Among certain groups, Z is reported to be related most closely with verbal intelligence.

SISSON, B. D., TAULBEE, E. S., AND GASTON, C. O. Rorschach card rejection in normal and psychiatric groups. *J. Clin. Psychol.*, 1956, *12*, 85-88.

Forty-four institutionalized mentally defective children rejected Rorschach cards approximately twice as frequently as the two hundred normal children tested.

SLOAN, W. Mental deficiency as a symptom of personality disturbance. *Amer. J. Ment. Defic.*, 1947, *52*, 31-36.

Comparison of the Rorschach protocols of two matched groups of children, ranging in IQ scores from 44 to 79 and 80 to 100, led the author to conclude that defective subjects deviate most frequently on total Z score, A%, F+%, F% and R, and that analysis of these patterns would be helpful in diagnosis of mental deficiency.

SMITH, S. R. The Rorschach examination and general intelligence: A validation study. Unpublished Ph.D. disseration. Univ. California, 1951.

SOMMER, R. Rorschach animal responses and intelligence. *J. Consult. Psychol.*, 1957, *21*, 358.

For a psychiatric population there was no overall relationship between the number of animal responses (total number of responses taken into account) and the patients' Wechsler-Bellevue verbal IQ scores. A small, but significant positive relationship was, however, found between IQ and animal movement responses.

SOMMER, R. Rorschach M responses and intelligence. *J. Clin. Psychol.*, 1958, *14*, 58-61.

It was found that the relationship between the Rorschach M response and the Wechsler verbal IQ was suppressed when both H and R were held constant. In addition, M responses for groups of IQ's of 80, 100 and 120 were ranked by judges of varying degrees of psychological sophistication. With verbatim M responses, all judges exceeded chance, with grammar and vocabulary cues removed, only psychologists produced significant judgments, and when M responses were judged only by the sex of the mover and type of movement, none of the judges made accurate predictions above the chance level.

SPANER, F. E. An analysis of the relationship between some Rorschach Test determinants and subtest scores on the Wechsler Bellevue Adult Scale. Unpublished Ph.D. dissertation, Purdue Univ., 1950.

SPIEGELMAN, M. Rorschach form-level, intellectual functioning and potential. *J. Project. Techn.*, 1956, *20*, 335-343.

The following correlations were found between the Wechsler-Bellevue verbal IQ scale and Rorschach categories for 122 psychiatric patients: Average form level equals .55, R equals .32, M equals .30. In addition, the literature on assessment of intelligence from the Rorschach as compared with IQ testing is reviewed.

STARK, S. A note on time, intelligence, and Rorschach movement responses. *Percept. Motor Skills*, 1962, 15(2), 267-272.

The author presents a view that Rorschach movement responses may be regarded as indicative of aptitude for creative foresight and planning, two variables which are beginning to be included in a redefinition of intelligence.

SUNNE, D. Rorschach Test norms of young children. *Child Develop.*, 1936, 7, 305-313.

A total of 3435 children were tested with the Stanford-Binet, Yerkes, Goodenough Draw-A-Man and the Rorschach. Detailed Rorschach scores by categories and MA's are presented.

SWIFT, J. W. Rorschach responses of eighty-two preschool children. *Rorschach Res. Exch.*, 1945, 9, 74-84.

Eighty-two children of a mean CA of 4-8 and mean IQ of 124.6 were administered the Rorschach. P, W% and F% significantly correlated with MA.

TAMKIN, A. S. Intelligence as a determinant of Rorschach card rejection. *J. Clin. Psychol.*, 1959, 15, 63-64.

The mean Wechsler-Bellevue IQ of thirty-seven psychiatric patients who rejected no Rorschach card was significantly higher (P equals .05) than the mean IQ of twenty-nine patients who rejected one or more cards. The author suggests, therefore, that card rejection may be largely due to the structural complexity of the cards rather than the emotional evocativeness.

TANAKA, F. Rorschach no undo hanno to chino tono kankei (Rorschach movement responses in relation to intelligence) *Jap. J. Educ. Psychol.*, 1958, 6, 85-91, 132-133.

From the Rorschach protocols of one hundred delinquent boys and their WAIS IQ scores, a positive correlation was found between M and IQ, M correlating higher with verbal than nonverbal IQ's. No relationship was found between FM and IQ.

TATOM, MARY H. Relationships between Wechsler-Bellevue subtests scores and certain Rorschach Test factors in clinical patients. Unpublished MA thesis, Catholic Univ., 1949.

TAULBEE, E. S. The use of the Rorschach Test in evaluating the intellectual levels of functioning in schizophrenics. *J. Project. Techn.*, 1955, 19, 163-169.

The Rorschach and Wechsler-Bellevue were administered to sixty hospitalized schizophrenics. Neither R, Z, M, F% individually or collectively or estimates of IQ from the protocols made by experienced clinicians correlated significantly with IQ scores.

TOLOV, A., GLASS, H. L., AND MARMELSTEIN, M. D. Rorschach card rejection as a correlate of intelligence in children. *J. Project. Techn.*, 1960, 24, 71-73.

The Rorschach records and intellectual evaluations of 268 emotionally disturbed children, ages four to eighteen, failed to confirm the hypothesis that intelligence and rejection of Rorschach cards are correlated in emotionally disturbed children.

TRIER, THOMAS R. Vocabulary as a basis for estimating intelligence from the Rorschach. *J. Consult. Psychol.*, 1958, 22, 289-291.

It was found that fairly accurate IQ's could be estimated on the basis of the vocabulary in Rorschach protocols.

TUCKER, J. E. Rorschach human and other movement responses in relation to intelligence. *J. Consult. Psychol.*, 1950, 14, 283-286.

The correlation of Rorschach M responses and Wechsler-Bellevue full scale IQ scores of one hundred adult male neurotics yielded a correlation of plus .26 between M and IQ and plus .35 between FM + m and IQ. The difference in the two types of responses as an estimation of IQ was not statistically significant.

VAN KREVELEN, D. A. Der Rorschach-Test in Fröbelalter. (The Rorschach Test in childhood.) *Beih. Schweiz. Z. Psychol.*, 1948, 13, 87-94.

It was found that of the twenty children, ages four to six, tested with the Rorschach and Stanford-Binet, the more intelligent child responded with an excess of large details, more F+ and Ms.

VARVEL, W. A. The Rorschach Test in relation to perceptual organization and to intelligence. *Psychol. Bull.* (abstract), 1941, 38, 705.

Intercorrelations of the Rorschach categories and the correlation between these categories and IQ scores as obtained from the ACE are discussed.

WEBER, A. Der Rorschach'sche Formdeutversuch bei Kindern. (The Rorschach Test as applied to children.) *Schweiz. Arch. Neurol. Psychiat.*, 1944, 53, 47-61.

A description of children's response is presented. The author concludes that the Rorschach is as good an indicator of intelligence for children as it is for adults.

WEWETZER, K. H. Zum Problem der faktorellen Gültigkeit projektiver Testverfahren. (The problem of factorial validity in projective techniques.) *Schweiz. Z. Psychol.*, 1961, 20, 238-252.

It is concluded that for the two hundred children tested, the factorial structure of the Rorschach was largely dependent on the subject's intellectual levels.

WILLIAMS, H. L., AND LAWRENCE, J. F. Further investigation of Rorschach determinants subjected to factor analysis. *J. Consult. Psychol.*, 1953, 17, 261-264.

An intelligence factor was extracted in this factor analytic study involving one hundred psychiatric patients. This confirms the view that certain Rorschach determinants covary with intelligence. M was found to be highly loaded on the IQ factor.

WILLIAMS, M. An experimental study of intellectual control under stress and associated Rorschach factors. *J. Consult. Psychol.*, 1947, 11, 21-29.

Twenty-five students were administered the Rorschach and the Wechsler-Bellevue Digit Symbol Subtest, first under standard and then under stress conditions. A relationship was found between intellectual performance in a stress situation and intellectual control as measured by the Rorschach.

Wilson, G. P. Intellectual indicators in the Rorschach Test. Unpublished Ph.D. thesis, U. of Texas, 1952.

Wishner, J. Rorschach intellectual indicators in neurotics. *Amer. J. Orthopsychiat.*, 1948, *18*, 265-279.

It was found that of the seventeen reputed IQ indicators in the Rorschach the most significant were R, number of W and Z, and that F+% did not correlate significantly with any Wechsler-Bellevue score. The subjects were forty-two neurotic patients.

Wittenborn, J. R. Certain Rorschach response categories and mental abilities. *J. Appl. Psychol.*, 1949, *33*, 330-338.

The results of analysis of Rorschachs and several mental ability measures of sixty-eight Yale students indicated that no linear relationship existed sufficient to warrant IQ estimation from any of the Rorschach scoring categories used.

Wysocki, B. A. Assessment of intelligence level by the Rorschach Test as compared with objective tests. *J. Educ. Psychol.*, 1957, *48*, 113-117.

Significant correlations ranging from .272 to .450 were found between verbal and nonverbal IQ tests and R, W%, human M%, F + % and A% responses from an administration of the group Rorschach to 217 subjects. By combining several scores, the multiple correlation was positively increased up to .81.

Wysocki, B. A. A factorial study of Rorschach protocols. *Percept. Motor Skills*, 1960, *10*, 105-106.

Nine Rorschach categories and two IQ test scores of 286 adult subjects were intercorrelated and factorialized. Among the factors extracted were intelligence level and intellectual control *versus* emotional impulsiveness.

Wyss-Ehringer, G. Intelligenzquotient und Rorschach-Versuch. (Intelligence Quotient and the Rorschach Test.) *Wiener Z. Nervenheilk.*, 1951, *4*, 134-155.

Appendix

Response No.	Beck Scoring			Klopfer Scoring		
1	W	FY+	A, P	W	FC'	A, P
2	Dd	FT+	Bell	D	Fc	Obj
3	D	F−	Bt	d	F	Pl
4	D	M+	Ad, P	W	M	Ad, P
5	D	FC−	Bt	D	FC	Pl
6	D	M+	H, P	W	M	H, P
7	D	CF+	Bld	D	CF, mF	Bl
8	W	FT+	Ad, P	W	Fc	Aobj P
9	W	F+	A, P	W	FM	A, P
10	D	F+	Ay	D	F	Obj
11	W	F+	A, P	W	F	Aobj P
12	D	M+	Hd, P	W	M	Hd
13	D	F+	A, P	D	F	A, P
14	D	F+	A	D	FM	A
15	D	F+	A, P	D	F	A, P
16	D	FC+	Fd	D	CF	Food
17	D	FC+	Bt	W	FC	Pl
18	Ws	F+	Ad	W, S	FM	Ad
19	Ws	F+	A, P	W, S	F	A, P
20	D	F+	Ad, P	D	FM	Ad, P
21	D	FC+	An	D	FC	At
22	W	F+	A, P	W	F	A, P
23	D	F+	Hd	D	F	Hd
24	D	F+	Hh	D	F	Obj
25	Ds	F+	Hd	S	F	Hd
26	W	M+	Hd, P	W	M	(Hd)
27	W	FC+	Art, P	W	FC	Crest
28		No score		W	Cn	Color
29	Ds	FC+	Hh	DS	FC	Obj
30	D	M+	H	D	M	H
31	D	F+	A, P	D	FM	A
32	W	FC+	Ls, A	W	FC	Na
				D	F	A
				D	FC	A
				D	CF	Coral
				D	F	A
33		No score		W	Cn	Color
34	Ds	F+	An, P	DS	F	At
35	D	FC−	An	D	F/C	At
36	D	M.FC+	Ad	D	Fm, FC	Aobj
37	Dd	FC+	A	d	Fc	A
38	D	FY−	A	dd	FC'	A
39	D	TF−	A	D	cF, FM	A
40	Dds	F+	Ad	S	F	Ad

Response No.	Beck Scoring			Klopfer Scoring		
41	Dd	F+	Al	de	F	Obj
42	Dd	F+	Hd	dd, de	F	Hd
43	Dd	F−	A	dd	FM	A
44	D	FY+	Ad	D	FC'	Ad
45	Dd	M−	Hd, Ab	dd	M	Hd, Ab
46	D	M+	Hd	d	M	Hd
47	D	F−	Ad	d	F	Ad
48	Dd	FY+	Cg	dr	Fc	Obj
49	Dd	F−	Nipple	dd	Fc	Obj
50	W	C	Paint	W	CF	Paint
51	D	F+	Hd	dd	F	Footprint
52	Dd	F+	A	d	FM	A
53	D	FC−	An	D	FC→M	At
54	D	TF+	Ice	D	cF	Ice
55	Ws	FY+	A, P	W, S	FC'	A, P
56	Dd	M+	Sex	dd	Fm, M	Sex
57	D	M+	H, P	W	M	H, P
58	Ws	M,CF−	Sex, Bld	W, S	M, CF	Sex, Bld
59	D	FY+	A	D	FC'	A
60	D	FY+	Sc	d	FC'	Obj
61	Ws	M+	Ab (Hd)	W, S	M	(Hd)
62	W	M+	Hd, P	W	M	Hd
63	W	FT−	Hh	W	Fc	Obj
64	D	CF−	Bld	D	CF, cf, C'F	Skin, Bld
65	D	F+	Hd, P	d	F	Hd
66	D	FC+	A	D	FC	A
67	W	F+	Pr	W	F, Fm	Obj, (A)
68	W	FV+	Ls	W	FK	N
69	D	F+	Hd, Cg, P	D	F, →M	Hd
70	W	FT+	Ad, P	W	Fc	Aobj
71	D	F+	Hd	dd	→M	Hd
72	W	C	Paint	W	CF	Paint
73	W	M.FY+	H, P	W	M, FC'	H, P
				D	F	A, P
74	D	M+	Hd, P	D	M	Hd
75	D	FC+	Bt	D	FC	Pl
76	D	F+	A, P	D	FM, FC	A, P
	D	FC+	A			
77	D	M.CF+	H, P	W	M, CF	H, P
78	Ws	M.FY+	Ad	W, S	M, FC, Fm	Ad
79	W	M.FT+	H	W	M, Fc	H

Response No.	Beck Scoring			Klopfer Scoring		
80	Dd	CF−	Bld	dd	CF−	Bld
81	D	F+	Sex	D	F	Sex
82	Dd	F+	A, Sym	D	FM	A
83	D	F+	Ad	D	→FM	Ad
84	Dd	M−	Hd	dd	M	Hd
85	Dd	F−	Ad	dr	FM	Ad
86	D	YF+	Cl	D	KF	Cloud
87	Dd	F−	Umbrella	dr	F,→Fm	Obj
88	D	M+	Ad, P	D	FM, m	Ad, p
89	W	CF−	Chart	W	CF	Obj
90	D	YF−	An	D	Fk	At
91	Ds	F+	Sym	S	F	Obj
92	D	F+	A	D	→FM,Fc	(A)
93	Dd	F+	Steps	de	F	Steps
94	Dd	F+	Saddle	dd	F	Obj
95	Dd	F+	Hh	dd	F	Obj
96	Dd	YF−	An	dr	kF	At
97	Dd	F+	A	dd	FM	A
98	Dd	F+	Bt	dd	F/C	Pl
99	D	C	Pr	D	CF	Hobj, Bld
100	D	F+	A	D	FM	A
101	Dds	Y	Mist	d, S	K	Mist
102	D	FY+	Hh	D	FC'	Obj
103	W	CF+	Bt	W	CF	Pl
104	Dd	F+	A	D	F	A
105	W	F+	A	W	FM	A
106	W	M+	H, P	W	M	H
107	D	F−	A	D	F	A
108	Ws	F−	Hh, Pr	W, S	F	Obj
109	Dd	F−	Imp	de	F	Obj
110	D	YF−	An	D	kF	A, At
111	W	M.FY+	H, (P)	W	M, KF	H
112	D	FY+	Hh	dd	FC', Fc	Obj
113	D	M+	Hd	d	M	Hd
114	D	FT+	A, P	D	FM, Fc	A
115	D	F+	A	W	FM	A
116	D	FY−	An	D	FC'	At
117	Dd	F+	Hd	de	F	Hd
118	W	FT+	A, P	W	Fc, Fm, FM	A, P
119	W	V	Na	W	K	N
120	Dd	M−	Hd	dr	M	Hd
121	D	FC+	A	D	FC, FM	A, P
122	DW	FV+	Ad, Bt	W	FM, FK	Ad, Pl
123	W	CF.YF+	Fi	W	mf, CF, KF	Expl.
124	Ds	M.YF+	Sex	D, S	M, cF	Sex
125	D	FY.FV+	Ar	d	Fc, FK	Arch
126	W	M.FT+	H	W	M, Fc	(H)
127	D	FT+	Cg, P	D	Fc	Obj
128	D	YF+	Ls	D	cF	N, Pit
129	W	FC+	An	W	F/C	At
130	W	Y	Ink	W	C', K	Ink
131	W	C.T	Fd	W	CF, cF	Food
132	D	VF+	Bt	d	KF	Pl
133	Dds	F+	A	dd, S	F	A
134	Dds	FV+	Ge	dr, S	kF	Geo
135	D	F−	A	D	F	A
136	D	CF.YF+	Bld	D	CF, FK	Blood
137	W	F−	A	W	Fc−	(A)
138	D	CF−	Bt	D	Fm, FC	Pl
139	D	M.FY+	H	D	M,F←→C'	(H)
140	Ws	M.FY+	Hd	W, S	Fm, Fc	(Hd)

Response No.	Beck Scoring			Klopfer Scoring		
141	D	FC.FY+	Ad	D	FC	Ad
142	W	M+	H, Ab	W	M	(H), Abs
143	D	M.YF+	Fd	D	mF, cF	Food
144	W	T.V	Na	W	cF, FK	N
145	W	C.V	Ls	W	CF, FK	N
146	W	FT+	Bt	W	Fc	Pl
147	W	FY+	Tr	W	Fm, KF	Obj
148	Ds	YF−	An, Sex	W	kF	At, Sex
149	W	YF−	Sc	W	FM. Fc	A
150	W	FC.FV+	Ls	W	FC. FK	N
151	W	C	Ab	W	Csym	Abs
152	D	FC.FY−	A	W	FM, CF, FC'	A
153	W	YF+	Cl	W	KF, mF, C'F	Cl
154	Ws	FV+	Ls	W, S	FK	N
155	D	FC+	A	D	FM, FC	A
156	D	M.FY+	H	W	M, FC'	(H)
157	Ws	M.FY−	Hd	W, S	M, FK	Hd
158	D	M+	Hd	d	M	Hd
159	D	CF.TF+	Bld	D	CF, cF	Bld
160	W	M.CF+	H, Fd, P	W	M	H. P
				D	CF, mF	Food
161	D	F+	A	D	FM,→M	A
162	D	FC+	A	D	Fm, FC	A
163	Dds	M+	H	S	M, Fm	H
164	Ws	YF.VF+	Cl	W, S	KF, FK	Cl
165	D	M.FY+	Hd, P	D	M, FC'	Hd
166	Ds	M−	Hd	S	M	Hd
167	D	FT−	Na	d	Fc, Fm	N
168	W	C.T	Fd	W	CF, cF	Food
169	W	CF+	Ls	W	CF, mF	N
170	W	CF+	Tr	W	mF, CF	Obj
171	D	M.FC−	Sex	D	Fm, FC	Sex
172	D	M−	A	D	M	A
173	D	M.CF+	H, Ab	D	M, mf, CFsym	(H), Abs
174	D	M.FV+	A	W	FM, FK	A
175	Dd	F−	An	dr	F−	At
176	Dd	M−	Sex	dd	Fm	Sex
177	D	F+	Ge	D	Fk	Geo
178	Ws	FY+	An	W, S	Fk	At
179	D	FY+	Pen	D	Fc	Pen
180	DW	F+	A	W	F	A
181	Dd	YF+	An	D	kF	At
182	W	FC+	An	W	F/C	At
183	Ws	F+	Ls	W, S	FK	N
184	Ws	M.FC+	Ad, Bld	W, S	FM, CF	Ad, Bld
185	D	CF.TF	Fd	D	CF, cF	Food
186	Dd	YF−	Na	d	C'F	N
187	Dds	FY+	Fd	dr, S	FC'	Food
188	W	FT+	Ad	W	Fc, FC'	Aobj
189	W	YF+	Cl	W	KF	Cl
190	Dds	Y	Na	S	C'	N
191	W	F+	A, P	W	F, FM	A, P
192	D	FY+	A	D	FM, FC'	A
193	W	YF+	An	d	Fk	At
194	Ds	FC+	Hh	dd, S	FC	Obj
195	D	CF+	Ab	D	CSym	Abs
196		No score		W	Cn	Color
197	D	F−	Rl	dr	F	Obj
198	D	FV−	Ls	D	Fk	Geo
199	W	FT+	Ar	W	Fc	Obj (Hd)
200	W	M.FV+	H	W	M, FK	(H)

Response No.	Beck Scoring			Klopfer Scoring		
201	D	FY+	A	D	FM, FC'	A
202	D	FC+	Bt	D	Fm, FC	Pl
203	W	CF−	Basket, Ab	W	CF sym−	Obj, Abs
204	D	M+	H, P	W	M, m	H, P
205	W	M.CF−	Ab	W	m, CF−	Obj
206	D	CF+	Fi	D	CF, mf	Fire
207	Dd	FT+	Mu	dd	Fc, FC'	Obj
208	Dd	F+	Ad	dd	FM	Ad
209	Dds	M	(Hd)	d, S	M	(Hd)
210	W	FY+	Cg, P	W	Fm, FK, FC'	Obj
211	Ds	FY+	Ar	S, d	Fc	Obj
212	W	M. Ft. FV+	(H)	W	M, Fc, FK	(H)
213	D	M.FC+	Cg	D	m, FC	Obj
214	D	M−	Sex	D	Fm	Sex
215	D	C.Y	Bld	D	CF, cF	Bl
216	W	FV+	A, P	W	FM, FK	A, P
217	D	FT+	Cl	D	KF, cF	Cl
218	W	CF−	An	W	CF−	At
219	Dd	F+	Al	dr	F	Obj
220	W	T	Ab	W	c	Abs
221	Dds	F+	Crown	S	F	Crown
222	Dd	F+	Hd	d	F	(Hd)
223	Dds	FY+	Glass	S, dd	FC'	obj
224	Dd	M+	Hd	d	M	Hd
225	Dd	FY−	Tooth	dd	Fc	Hobj
226	Dds	F+	H	S	F,→M	(H)
227	Dd	F+	Pin	dr	F	Pin
228	D	F−	An	D	F	At
229	D	F−	Boat	dd	Fm	Obj
230	Dd	M+	H	dd	M	H
231	Ds	F+	Hd	S	F	Hd
232	D	F+	Ad	d	F	Ad
233	Dds	FY+	Fd	S	FC'	Food
234	Dds	F+	A	S	F	A
235	Dd	F+	Ad	dd	F	Ad
236	Ds	F−	Bell	D, S	F	Bell
237	Dds	F+	Paddle	dr, S	F	Obj
238	W	F−	A	W	F	A
239		No score		W	Cn	Color
240	D	FC−	A	D	M, F←→C	A
241	Dds	M. FY	H	S	M, FC'	H
242	Dd	FY−	Pr	dr	Fc, FC'	Obj
243	Dd	F+	Ls	dd	F	N
244	Ds	M+	Top	S	Fm	Top
245	Dd	F+	Hh	dr	F	Obj
246	Dd	F−	A	di	F−	A
247	Dd	F+	Spear	dd	F	Spear
248	Dd	F+	Hh	dd	F	Obj
249	Dd	M.Fc+	H	dr	M, FC	H
250	Dds	F+	Ar	S	F	(H)
251	Dds	M.FY+	H, Ar	dd, S	M, FC'	Hobj
252	Dd	F−	Ad	di	F	Ad
253	Dd	CF.YF+	Fi	dd	CF, mF, KF	Fire
254	Dds	FV+	Ls	S, dr		N
255	Dds	F+	Hd	S	F	(Hd)
256	Dd	F+	An	dd	F	At
257	Dd	F+	Ad	dd	FM	Ad
258	Dd	M−	Hd, Tongs	dd	M−	Hd, Tongs
259	Dd	M−	H	dd	M, m	H
260	Dd	FC+	Fd	dd	FC	Food
261	Dd	CF.YF+	Fi	dr	CF, mF, KF	Fire
262	D	F+	A	D	FM	A
263	D	FC+	Ls	D	FC, Fm	N
264	Dd	YF−	An	dd	cF	At
265	D	FV−	A	W	FM, FK	A
266	W	F−	Cg	W	F−	Obj
267	Dds	M−	Ab	dr, S	Fm−	Abs
268	W	M. FV. YF	H, P	W	M, FK, FC'	H
269	D	FT FC−	A	D	FM, Fc, F←→C	A
270	D	FT. FY+	Na	d	Fm, Fc, FC'	N
271	W	CF.FT	Bld	W	CF, m, cF	Bld
272	D	M. FY+	H, P	W	M, KF, FC'	H, P
273	Dd	C.Y	Mist	dr, S	CF, KF	Mist
274	W	CF. FV+	A, P	W	FM, CF, FK	A
275	Dd	FY. FT+	Candle	dr, S	Fm, Fc	Candle
276	W	CF+	Ar	W	mF, CF	obj
277	W	CF. YF+	Smoke	W	CF, mF, KF	Smoke
278	D	M. FY. FT+	Hr, P	D	M, FK, Fc	H
279	W	Y. T	Ice	W	C', c	Ice
280	W	Y	Smoke	W	K, C'	Smoke
281	W	Ft. FY	Ad, P	W	Fc, FC', Fm	aobj
282	W	CF. VF	Light	W	CF, FK	Light
283	W	FY+	A, x-ray, P	W	Fc, FK	Aobj
284	D	YF+	Gem	D	CF, FK	Obj
285	D	M. FY. FC+	H, P	W	M, CF, Fc	H, P
286	W	T	Wool	W	c	Aobj
287	D	FC+	A	W	FC, FM	A
288	W	YF+	Cl	W	KF, mF	Cl
289	W	M−	Ls	W	mF	N
290	Dd	Y	Ab	di	Fc	Abs
291	W	Y	Ab	W	M, K	Abs
292	D	CF. FV	Ls	D	CF, FK, Fm	N
293	W	M+	Hd, Hh	W	M	Hd, Obj
294	Dd	FC+	Ls	dr,→D	Fm, FC	N
295	W	M, CF+	Sex	W	M, Fm, CF	Sex
296	W	M, CF+	Paint	W	m, CF	Art
297	W	M.TF−	Tr, ice	W	mF, CF	Obj, ice
298	W	M. CF	Hd, Ab	W	M, m, CF	Hd, Abs
299	W	M.FY. FC− contamination	H	W	M, Fc, FC−	(H)
300	W	M.FY+	H, Ab	W	M, Ksym	H, Abs

Index